Kennikat Press
National University Publications
Series in American Studies

THE DEPRESSION
in the
SOUTHWEST

edited by

DONALD W. WHISENHUNT

National University Publications
KENNIKAT PRESS // 1980
Port Washington, N.Y. // London

Manufactured in the United States of America

Published by
Kennikat Press Corp.
Port Washington, N.Y. / London

Library of Congress Cataloging in Publication Data
Main entry under title:

The Depression in the Southwest.

(National university publications)
Includes bibliographical references index.
1. Depressions—1929—United States—Addresses,
essays, lectures. 2. Southwestern States—Economic
conditions—Addresses, essays, lectures. 3. Texas—
Economic conditions—Addresses, essays, lectures.
I. Whisenhunt, Donald W.
HB3717 1929.D45   309.1'76   79-18845
ISBN 0-8046-9258-0

CONTENTS

PREFACE

The Great Depression of the 1930s, one of the most significant periods in American history, has received increased attention from historians in recent years. Despite the cliché, it is true that the decade between 1929 and 1939 was indeed a watershed in American history. American social, cultural, political, and economic life could never be the same after such an era. Despite the arguments about a "Roosevelt revolution," few can deny that the economic crisis and resulting increase in governmental activity transformed the United States in a dramatic way, the effects of which we are still experiencing.

Many studies have been made in recent years (and more are needed) of the depression on localities—states, regions, cities—and on special groups—labor, churches, ethnic groups. Franklin D. Roosevelt and the New Deal, perennial topics of interest, have been studied in depth in the same locations and in relation to the same groups. The studies prove that the impact of the depression varied from place to place and from group to group. The reaction to the crisis and the solutions attempted by the New Deal also vary, depending upon the subject of the study.

This book is designed to look in depth at one part of the United States in this momentous era. Although we refer to the Southwest, the focus of the following essays is on Texas and the states surrounding it on all sides. This area was chosen because it contains almost all characteristics to be found in the United States as a whole. Included in this region are urban areas, rural poverty, ethnic and racial minorities, drought areas, coastal regions, and deserts. Certain portions of the Southwest experienced events that were not typical of all the United States—an oil boom in the midst of the depression and the disastrous erosion in the Dust Bowl.

Missing from the Southwest were heavy industrialization and intense labor organization, both of which elsewhere were directly affected by the depression and the New Deal remedies. In that sense, the Southwest was not typical of the United States as a whole. Another factor that is also atypical was the amount of political power concentrated in these few states in the thirties. It is significant that political leaders from the Southwest were more than proportionally instrumental in making the laws and shaping the direction of the nation in such a critical period for people quite different from themselves all over the country.

The essays in this book were written especially for this study by eight scholars who teach at universities in the area; most of them are the products of educational institutions of the Southwest. They are relatively young scholars, and, with one or two exceptions, do not have established national reputations. Nonetheless, they all have been productive in this field of study and will be better known in the future.

There is not a central theme to this series of essays beyond the general idea of the depression in the Southwest. Each of the contributors, a specialist on one phase or another in this period, was asked to write about what he knows best. The result is a series of essays that illuminate the decade as well as any collection available.

There was no thematic plan involved. The first three essays are concerned with the economic impact of the depression and the activities of federal agencies in coping with it. The first, by Kenneth E. Hendrickson, Jr., of Midwestern State University, is a thorough study of the Civilian Conservation Corps (CCC) in six southwestern states. The organization, administration, impact, and day-to-day operations of the CCC are analyzed and evaluated. Professor Hendrickson concludes that despite occasional difficulties, the CCC was one of the most popular and successful agencies of the New Deal.

The Dust Bowl and its effect on the southern Great Plains is the subject of the next essay, by Professor Garry L. Nall of West Texas State University. The high plains region, one of the most productive areas of the world, was devastated by the economic crisis of the depression and the period of extreme drought that followed close behind. One of the major efforts of the New Deal was to counteract these events—it is this effort that Professor Nall chronicles.

Cattlemen of the Southwest prided themselves on being independent and more free of governmental interference and control than other economic groups. C. Roger Lambert of Arkansas State University puts that myth to rest in the next essay. He show the impact of the depression on cattle raisers and explains their gradual transition from individualists who would remain aloof from government aid to a group demanding more and more assistance.

The fourth essay, by the well-known music historian Bill C. Malone of Tulane University, illustrates developments in country music during the depression. Especially significant is the fact that music was an escape or diversion for a people affected by conditions they could neither comprehend nor cure. Ironically, commercial country music was a growth industry in the thirties, and its major customers were among those hardest hit by the depression. Professor Malone also examines how the music reflected the conditions of the times.

The next essay, contributed by the editor, is an effort to study the reactions of the people to the depression—especially what they considered the cause of the depression to be. By focusing on one state and analyzing in detail all available evidence of opinion, the essay concludes that southwesterners were agrarian in mentality and were practitioners of the "conspiracy theory" of history.

The final three essays focus upon two states in the region. The first, by Professor Lionel V. Patenaude of the University of Texas at San Antonio, is a summary of the New Deal in Texas. Professor Patenaude concentrates on the role of Texans in national affairs during the New Deal and on the impact of the New Deal upon the pivotal state of Texas.

Professor Stephen F. Strausberg of the University of Arkansas does the same for his state. This is particularly significant since Arkansas was probably the poorest state in the area and the most rural. Because of these facts, the impact of the New Deal in Arkansas was somewhat different and more profound in some ways than in other states.

The final essay, by Professor William J. Brophy of Stephen F. Austin State University, is a study of blacks in Texas during the depression. The conditions of blacks were similar in other states; Texas, therefore, serves as a good example of the treatment and condition of America's largest racial minority.

Numerous other topics could have been included in this book. But the studies included tell us some things we did not know, and, probably more important, they confirm much of what we already suspected and verify some of the conclusions already reached about the depression on the national level.

More work needs to be done on the depression era at the local level. We sincerely hope that these essays will add to local knowledge and will encourage additional research.

THE DEPRESSION IN THE SOUTHWEST

KENNETH E. HENDRICKSON, JR.

1.

THE CIVILIAN CONSERVATION CORPS
IN THE SOUTHWESTERN STATES

The Civilian Conservation Corps (CCC) was one of the most successful of New Deal relief agencies. Despite the fact that it was conceived and developed in a very short period of time, the CCC was nevertheless effective from the beginning. Before it was disbanded in 1942, it provided outdoor employment for 2,500,000 young men, with as many as 519,000 enrolled at a given time. These workers operated from some 3,000 camps located throughout the United States, and they accomplished a great many tasks in the areas of conservation and reclamation which had for many years been left undone. This study focuses upon the operations of the CCC in the six southwestern states of Arizona, New Mexico, Texas, Oklahoma, Arkansas, and Louisiana.

President Franklin D. Roosevelt decided to proceed with his plan to put an army of unemployed young men to work in the nation's parks and forests on March 14, 1933. Authorizing legislation was soon introduced in the House and Senate and referred to committees, where hearings quickly began. Protests came from organized labor, socialists, and a few other groups, but the Roosevelt Democrats steered the bills through skillfully and the President signed a compromise measure on March 31. Among congressmen and senators from the Southwest only one voice— that of Huey Long—was raised in opposition.[1]

As originally conceived, the administrative structure of the CCC was exceedingly cumbersome, and observers have long marveled that it could have operated effectively. That it did is a credit to those dedicated administrators at the federal and state levels who bore the responsibility for its functions, who overcame the inevitable foibles of bureaucracy and plunged ahead toward a worthwhile goal. The Corps was, it will be remembered, a bureaucratic monstrosity in which the Labor Department enrolled the men, the War Department ran the camps, and the Agriculture and Interior Departments, along with various state agencies, supervised the projects.[2] Of course, there were administrative problems, personality clashes, and jurisdictional and ideological wrangles, as well as financial difficulties, but none with the magnitude of those which beset many other New Deal programs.

What follows is a composite discussion of the CCC in the six south-western states illustrated by examples of specific events which occurred in those states. We should begin, however, by introducing the leading administrators of the program, for there will be occasion to mention some of them frequently. The national director was Robert Fechner of Tennessee, a former official in the Machinists' Union. He was a stolid and unimaginative man who viewed the mission of his agency in the narrowest possible context. He also possessed an abrasive personality which caused frequent irritation among his close associates; but on the other hand he was totally dedicated to his task and served ably. He literally gave his life to the CCC, dying on December 31, 1939, of exhaustion and heart failure.

Fechner's assistant director, who succeeded him after his death, was James J. McEntee, also of the Machinists' Union, who was considerably less able and more abrasive than his chief. Unfortunately, he became director at a critical time in the history of the Corps when it required much more skillful and dynamic leadership than he was able to give.

Vital to the success of the CCC was the work of the Selection Division in the Department of Labor. The main responsibility here was entrusted to W. Frank Persons, a lawyer and social worker who headed the United States Employment Service and who possessed administrative skill and humanitarian qualities of a high order. After 1935 he was ably assisted by Dean A. Snyder, formerly the state selection director of Ohio, who shared his abilities and views. In 1937 they were joined by Neal Guy of Texas, another former selection director of high ability.[3]

In the Department of Agriculture many of the CCC projects came under the supervision of the Forest Service, where the major policy maker was Fred Morrell, who quite naturally conceived of forest conservation as the primary mission of the Corps; but equally important was the Soil Conservation Service, led by Hugh H. Bennett. Indeed, most of the CCC projects in the Southwest came under the auspices of the Soil Conservation Service. In the Interior Department the Park Service was most important. Here Morrell's and Bennett's counterpart was Conrad Wirth, whose views were very similar to theirs except that he proceeded from the standpoint of his own agency.[4]

For the Army the most important voice was that of Colonel Duncan K.

Major, a member of the CCC Advisory Council. However, the Army administered the camps through the Corps Area Headquarters, so state administrators had most of their direct contact with the various Corps Area Commanders who served between 1933 and 1942. The states covered by this study lay in three Corps Areas, the fourth, seventh, and eighth; thus, we are concerned with the relationship of civilian administrators to three distinct military groups in which there were frequent personnel changes. Overall, it can be said that these relationships were cordial and effective; a fact of no little significance since it was not true in all parts of the country, and since the highest leadership in the Army was not always totally committed to the success of the CCC.[5]

One other federal agency heavily involved in CCC operations was the Office of Education. The educational offerings of the CCC were important though controversial components of the overall program. The Office of Education under George T. Zook and John W. Studebaker tried valiantly throughout the existence of the CCC to make it a sort of "University in the Woods," and in so doing engendered a great deal of friction between themselves and the representatives of the technical services, who always complained that their contributions to the training of the enrollees received too little credit.[6]

At the state level there were two groups of administrators of virtually equal importance. First were those who operated the relief agencies and who were called upon to act as selection officers in cooperation with the Department of Labor. In the beginning these included Florence M. Warner in Arizona, Margaret Reeves in New Mexico, Lawrence Westbrook in Texas, Carl Giles in Oklahoma, W. R. Ryers in Arkansas, and Frank H. Peterman in Louisiana. All these men and women were delighted at the prospects posed by the CCC and indicated their willingness to cooperate with the federal government. As the years passed, of course, there were many personnel changes for political or administrative reasons, and the intensity of dedication to the CCC fluctuated; but generally speaking state relief officials supported it throughout its existence.[7]

Since many CCC projects were developed on state land, the people in the state park, wildlife, and conservation departments were also of major importance. They exhibited varying degrees of competence from state to state, but they were practically unanimous in their enthusiasm for the CCC concept. A typical response was that of State Forester V. H. Sonderegger of Louisiana, who anticipated the work of the CCC in his state eagerly and who provided able assistance in the formulation of work projects during April 1933. Another was George R. Phillips, the state forester of Oklahoma, who saw at the beginning how valuable the CCC would be to his state in many different ways, including reforestation, fire prevention, and erosion control. Hugh G. Calkins, assistant regional forester in New Mexico, expressed similar views and declared further that New Mexico could easily employ from four to ten thousand men for a year in the forests of the state. The one reservation expressed by the technical people was that CCC boys might be asked to undertake work beyond their capacity.[8]

The CCC also met the approval of private enterprise. Timber, lumber, and conservation men all over the Southwest supported the idea. Very few protests emanated from organized labor, and even the farmers were pleased when they began to realize what benefits the work of the CCC would offer them. The press, a reasonable barometer of opinion, indicated general public approval, or at least a willingness to give the experiment a try. A survey of several papers in diverse areas of the Southwest gave no indication of open hostility, although to be sure the CCC was received by many with something less than ecstasy.[9] An April 10, 1933, editorial in the *Baton Rouge Times* was typical.

The recent enactment of President Roosevelt's plan for a CCC . . . is an emergency measure which will be watched with hopeful interest. Those who have voiced objections . . . on grounds that the actual return will hardly justify the investment have overlooked two distinct merits of the measure. This work can be started and expanded with very little preliminary delay in comparison to . . . other permanent public works . . . . Then this type of labor will not be involved with union labor or the wage scale.[10]

The *Albuquerque Journal,* lukewarm to the New Deal despite the fact that New Mexico was stone broke and needed help desperately, said the CCC was a good idea, but not new. Work camps already existed in a number of states—like California. Such programs make a much needed contribution, said the editor, but should be swiftly curtailed once prosperity returned. A little more realistically, the *Daily Oklahoman* declared that such programs as the CCC would be a "great step" in providing relief to the poverty-stricken people of the Sooner State, and said nothing about curtailment. *Happy Days,* the "official" CCC publication, pointed up the general interest in the Corps by commenting that even though it had to compete in the Oklahoma papers with Alfalfa Bill Murray, Pretty Boy Floyd, Wiley Post, and Will Rogers, it nevertheless received substantial coverage.[11]

The first business of the CCC in that dark spring of 1933 was twofold: the selection of projects and campsites, and the selection of men. State officials were called to Washington for orientation conferences, while at home the scramble for campsites began and soon became highly competitive because each state was assigned a quota. Groups and individuals from virtually every corner of every state contacted officials in Washington and their own capitals with suggestions for projects and camp locations. They bombarded their congressmen with requests for assistance, and the latter almost always responded favorably.[12]

As some had feared, many of the early proposals revealed haziness of understanding as to the purpose and capabilities of the Corps. They often contained requests for highly technical and expensive work which the young and inexperienced men who would comprise the bulk of CCC personnel could not possibly perform. Fred Morrell of the Forest Service expressed his dismay over such proposals to E. O. Siecke of the Texas State Forest Service. "I have received an enormous quantity," he wrote, "of baby blue bound projects from Texas quite in consonance with the style and majesty of the state itself." He vowed to approve only those projects which seemed reasonable and logical—and he did. His task was made easier by the fact that as time wore on most proposals which came in were quite within the capabilities of the Corps to handle.[13]

The actual task of campsite selection once projects were approved lay in the hands of the federal or state technical service personnel, who worked closely with the Army. This process required the selection of an adequate site, the construction of facilities, and provisioning. It also required rather precise timing among a number of government agencies, which occasionally went awry so that men sometimes arrived at campsites before the latter were ready for occupancy; but on the whole the process went remarkably well, and a few camps were ready before the end of April.[14]

As the process of campsite selection went on apace, the more tedious but equally vital process of enrollee selection began. It was enormously complicated because it required quick identification of hundreds of thousands of eligible young men, and because the administrative machinery used for the job was often inadequate. At first it was decided that with certain exceptions the age limits for participation in the CCC would be 18 and 25, that the enrollees should be unmarried and come from families on relief, and that the period of enrollment should be six months. Later it was extended to one year, and the age limit was reduced to 17. The men were to be paid $30.00 a month, of which $25.00 would be allotted to a dependent, if there was one. Also, from the beginning a small number of veterans and local experienced men were permitted to enroll, but they constituted a tiny minority of the total. The veterans were placed in camps of their own, but the local experienced men, or LEMs, as they were known, were integrated with the younger men in the regular camps. The idea was that their maturity, experience, and familiarity with the outdoors would assist the boys in orienting themselves to a new way of life, and it seems to have worked reasonably well.[15]

The state relief officials found selection to be an enormous task. Most relief boards were understaffed, and they found themselves swamped with applications. They had to determine eligibility and meet quotas and deadlines amid the clamoring of thousands of young men for admission, and of course many who applied were ineligible for one reason or another. Some came from families not on relief, some misrepresented their age, and some claimed to be unmarried when in fact they had wives and children. Many were deadbeats—men of low character and reputation in their communities—whose presence in the camps might pose a threat to stability and productivity. They all had to be picked over, sorted, processed, and assigned, and it created a mountain of work and confusion. There were frequent misunderstandings, innumerable mistakes, and cases of inconsistency and even injustice, but somehow the process worked, and before the end of April 1933 the first enrollees began to arrive in the camps.[16]

The enrollment system worked somewhat as follows. An applicant would present himself at the local enrollment center—usually the county welfare office. He would answer a series of questions designed to establish his eligibility, and if possible his home would be visited by a welfare worker. If it was determined that he was eligible, the applicant would be given a physical examination and a series of inoculations; he would then be sent off to a "reconditioning camp" at an Army post such as Fort Bliss, Fort Sam Houston, or Fort Sill, where he would be "oriented to the outdoor life." After about two weeks of that he would go to camp. Usually the enrollee would remain in his home state, but this was not always true. Some states, like Arkansas, enrolled many more men than they could use in their own projects, and sent a large number off to faraway places like South Dakota, while others, like Arizona, needed thousands of imports in order to man their allotted camps. This inconsistency frequently caused problems, for men objected to being sent away from their home states, especially when they had to face racial or cultural differences.[17]

As time passed, the selection procedure became routine and there was much less confusion. Still, it was occasionally marred by difficulties arising from personality clashes, patronage wrangles, financial embarrassment, changing jurisdiction, or some combination of these. Texas provides one good example. From 1933 to 1939 selection in Texas was directed by the Texas Relief Commission (TRC), first under the leadership of Colonel Lawrence Westbrook and then of Adam R. Johnson. In 1936 the state cut appropriations for the TRC in an economy drive. The cuts made it very difficult to handle even the routine business of selection since an adequate staff could not be supported, and thus much greater responsibility devolved upon the county welfare agencies without adequate control. By the end of June 1936 funds were nearly exhausted, and a special session of the legislature extended the life of the TRC by providing a special appropriation. However, it was so small that only the barest minimum of work could be carried on.

In the regular 1937 session of the legislature, a bill was introduced creating a State Department of Public Welfare (DPW). This was followed, of course, by much discussion of funding needs, personnel, and appointments, but at length the bill was passed and the Texas Department of Welfare became a reality in 1938. However, it existed only on paper, for it had a minuscule appropriation of $25,000. Meanwhile Adam R. Johnson, director of the Texas Relief Commission, expended as little time, effort, and money on the CCC as possible, while his assistant, Neal Guy, who was directly responsible for selection, worked heroically attempting to manage the largest state program in the nation on the smallest budget. Toward the end of 1937 he gave up in disgust, resigned, and went to work for the CCC Selection Division in Washington.

Until September 1939 the lame duck TRC continued as best it could to handle selection. Johnson continued as chief administrator, and Guy was replaced by Charles J. Sweeny. On September 1, 1939, the legislature finally activated the welfare department with an adequate appropriation. Adam Johnson was named director, but a number of new administrators were added, and there was much concern in Washington over the need to maintain high quality selection procedures.

As it turned out, the legislation caused some problems. Although Sweeny was a competent administrator, he was surrounded by political hacks who were either antagonistic, incompetent, or both. Worst among the enemies of the CCC in this group was Kenneth Wendler, long an outspoken critic of the program, who was named assistant director of the DPW. Next in line were Mrs. Zuleika Hicks, who bore personal and political grudges against Sweeny, and Odie Manatra, who was simply incompetent. To make matters worse, under the new welfare system the state department was given no administrative authority over the counties but could only advise them. Thus, no machinery existed to control the selection procedure at the local level.

Despite such handicaps the program continued in the state, and its popularity did not diminish, although the quality of the enrollees declined and desertion continued to be a major problem. Finally, in late 1940, Adam Johnson was replaced by J. S. Murchison, who immediately fired Hicks and Manatra, much to the relief of Sweeny. "This should result in better working conditions at least," he wrote, "unless the new appointees are worse 'heels' which is not probable."[18]

Another example of administrative difficulty at the state level is the case of Arkansas, where in the mid-thirties the Department of Public Welfare was presided over by Miss Gussie Haynie, an appointee of Governor J. Marion Futrell. Miss Haynie was clearly unenthusiastic about the CCC, but since relief was so necessary and the program so popular she could not afford to ignore it completely. However, she was able to make life thoroughly miserable for Selection Director Ed Bethune, whose office fell under her jurisdiction. She kept his salary low, refused to provide him with adequate staff support or even adequate office space, and responded to his entreaties with bland promises which she never intended to fulfill. Bethune relied heavily on the Washington office for support, hoping his friends there would pressure Miss Haynie to become more responsive to his needs. They were successful to a degree, but Bethune was rewarded more with promises than with substantive support. "No matter how hard I work or how much I accomplish," he complained, "there is no appreciation or consideration from Miss Haynie . . . ." But he concluded, "I will carry on hoping things will get better."

In 1937 Carl E. Bailey succeeded Futrell as governor of Arkansas, and the wheels of political fortune turned round and brought the change for which Bethune had waited so long. Miss Haynie was removed from her position and replaced by John R. Thompson of Fort Smith. Thompson was infinitely more enthusiastic about the CCC than Miss Haynie and much more sympathetic and encouraging to Bethune. For the next two years the administration of CCC selection in Arkansas was among the best in the nation. After 1940, however, as in most other states, the program went into decline in the face of mounting pressures. Bethune stayed on as selection director until April 1942, at which time he resigned to run for state auditor.[19]

In some states the difficulties caused by the inadequate staffing of relief agencies were never fully resolved, so that even in the absence of political or personal bickering it was hard to achieve a very high level of efficiency. Arizona and New Mexico are excellent examples. In the former, as late as 1937, selection was handled by one person, Miss Noretta Graf, who was secretary to the commissioner of the Board of Social Security and Welfare. Miss Graf had no assistance and simply did not have time to do her job properly. She could not handle promptly the vast number of applications she received, nor could she provide adequate follow-up. Only late in the life of the CCC were these conditions improved when the Arizona State Department of Public Welfare was created. In New Mexico the situation was similar. Here the work of selection fell to Miss Laura Waggoner, secretary to Faye Guthrie, head of the Relief and Security Authority. Miss Waggoner did a competent job, and Guthrie gave her all the support he could, but their extremely limited budget made it almost impossible to reach all the eligible young men or provide adequate follow-up.[20]

Another source of difficulty in administering the CCC at the state level grew out of the allotment system. Under the original regulations, it will be recalled, the CCC enrollees were paid $30.00 per month and were required to allot most of it to a dependent. Many enrollees were disturbed by this requirement, and it soon became clear to relief officials in the states that the $25.00 allotment was too large. No one could meet even his incidental expenses on $5.00, and it was suspected that this problem was becoming a significant deterrent to enrollment. Yet to reduce the allotment would increase the relief burden of the states, and this state officials were reluctant to do. Thus, they faced a serious dilemma. On the one hand, they desired to maintain the highest possible federal contribution, but on the other hand they desired to maintain the highest possible enrollment. For a time they hesitated to take any action, but at length in 1937 most states chose the stopgap measure of allowing the enrollees to choose their own allotment. This approach proved highly unsatisfactory, and in 1938 the mandatory allotment was reduced to $22.00. Later it was lowered to $15.00 when the improving economy made the allotment less significant.[21]

Although the CCC was generally popular, desertion soon became a problem. It was a noticeable factor by 1935 in all the states, and in some reached crisis proportions by 1937. All the selection directors gave much attention to these problems and reported their findings to Washington, citing inadequate camp conditions, the competition of other federal relief programs such as the WPA and NYA, improving agricultural conditions, and later, war hysteria as major contributing factors. Some selection directors did much more than report conditions. J. L. Hill in Oklahoma, for example, recommended that hazing of new enrollees should be prohibited, that weekend leaves should be minimized, that officials of the technical services should be encouraged to be more cooperative in portraying camp conditions accurately, and that more attention should be given to the need to place discharged enrollees in private jobs. Another director, J. S. Murchison of Texas, emphasized the need to improve vocational training in the CCC. Such a step would have a threefold effect, he argued. It would stimulate wider interest in the program, encourage boys of the "better type" to apply, and induce them to stay longer once enrolled.[22]

All the directors believed that favorable publicity was vital to the continued success of the program, particularly after the beginning of the war, but none was so innovative as Ed Bethune of Arkansas. In the spring of 1941 he planned and carried out a CCC Appreciation Day which attracted nationwide attention. Bethune selected Camp Dutch Creek near Waldron as his showplace, and invited representatives of local, county, and state government in addition to many important private citizens to come and see the Corps in action. On April 17, 1941, he conducted a grand tour of the Dutch Creek Camp and its projects in a caravan of more than two hundred vehicles. His guests witnessed soil conservation work in progress, saw surveyors and bridge builders at work, saw a firefighting demonstration, and on-the-job training. In camp they saw the living, dining, and recreational facilities of a model installation, witnessed the enrollees hungrily consuming a wholesome meal, listened to stirring band music, and finally were treated to a gigantic barbecue and dance that night. According to the newspaper accounts and Bethune's own report, the event was an enormous success, and it was imitated by others with equal success, especially in Oklahoma and Louisiana.[23]

The selection officials also engaged in numerous additional publicity activities. They traveled about their states speaking to civic clubs and other organizations, held frequent orientation sessions for parents and applicants, encouraged favorable radio and newspaper reports, and above all sought to improve camp conditions in cooperation with the Army and the technical service personnel.[24] This was all done not only to reduce desertion and improve the image of the CCC, but to create the impression that the primary mission of the Corps was not now relief but conservation and character building. But it was a losing battle. By the early forties the CCC was beset by forces much too great to be overcome by favorable publicity. Among these were the war, the improving economy, and above all the general feeling that all such federal relief programs had outlived their usefulness and it was time to get on to other things.

That politics played a role in the life of the CCC cannot be denied, although the role was a minor one when compared to other episodes in New Deal history. State politicians were favorably inclined toward the Corps, and congressmen loved it for its patronage potential as well as for the obvious contribution it made to the people. Whenever cuts were proposed in the strength of the CCC, and this occurred on several occasions between 1935 and 1940, their outcry was loud and bitter. There was one instance, prior to the war, however, when congressional support of the CCC wavered. That occurred in 1937 when an administration-sponsored bill was introduced to make the Corps permanent. Although it had the hearty support of some, like Jed Johnson of Oklahoma, many others opposed it. Johnson led the pro-permanence forces with eloquence and dignity, but both in committee and on the floor the majority favored extension for two years only. This view was embodied in an amendment offered by Fritz Lanham of Texas, who argued that to make the CCC permanent would be to admit that the economic crisis might never end. Johnson argued forcefully against the proposition, but in the end the

Lanham Amendment passed by a vote of 398 to 12; even Johnson voted for it in an apparent bow to the inevitable. Indeed, no one in the congressional delegations of the southwestern states opposed it. They joined with the overwhelming majority who favored the extension of the CCC, but not permanence.[25]

In common with most leading newspapers across the country, those in the Southwest interpreted the passage of the Lanham Amendment as a blow struck for congressional independence in defiance of President Roosevelt's "court-packing" scheme. The worth of the CCC was not the real issue. The *Arkansas Democrat*'s reaction was typical. The editor proclaimed that while many of the President's recent ideas had generated much criticism, almost no one attacked the CCC. The Corps, he said, had done a remarkable job during its first four years. It was a wise investment and it deserved to be made permanent.[26]

Much as they liked the patronage aspect of the CCC, congressmen often complained when it appeared that political maneuvering had descended to the camp level. In 1934 Senator Thomas P. Gore of Oklahoma informed Assistant Director McEntee that there was "politicking" going on in the camps in connection with the congressional run-off election between Will Rogers and Henry Johnson. He did not like it. At the same time Bronson Cutting of New Mexico told Fechner he had "reliable" information that organized efforts were under way to register the CCC personnel in the state to vote. Many of these people were not citizens of New Mexico, he warned, and he demanded that Fechner should give the matter "close attention." The director offered assurances that he would.[27]

More bizarre was the episode which unfolded two years later in Arkansas. In July 1936 an enrollee named R. E. Smee at Camp F-9 near Cass wrote a young man named Armstrong Evans of Booneville that he controlled the votes of the enrollees in the camp and would "deliver" them if Evans so desired. Subsequently Charles I. Evans, Armstrong's father and a state senator, complained to Fechner that someone had paid the poll taxes for the boys in Camp F-9 though "they are not *bona fide* residents and should not be allowed to vote."

Evans demanded an investigation of the matter. It turned out that father and son Evans supported opposing candidates for prosecuting attorney in their county. Smee and young Armstrong were friends—thus Smee's offer and the elder Evans's complaint. On the surface it appeared to be political manipulation of the worst sort, but upon closer investigation J. S. Billups concluded that the boys in Camp F-9 who met the age and residence requirements were entitled to pay their tax and vote and that Smee had done nothing illegal. There was no evidence that anyone had paid the poll tax for the enrollees.[28]

In spite of such administrative and political squabbles, the work of the CCC in the Southwest went on without interruption for nine years and made significant contributions to the social welfare and environmental development of each southwestern state. The greatest contribution of the program, of course, was relief. In nine years it gave employment for varying periods of time to 403,949 young men at a cost of $403.9 million in the states of the Southwest. These men provided allotments to their families amounting to more than $97 million, and since CCC enrollees tended to come from large families, averaging eight in number, it is reasonable to say that the CCC provided financial assistance to something like three million people.

The greatest contributions of the CCC to the environment were in the areas of soil conservation and forest and park improvement. The young men improved or initiated the development of nearly one hundred parks in the Southwest. They planted more than 333 million trees to enhance the forests and built over 2 million check dams to impede erosion. They also assisted in teaching thousands of farmers such soil-saving techniques as terracing, contour plowing, and crop rotation, and in all were directly responsible for the salvation of hundreds of thousands of acres of invaluable farm and grazing land.[29]

Some of the individual projects were spectacular. In Arizona, for example, an enormous tract of land which lay between the Colorado River and the Utah border was opened to grazing through the construction of trails into inaccessible areas and the development of livestock water supplies. The Spring Canyon dam near Hatch, New Mexico, was the largest structure of its kind ever built by the Soil Conservation Service. All the labor was supplied by 150 CCC enrollees, who expended 58,600 man hours to complete it. The dam was 408 feet long and 54 feet high, and it created a 550-acre lake behind it. In Texas one of the outstanding projects was the development of the Palo Duro Canyon Recreational Area, while in Oklahoma it was the Wichita Mountain Wildlife Refuge and Park. The CCC in Louisiana conducted forest stand improvement operations in the Kisatchie National Forest and in the state forests which advanced the conservation program by an estimated twenty years.[30]

There were more than 220 camps operated in the southwestern states during the nine-year lifetime of the CCC, some in or near towns where they often became a recognized part of community life, and some in remote areas where they went unnoticed. Regardless of their location, the camps were similar and life within them conformed to a general pattern, but there was enough variation that generalizations about camp life are difficult and always subject to exceptions. A typical camp during the heyday of the CCC had from 150 to 200 enrollees and was operated under the direction of a reserve army officer who was directly responsible to the Corps Area Commander. The Camp Commander usually had from one to four military assistants, and in addition there would be a camp doctor, a technical project supervisor, four or five project leaders or foremen, and an educational adviser. The project leaders were usually patronage appointees and were not responsible to the Army; however, all other administrative personnel, including the educational adviser, were subject to military authority as exercised by the Camp Commander. As for the enrollees, they were quite literally responsible for their actions to various government agencies, depending upon the time of day. If this sounds ridiculous, do not be too quick to scoff. According to eyewitness testimony it was not uncommon for CCC officials from Washington upon entering a camp for inspection to begin their tour by asking, "Where are the men?" and "What time is it?" The answers would tell them if the enrollees were where they should be and who was in charge of their activities.[31]

A day in camp typically began with reveille at 6:30 a.m., followed by physical training and a hearty breakfast. CCC food was plain, but very nourishing and served in large quantities. Most enrollees seem to have enjoyed it, for compliments far outweigh complaints in their letters, and it is clear that many were delighted with the weight gain and more vigorous feeling they experienced as a result of their new diet of good food and hard work. After breakfast and roll call the enrollees set out for work under the direction of their project leaders, and while it is true that their activities consisted for the most part of routine labor, there was occasional excitement, as when they were called upon to fight disasters such as floods and forest fires. At the end of the day there were almost always additional activities to occupy their time if they so desired since most camps offered educational, recreational, and athletic programs. Athletics ranged from intramurals to highly competitive programs in track, baseball, basketball, and football. There were district, state, and Corps Area championships in all sports, with some of the competition at a very high level. Major league scouts even followed CCC baseball, ever on the lookout for budding professionals.

Many enrollees became interested in journalism and wrote extensively for the camp newspapers or for *Happy Days*. The latter was the "official" CCC national newspaper. Founded by two enterprising journalists from Ohio, it received no government funding but was otherwise encouraged. It survived throughout the life of the CCC and served as a major propaganda tool emphasizing the heroic and romantic aspects of camp life. Today it is a major source for the study of several important facets of CCC history.

It is almost as difficult to generalize about enrollees' attitudes toward the CCC as it is about any other aspect of camp life, but clearly most young men enjoyed the experience. From all over the Southwest throughout the nine-year history of the CCC came the reports of those who felt the program was changing their lives. They related feelings of renewed hope, improved health, and higher spirits. Not only were they contributing to the welfare of their families, but through the educational and training programs available in the camps they were improving their own potential for the future.[32]

The enthusiasm of the young men in the camps was often matched by their parents, particularly during the early days of the program. Maude Barrett, Louisiana state relief director in 1933, interviewed a number of families in selected parishes and found the overwhelming majority were pleased with CCC. In Terrehone Parish, for example, Mr. and Mrs. James Redmond said their son Thomas was healthier than ever before. His allotment supported the entire family; they were able to pay all their bills and live on cash. The general impression conveyed by almost all the families interviewed in Terrehone, Rapides, and Orleans parishes was the same.[33]

Of course, high morale and enthusiasm were not without their counterpoint. We have already seen that desertion became a serious problem after 1935, but even those who stayed on sometimes addressed complaints to administrators or to their parents telling of bad food, overwork, boredom, or mistreatment by camp leaders. In all such cases the CCC immediately sent investigators to the scene; the results varied considerably. For example, in 1938 enrollee A. B. Nicholson wrote to Fechner from Camp SCS-20 near Yukon, Oklahoma, complaining of bad food and other unsatisfactory conditions. The director sent F. B. McConnell to the campsite to investigate, and he discovered that conditions were entirely adequate. It appeared that Nicholson simply had a personal grievance against Camp Commander Captain Paul M. Brewer and was attempting to stir up trouble. Nicholson was asked to submit to a mental examination at Fort Sill, but refused, deserted, and was never heard from again.

In a similar case Congressman Mike Monroney forwarded a complaint to Assistant Director McEntee from the enrollees in Camp SCS-10 near Wynnewood, Oklahoma. They claimed that Camp Commander Captain Roy Hamilton treated them unjustly; that he had "abused and insulted them for years." McConnell investigated and found the complaints to be unjustified. The mess was good, Hamilton was a firm but fair disciplinarian, and the camp had received a superior rating under his command. It appeared to be another case of personal grudges, and McConnell recommended that no action be taken.[34]

Regrettably, complaints against camp authorities could not always be dismissed in such fashion. In early 1940 enrollee J. C. Reddock wrote of the abusive practices of his commander Lieutenant Walter Scoggins at Camp NP-1 near Marathon, Texas. These charges were investigated by Charles H. Kenlan of the national office, who quickly ascertained that they were true. "Scoggins is downright mean," he concluded in his report, and as a result the commandant was soon removed. In another instance it was found after the investigation of an anonymous complaint that officials in Camp SCS-15-N, near Whitewater, New Mexico, had made arrangements with local authorities to pick up and hold enrollees in town whenever it seemed necessary or desirable, as in cases of rowdiness or drunkenness. Investigator A. M. Stockman viewed such a practice with alarm since it reflected weakness on the part of camp officials. Such routine matters were usually handled at the camp level, and Stockman believed that to leave troublesome enrollees to the mercies of townsfolk could be dangerous.[35]

Happily, complaints make up a very small portion of the voluminous files of camp records and statements left by CCC enrollees. Still, they were significant because they affected the administration of the program, and the bad publicity they often generated was a deterrent to many potential enrollees.

Perhaps the most unsatisfactory aspect of CCC performance was the treatment of Negroes. The act which gave the Corps its existence was obviously intended to prohibit discrimination, but this intent was disregarded in practice. The plight of the Negroes was certainly desperate. The depression had plunged them further than ever before into a quagmire of economic misery, and the unhappiness of their lives, great even in the best of times, was magnified a thousandfold. In 1933 unemployment among Negroes was double the national average, and over two million were on relief.

Reports from the South showed clearly in the spring of 1933 that Negroes were experiencing discrimination in spite of the law. In Arkansas, for example, Senator Hattie Caraway received complaints as early as the first week in May that "no colored boys" were being accepted into the CCC, and Roy Wilkins of the NAACP was outraged when he was told that not only were no Negroes enrolled in the state but that when some young black men presented themselves as applicants they were told by local officials that there were "no orders from Washington to recruit Negroes." The fact is that very few Negroes, if any, were enrolled in Arkansas in the early days of the CCC program; W. A. Rooksberry, the first selection director, tried to sidestep the issue. He reported to Persons that selection was being handled by the various county relief committees under the general instructions issued at the beginning of the program. No instructions had been given which might be construed to encourage discrimination. However, most of the early camps were established in the Ouachita and Ozark National Forest areas, and forestry officials had warned of the dangers of placing Negroes there due to the "known race prejudice" of the mountain people. Rooksberry promised that at least one Negro company would soon be enrolled for placement in southern Arkansas.[36]

In Oklahoma the situation was very different. Not only were a few Negroes enrolled during the early stages of the program, but they were placed in camps with white boys. This practice was initiated and continued until early 1935 because there were allegedly too few Negro applicants to establish even one all black company. By 1935 complaints were numerous. In January M. J. Miller wrote to Persons, in charge of national selection, to inquire if Negroes could be segregated in Oklahoma. He explained that "everybody" in the state he talked to desired it, and that if segregation could be accomplished more Negroes could be enrolled. He reported that complaints and tension were mounting and that more and more white boys were refusing to stay in camps with Negroes. Fechner was angry when he learned that the CCC camps in Oklahoma were integrated, and he demanded a full report of the situation. He found that 125 Negroes were enrolled in the state and that at least one congressman and several other people had already requested the establishment of a Negro camp. Now a serious effort was generated, and the first black camp was installed at Fort Sill in July. In August another was established near Konowa, but there were to be no more for some time.[37]

State and local selection officials in Louisiana claimed that Negroes were enrolled in their state beginning with the very first round, but the fact was that they were very few in number. It was also true that Louisiana officials sincerely believed that no Negroes should be chosen because the amount of money they would derive from the CCC would be "so much more than they are accustomed to having." They also believed that most Negroes were "just not interested in the CCC," and despite constant entreaties from Washington and demands emanating from the NAACP and other groups a fair proportion of Negroes was never chosen in the state. The population of Louisiana was 36 percent black, but the proportion of black CCC enrollees never exceeded 12 percent.[38]

In Texas state officials were as hostile to Negro enrollment as in any state of the Deep South. Thus, by 1935 there were only twelve under-strength camps in the Lone Star State and thousands of young Negroes clamoring for admission. Conditions in Texas finally drove Fechner to action; he decided to limit black enrollment by ordering that no further Negro camps be established and that henceforward Negroes were to be selected only as replacements in existing camps. This order was to apply not only to Texas, but to the entire nation, and as a result there were never enough places for eligible Negroes in the CCC. Later, officials in most states attempted to secure expanded Negro quotas, but with little success. As late as the summer of 1941 there were still many more Negro applicants in Arkansas, Louisiana, Texas, and Oklahoma than places to accommodate them, and selection officials were told to do what they could to discourage prospective Negro enrollees. Later that year the restrictive policy was finally eased, but the result was inadequate to meet the need.[39]

Ironically, those Negroes fortunate enough to be accepted did not always find the CCC a pleasant experience. Jimmie Lee Robinson, for example, addressed a plaintive letter to President Roosevelt on September 21, 1935, asking that he and his friends be transferred to another camp. They were stationed at Palo Duro Park near Canyon, Texas, and had no place to go on weekends because the residents of the city refused to permit them to enter. "We could go to Amarillo," said Robinson with pitiable naiveté, "but we are seldom issued passes." An investigation of this complaint revealed that Robinson and his companions were unjustly confined and that the camp suffered from incompetent leadership. The investigator recommended that "more experienced officers are needed."[40]

In another case in Louisiana Chester Gage became involved in a dispute with his educational adviser Robert Hartman and was discharged from the Corps. Shortly thereafter he was arrested on a misdemeanor charge and placed in jail in Bossier City, only to be released in the custody of white men who took him out to the country and beat him senseless for his "uppity ways." An investigation of the incident revealed that since the beating occurred after Gage was discharged from the Corps, CCC officials had no jurisdiction and no action was taken in Gage's behalf.[41]

One of the most serious racial incidents occurred in Arkansas in 1938. A group of black enrollees became embroiled in a gang fight with white WPA workers at a gravel pit near Forrest City. During a subsequent investigation in camp a foreman, Robert Bradley, beat one enrollee, John Smith, for "impudence" and another, Freeman Montague, was accused of theft and put in jail. Smith and Montague wrote to Fechner asking for an investigation, and J. S. Billups was ordered to the camp. He found that conditions there were horrible and that beatings were common. This accounted, he thought, for the flare-up at the work site. The situation was very delicate, however, because the white civilians in the camp had friends high up in Arkansas state politics. Bradley, for example, was a friend and appointee of Senator Hattie Caraway. Billups concluded that little could be done, but he recommended that Negroes on the Corps jobs should always have highly competent white supervision in order to avoid recurrences of such incidents as the gravel pit brawl. Racial tensions continued in the Forrest City area, and as long as two years later relations were so strained between the camp and the town that it became necessary to transfer the Negroes to another location in an out-of-the-way forest area.[42]

Despite fear, prejudice, and occasional violence such outbreaks were rare, and the Negroes in the CCC made significant contributions. In most cases Negro camps located near white communities caused no trouble, and in fact when some of them were abolished in the late thirties as a result of financial cutbacks, the townsfolk often complained as loudly as in the case of white camps, particularly if the project was incomplete.

Many Mexican Americans served in the CCC, but the number is difficult to ascertain because they were placed in integrated camps and were not identified by race. Nevertheless, there is some evidence to indicate the existence of racial problems involving them. In New Mexico, for example, enrollees from out of state were frequently unhappy about the prospect of sharing a camp with the "greasers." It was also clear that the Army authorities in New Mexico were not vitally concerned with the physical well-being of the Mexican American enrollees. Most of these young men came from backgrounds of extreme poverty and were almost always undernourished and frequently illiterate when they arrived in camp, yet the Army seemed to be much more interested in the efficient administration of the camps than in the improvement of human beings.[43]

There is also evidence that racial tensions in mixed camps occasionally led to violence. In the most unfortunate of such incidents enrollee Ray C. Densmore was beaten to death when a recreational boxing match degenerated into a riot. There was an investigation which traced the causes of the outburst directly to race and language difficulties, but those responsible deserted and no charges were ever filed.[44]

Indians were enrolled in the CCC under special conditions, beginning in July 1933. Enrollment was opened to all Indians over 18 whether or not they were married. The Bureau of Indian Affairs in the Department of the Interior selected the men and administered the work, and the Indians were not subject to the formal regulations of the CCC. They had their own camps, most of which were on reservations; they were allowed to select their own projects and administer their own affairs. To provide leadership the tribal councils selected project supervisors and job foremen who were trained at special camps such as those in Arizona and New Mexico and then were sent home to pass on their new knowledge and skills. The Indians received the $30.00 per month allowance with no allotment requirement and were allowed to participate in the CCC educational program. The CCC was popular among the Indians, and it was successful. By 1942 more than 88,000 had participated, most of these in Arizona, New Mexico, and Oklahoma.[45]

As suggested earlier, one of the most interesting, most controversial, and in some ways least satisfactory aspects of the CCC program was its educational phase. From the beginning certain officials at both the federal and state levels felt strongly that the opportunity to provide education as well as work for the enrollees should not be wasted. Among those most strongly committed to education at the federal level was Frank Persons, but at the outset there was opposition from the Army which was powerful enough to nearly destroy any chance the program might have had. In late 1933, however, Chief of Staff General Douglas MacArthur submitted a proposal which envisioned an educational program for the CCC to be administered by the Army, but operated through the Office of Education. It was a cumbersome plan at best, but was accepted since there was no alternative acceptable to the Army.[46]

As the program developed, it became clear that the men at the Office of Education, particularly Commissioner George S. Zook, his successor Dr. John W. Studebaker, and C. S. March and Howard Oxley, CCC education directors, were somewhat unrealistic and visionary in their approach. Whereas most officials in the technical services conceived of "education" primarily as a process of work training, the educators tended to see it not only as an opportunity to provide basic literacy and vocational training to those who desired them, but also a "complete educational experience" such as would be available in the public schools. There was friction from the beginning between the educational advisers who were placed in the camps by the Office of Education on the one hand and the Army and technical service personnel on the other. By 1937 the conflict reached crisis proportions. The technical service people, particularly the foresters, were bitter over what they considered lack of recognition for their contributions to the education of the enrollees. Their contribution, of course, was in the form of on-the-job training which occurred while the enrollees were at work and was not considered an official part of the education program. As a direct result of the tension Fred Morrell, Conrad Wirth, and Adjutant General George P. Tyner appealed to Fechner to approve a new distribution of responsibilities with regard to education. While this proposal was under consideration, Fechner received another from Dr. Studebaker, which, if adopted, would have made the Office of Education independent of Army control in the administration of the Corps program. Fechner approved the Studebaker plan, but it never went into effect because it was discovered that under existing law funds could be expended only under the old structure. Thus, the original organization was continued and conflict persisted.

In December 1937 Morrell and Wirth sent another proposal to Fechner, this time calling for the complete dismantling of the educational program. They claimed the effort to provide academic training in the CCC camps was a failure and that on-the-job training should now be emphasized. This proposal, together with the continuing tension between the technical services and the Office of Education, led Fechner to appoint a special committee to investigate the entire matter and make proposals for adjustment. The committee's report, submitted in January 1939, was very critical. It called for the removal of the program from the jurisdiction of the Army, more emphasis on vocational training, and better training of educational advisers. In short, the report virtually duplicated the previous recommendations made by Morrell and Wirth. Fechner ignored most of these recommendations, but he did approve the notion of better training for camp teachers and more emphasis on vocational education.[47]

It is almost impossible to summarize the operation of the educational program at the state level, because there were such great differences from time to time and place to place. Still, by examining the educational adviser's report files, newspaper stories, and certain files of official correspondence, it is possible to construct a reasonable picture of the system in operation. Clearly, since facilities were often primitive at best, much depended on the ingenuity and imagination of the educational adviser. Among the best to be expected was Camp SP-43-T near Goliad, Texas, which was established in 1935. Here Don Keane, the first educational adviser, interviewed all the enrollees about their interests and desires. He then visited all the prominent people of the community asking for help and was received sympathetically by most. Some teachers came from the public schools and others were provided by the Federal Emergency Relief Administration. From the beginning both academic and vocational courses were offered in order to meet the needs of individual students, and according to the *Goliad Advocate Guard* everyone was pleased with the results. As time passed, the program expanded to include numerous courses from arithmetic to zoology to blacksmithing to music. In addition to regular classroom activities there were special lectures, films, and on-the-job demonstrations. The level of the courses ranged from pre-literate to college review, and the last educational adviser in 1941 was satisfied that at least some of the enrollees were obtaining jobs in private industry as a direct result of the CCC training and education they received.[48]

Another example of an outstanding educational program was that in Camp SCS-11 near Jacksonville, Arkansas. Here, in 1939, the curriculum included twenty-nine subjects from arithmetic to woodworking. Films, first aid, and safety training were also available. The library had fifteen hundred volumes, and the camp subscribed to five daily newspapers. This camp was also one of two high school centers in the state, allowing enrollees to attend nighttime classes at Jacksonville High School for graduation credit.[49]

There can be no question that many of the young men in the CCC craved learning. They often complained when a camp had no educational adviser, and occasionally in such cases they took matters into their own hands. This happened, for example, at a camp near Redlands, New Mexico, where the men set up their own "college"—Yuma University—and exchanged whatever skills and knowledge they possessed among themselves. Men also complained when they failed to receive the on-the-job training they had expected at the time of enrollment.[50]

These examples, it must be quickly admitted, are atypical. The average camp educational program appears to have been very ordinary and very unimaginative. Often the educational advisers were incompetent and the camp commanders were hostile. As one officer put it, "These men are here because they want to work. If they had wanted to go to school, they would have done that instead."[51] In the average camp the curriculum was meager, the library was very small, and the facilities were unattractive; yet the educational program was by no means a failure. Even during the early years attendance was frequently over 70 percent, and the enrollees seemed to be attracted to both the academic and the vocational phases of the program. They were most interested in learning a skill, however, and after 1939 interest in the educational program reached its peak. Indeed, many young men joined the CCC thinking they were going to learn a trade. Often they did, and despite the existence of some less than adequate programs many seem to have been pleased with the results. In 1941 a number of Oklahoma newspapers solicited testimonials from ex-enrollees concerning the benefits they received from participation and from the educational program in particular. They were inundated with replies, of which the following statement by Clyde Gregory is typical:

The CCC is very beneficial in work of this kind [he was a riveter for Lockheed] in that you learn to work with a large group of men and you also learn to take orders. The CCC offered an excellent opportunity to become a welder which I took part in while in camp. When Hitlerism is destroyed I will be able to return to my home town as a competent welder.[52]

Most of the letters received by the newspapers—at least those published—contained sentiments similar to those of Gregory. The quality of the education and training offered by the CCC may have been low by professional standards—it undoubtedly was—but nevertheless the enrollees appreciated it deeply.

State and CCC authorities gave some attention to the need to place the enrollees in jobs when they departed from the camps, but their efforts were sporadic and not particularly effective. The number of men who went directly from CCC camps into jobs acquired as a direct result of their training in the Corps was small, certainly, but precisely how many did it can never be known since no records were kept. It is known that many state selection directors like Ed Bethune in Arkansas, Charles Sweeny in Texas, and J. L. Hill in Oklahoma worked with their state employment agencies to try to create placement services, while in other states, like Arizona, almost nothing was done. Bethune, indeed, developed a rather elaborate program, but in most states placement operations never rose above the hit-or-miss level, and the vast majority of young men leaving the Corps were on their own in hunting for a job.[53]

When the CCC celebrated its eighth anniversary in April 1941, the end was almost in sight, although most CCC administrators were loath to admit it. The war in Europe was then in its second year, and many observers believed that America would soon become involved. Opinion over the future of the CCC became divided, with some people arguing that CCC camps should become military training centers and others vehemently opposed to such an idea.

Director James J. McEntee, who succeeded Fechner in 1940 after the latter's death, at first favored military training but then abandoned that notion in favor of an effort to demonstrate how useful the CCC could be to the war effort through its educational program, which could be used to train enrollees in war-related skills. Simultaneously he attempted to de-emphasize the relief aspect of the Corps, which was now obsolete. The Corps, he said, should be retained for its contributions to society and its character-building potential, and all across the country CCC administrators and selection directors emulated him with massive recruiting drives and publicity campaigns.[54] In the Southwest, as elsewhere, this program took the form of voluminous newspaper releases, radio shows, camp open houses, and orientation meetings designed to show youth and their parents the benefits of CCC participation. The CCC remained popular as a concept, but the preservation effort was unsuccessful. The Corps could not overcome its image as a relief agency. Furthermore, the Army and the improving economy reduced the ranks of the unemployed so greatly that in many areas even reduced quotas could not be filled. Arkansas and Louisiana reported continuingly high numbers of applications, but in other states applications declined and desertions increased.[55] Still, the program probably could have been preserved and nursed through the war had it not been for the conservative inclination of Congress during the spring of 1942.

One of the provisions of the Appropriations Act of 1941-42 authorized the creation of a Congressional Joint Committee to investigate all federal agencies and recommend the elimination of those not essential to the war effort. Six of the twelve members of this committee were conservative southerners, among whom were Senators Harry F. Byrd of Virginia and Kenneth McKellar of Tennessee, both openly hostile to the CCC. Under their influence the committee recommended that the CCC be abolished not later than July 1, 1942, and McKellar introduced a bill calling for the abolition of both the CCC and the NYA. In hearings before the Senate Labor and Education Committee he produced witnesses who bombarded the Corps with vicious and abusive charges. One of the most irresponsible of these was Governor Leon C. "Red" Phillips of Oklahoma, who said that many convicts whom he interviewed for parole were former members of the CCC or NYA. Phillips's outrageous statements were patently untrue, and he was countered by others, including Senator Dennis Chavez of New Mexico, but the damage was done and McKellar's views clearly dominated the proceedings of the committee. However, the McKellar bill was never reported out. Instead, the end came by other means. On May 4, 1942, President Roosevelt asked for an appropriation of $49 million to operate the CCC during the fiscal year 1942-43, but the House Appropriations Committee defied him on June 3 voting not to comply. The fight then went to the floor, where friends of the Corps fought a final desperate battle to preserve it, losing on June 5 when the House voted 158-151 to provide $500,000 for liquidation. At first the Senate balked at this abrupt move, but on June 30 House-Senate conferees agreed on a compromise providing $8 million for the phase-out program. The Civilian Conservation Corps was dead.[56]

Most newspapers in the Southwest gave rather matter-of-fact coverage to the death throes of the Corps, although a few, like the *Fort Worth Star-Telegram* reported wishfully that perhaps after the war the CCC might be resurrected. Not all the papers commented editorially when the end finally came, but of those which did the *Albuquerque Journal* was typical. On July 2, 1942, the editor said he thought Congress did the right thing in terminating the CCC and trimming the WPA and NYA. He said those agencies were very beneficial during the depression, but now times were different. Jobs were plentiful, the war was expensive and demanded sacrifices, and social welfare agencies were no longer needed.[57] He cannot be blamed for his inability to see the future.

GARRY L. NALL

2.

THE STRUGGLE TO SAVE THE LAND
The Soil Conservation Effort in the Dust Bowl

During the decade of the 1930s the agricultural economy of the southern Great Plains, one of the richest farm regions in the United States, faced a crisis. Not only did the farmers and ranchers of the predominantly wheat and cattle country of western Kansas, eastern Colorado and New Mexico, and the panhandles of Texas and Oklahoma suffer from the effects of the Great Depression, but also they contended with drought and dust storms that virtually halted crop and livestock production. While a period of low prices and sparse rainfall represented a temporary phenomenon, the destructive effects of wind erosion to the soil threatened to reduce the agricultural potential of the area permanently.

First settled by cattlemen attracted by the vast grassland in the late nineteenth century, the southern Great Plains rapidly became a territory dotted with stock farms and ranches, as homesteaders and land seekers rushed into the region at the turn of the twentieth century. In adapting to the subhumid-semiarid conditions, farmers learned that drought resistant crops fared better on a long-term basis than did such a cash commodity as wheat. Yet the rise of prices for grain during the World War 1 era, the availability of tractors, one-way disc plows, and combines, and an extended period of favorable moisture conditions spurred farmers not only to increase the wheat acreage on land already in cultivation but to plow up extensive areas of native pasture for further expansion of the crop.

Throughout the five-state area non-resident farmers, city businessmen, and tenants joined the long-time agricultural operators in the expansion of wheat production. Typical of many localities in the region was Grant County, Kansas, where the average 1,509 acres sown in grain in the five-year period 1910-15 jumped to 140,626 acres in a similar time span twenty years later. In the Texas Panhandle the percentage of cultivated land in the crop rose from 25 in 1919 to 43 in 1929. Large producers such as Hickman Price in Texas and Simon Fishman in Kansas and Colorado, as well as small operators, found that raising wheat required relatively little labor or attention in comparison with other commodities. After planting their crops in the fall they placed cattle on the wheat pasture during the winter, harvested the grain in the late spring, and burned the stubble to allow for easier plowing in the summer. Even though prices faltered after 1929, wheat production continued to expand as long as climatic conditions remained favorable.[1]

However, trouble developed as drought, heat, and dust storms hit the Great Plains in 1931 and lingered on for almost a decade. In nine of the twelve years between 1929 and 1940, rainfall at Amarillo, Texas, failed to reach the normal 19.67 inches. In an eighteen-month period between September 1934 and March 1936, the moisture over the region averaged from 50 to 60 percent less than normal. Abnormally high temperatures throughout much of the decade added to the arid conditions, so that when spring winds blew, the dry, unprotected soil was easily lifted into the atmosphere, thus causing dust storms.

While southern Great Plains residents had witnessed dusters or black blizzards occasionally in the past, they had never experienced such frequency or encountered such destructive effects as they did during the 1930s. Between January 1933 and February 1936 the Amarillo weather bureau reported 192 dust storms. Sweeping across the landscape from any direction, the dusters, which lasted from a few hours to several days, turned daylight to darkness and made living conditions miserable. In describing the situation in Hansford County, Texas, in April 1935, Everett C. Greene wrote President Franklin D. Roosevelt: "Much of the time the dust is so dense that one does well to see fifty feet." A farm wife in Guymon, Oklahoma, Mrs. George L. Aycock, complained that "the ravages of these terrific dust storms, which have been increasing in velocity and frequency with the continued drouth, have become a daily occurrence and almost unendurable. . . ."[2]

As the blowing dust caused misery and suffering, H. A. Hildwein, the Curry County extension agent in New Mexico, clearly expressed the fears of farmers and ranchers throughout the southern Great Plains when he warned in March 1935 that unless efforts were made to control erosion, "thousands of acres of fertile agricultural land will be reduced to a nonproductive state, and perhaps permanently ruined for farming purposes."[3] Reports from all areas of the Dust Bowl revealed the serious toll that wind erosion had inflicted upon the land. In Las Animas County, Colorado, the winds "either blew the top soil away entirely or so piled it up that further cultivation is both dangerous and difficult."[4] In Deaf Smith County, Texas, approximately 1,500 miles of fencerows were covered with dust.[5] At Fort Hays, Kansas, landowners found that "fences, Russian thistles, weeds, shrubs, farm machinery, in the fields, farmland, wind-breaks, roads or [any] obstruction that might retard the wind velocity and prevent the soil to settle, were filled and covered with wind blown soil."[6] On the range land of Cheyenne County, Colorado, grassland that had once pastured thirty cows per section had suffered so much from erosion that the same acreage could handle only ten head. When Arthur H. Joel of the Soil Conservation Service conducted a survey in twenty counties in the heart of the region in 1936, he concluded that 97.6 percent of the land suffered from the effects of erosion, with 53.4 percent affected to a serious degree.[7]

Undoubtedly, the severity of the Dust Bowl conditions exceeded the ability of the individual landowners to prevent the destruction of their soil. Consequently, they turned to the federal and state governments for assistance. Yet on both political levels a lack of experience in erosion control, the dependence upon the cooperation of numerous agencies, the shortage of funds, and the failure to coordinate a plan of attack limited the success of the initial efforts. Effective measures came only when federal, state, and local officials joined with farmers and ranchers to imple-ment a long-range conservation program.

Government involvement in erosion prevention was relatively new when the first destructive dust storms hit the southern Great Plains in the 1930s. In the states a few agricultural agencies had made efforts to en-courage moisture preservation. Following research conducted at the experiment station at Spur, the Texas Extension Service launched a cam-paign between 1916 and 1933 which resulted in the terracing of more than seven million acres. Also, largely in response to the influence of H. H. Finnell, director of the agricultural experiment station at Oklahoma Pan-handle Agricultural and Mechanical College at Goodwell, farmers in that area terraced 177,000 acres in 1932. On the national level, Hugh Hammond Bennett of the Bureau of Chemistry and Soils in the United States Department of Agriculture achieved sufficient recognition in his crusade to awaken interest in erosion research that Congress provided funds in 1929. Within three years Bennett was supervising ten erosion investigations, one of which was located at Hays, Kansas. However, despite these efforts, the state and federal governments were initially ill-prepared to handle the scope of the Dust Bowl problems.[8]

While the state extension services personnel continued to encourage terracing and the scientists at the erosion investigation stations pursued their research, only a few federal or state officials displayed much concern over the conditions in the southern Great Plains. However, in August 1933 Secretary of Agriculture Henry A. Wallace and Federal Emergency Relief Administrator Harry Hopkins did direct Bennett to begin a survey of the soil situation in the distressed region. Bennett, in turn, dispatched H. V. Geib from the erosion investigation station at Temple, Texas, on a thirty-county tour of the Texas and Oklahoma panhandles, southwestern Kansas, southeastern Colorado, and northeastern New Mexico. Upon his return Geib reported that the most serious erosion had occurred in patches. He found very little damage in cultivated areas where wheat grew on heavy soils. However, in fields where farmers had planted row crops on silt loams or very sandy soils, no less than five inches of surface material had been removed. Geib also observed dust accumulations several feet in depth scattered in fields, pastures, and along fencerows. Upon receiving the analysis, Bennett commented to Hopkins: "The damage which has been done by wind erosion during the past year is of enormous proportions, much greater than generally supposed."[9]

Yet instead of responding directly to the problems of the Great Plains, Washington officials focused their attention upon the formation of a national soil erosion program. In October 1933 the Soil Erosion Service was established in the Department of the Interior, with Bennett as the head. Organized in association with the Public Works Administration as a means of channeling funds into the national economy, the agency launched a campaign to prove that erosion could be controlled. Operating on the premise that farmers would make efforts to protect their land through example, Bennett initiated demonstration projects across the nation. Under his supervision agency officials selected land tracts with erosion problems representative for the larger region and then prepared a comprehensive plan to correct the difficulties. Property owners within the designated area would then be asked to sign five-year agreements whereby, in exchange for providing certain labor and materials and by following prescribed land use practices, they would receive technical assistance for such measures as contouring and terracing fields, building dams, and erecting fences. The government would also provide seeds, trees, and shrubs along with any supplementary labor required. Upon completion of the preliminary arrangements the work would begin. Within six months after its founding the Soil Erosion Service had twenty-four projects underway.[10]

While none of the early demonstration projects was located in the Dust Bowl area, Bennett received several proposals for programs to deal with the wind erosion problems. Following his visit to the region in the summer of 1933, H. V. Geib suggested on two occasions that the Extension Service, the Federal Emergency Relief Administration, and the Soil

Erosion Service cooperate to implement practices of contouring, strip cropping, and terracing as well as removing marginal and submarginal land from cultivation. D. P. Trent of the Oklahoma Extension Service recommended a contour-listing program for the panhandle area of his state.[11] Yet Bennett took no action until Geib returned to the Texas Panhandle in April 1934 and reported, "It was almost unbelievable to see how many more fences were covered and how the bare spots of exposed subsoil in many fields have been greatly extended to cover such greater area." [12] Upon receipt of this observation Bennett decided to establish a demonstration project near Dalhart, Texas.

One of the first steps taken in organizing Dalhart Project No. 27 was the selection of H. H. Finnell to serve as supervisor as well as regional director for the Soil Erosion Service. During his eleven years as director of the experiment station at Oklahoma Panhandle Agricultural and Mechanical College, Finnell had formulated concepts on wind erosion control that coincided with the views of Bennett. Believing that such farm and ranch practices as burning stubble, overgrazing fields and pastures, and failing to protect crop residues had contributed to the erosion problem, he advocated the constant maintenance of a vegetative cover on the land whenever possible. Although not discounting the value of terracing and contour tilling as a means of retaining moisture, Finnell also felt that the education of farmers to plant erosion-resisting sorghums and grain cover crops and to protect the crop residue was more important. These ideas became the fundamental program for fighting wind erosion in the Dust Bowl.[13]

Finnell got an opportunity to test his ideas when he began work at Dalhart in August 1934. He selected a 27,000-acre tract which suffered from both severe wind erosion and hummocking in the Conlen community in eastern Dallam County. After farmers signed five-year cooperative agreements, Finnell supervised the terracing and contour plowing of the cultivated land and then planted erosion-resisting cover crops as well as wheat. In case the wheat failed, he was prepared to substitute sorghum for protective purposes. He also contour furrowed the 7,000 acres of grassland and planted 17,000 trees to provide windbreaks. Within a year Finnell claimed success, for all but 900 acres of the area was under control.[14]

However, the success of the Dalhart Project contrasted sharply with the worsening conditions in the southern plains. By the spring of 1935 reports from the five states in the region indicated that more than a demonstration project was needed. F. L. Duley of Mankato, Kansas, complained that dust storms were occurring daily in western Kansas. In Cimarron County, Oklahoma, the wind destroyed 80 percent of the wheat acreage, and similar damage existed in the Texas Panhandle. At Fort Morgan, Colorado, only 25 percent of the cultivated dryland farms escaped serious harm.[15]

In fact, conditions had reached such a bad state that when Finnell called a meeting at Dalhart on March 18, 1935, to discuss the situation, more than six hundred representatives from fifty-one counties of five states attended. At the conference unanimous support was given to a program presented by Finnell which he named the Dalhart Plan for Emergency Wind Erosion Control. He proposed that the federal government furnish funds to protect approximately 3 million acres of denuded wheat land. He suggested that acreage under contract with the Agricultural Adjustment Administration as well as abandoned lands be listed on the contour and seeded in sorghum or a suitable cover crop at the expense of the government, which would impose harvesting and grazing restrictions for one year. As for the remaining cultivated land, the proposal called for the Soil Erosion Service to conduct an educational campaign to encourage farmers to adopt similar practices.[16]

While the Dalhart Plan had merit, the Soil Erosion Service lacked the funds to finance an emergency listing program. Bennett, however, made arrangements with other federal and state agencies to provide assistance. In most states the extension service assumed the responsibility for arranging loans and grants from the Rural Rehabilitation program of the Federal Emergency Relief Administration and the Farm Credit Administration. The New Mexico Emergency Rehabilitation Administration provided gas and oil for farm vehicles, while engineers for the state highway department and irrigation districts laid out contour lines in fields. The New Mexico Extension Service worked with local farmer committees in the preparation of plans. F. A. Anderson of the Colorado Extension Service encouraged the establishment of county erosion district committees consisting of the county agent, the county commissioners, the county relief administrator, the Rural Rehabilitation supervisor, and farmers to take charge of the program. In Oklahoma D. P. Trent, the director of the extension service, obtained $76,400 from the Oklahoma Emergency Relief Administration for fuel plus funds from the Rural Rehabilitation Administration to pay field crews whose labor was overseen by district and county agents of the state extension service. In Kansas a grant of $250,000 from the state relief organization became available for the purchase of fuel by farmers engaged in the listing program.[17]

While the emergency listing undoubtedly alleviated some soil drifting problems, several complaints surfaced on the inadequacy of the temporary effort. Farmers charged that the 10¢-per-acre allotment for fuel fell far below the actual costs. The New Mexico director of extension decried the fact that relief funds were halted when rain showers came even though the moisture was insufficient to have much effect upon the distressed areas. Such dependency upon a variety of agencies and such lack of financial support clearly indicated that these temporary programs were inadequate remedies for achieving a satisfactory cure.[18]

By the spring of 1935 H. H. Bennett and Secretary Wallace had reached the conclusion that the presence of the Soil Erosion Service in the Department of Interior inhibited the agency's ability to do effective work. Upon their recommendation President Roosevelt transferred the Soil Erosion Service to the Department of Agriculture in March 1935, and then Congress enacted Public Law 46 creating the Soil Conservation Service in April.[19]

Conceived as a bureau within the Department of Agriculture that would coordinate a national erosion program, the Soil Conservation Service under Bennett's direction divided the nation into regions and appointed a conservator to act as chief administrator within each area. Originally the bureau chief planned to establish ten regions along state lines. However, when Congressman Marvin Jones, chairman of the House Agriculture Committee and representative from the Texas Panhandle, threatened to use his influence to block appropriations for the agency unless the Dust Bowl area was designated a separate region, Bennett created eleven, placing sixty-seven counties in Colorado, Kansas, New Mexico, Oklahoma, and Texas in Region 6.[20]

In October 1935 H. H. Finnell, whom Bennett selected as conservator for Region 6, opened the headquarters office in Amarillo, Texas. There he assembled a staff assigned to divisions of planning, agronomy, engineering, wildlife management, information, conservation surveys, and forestry. For the next seven years the Amarillo office became the center for implementing the programs of the Soil Conservation Service as well as cooperating with other federal, state, and local agencies in their struggle to curb the immediate and long-range effects of the Dust Bowl.[21]

The policy of operating demonstration projects which had originated under the Soil Erosion Service was continued and expanded in Region 6. By the fall of 1935 work had begun on nine projects, and within two years an additional four units were functioning. Although mixed farming and ranching operations existed on each tract chosen, the emphasis of the erosion control program was divided into two categories: cultivated acreage and grazing lands.

Work at the Hereford, Texas, demonstration project typified the efforts at such other sites as Seward County, Kansas, Guymon, Oklahoma, Clovis, New Mexico, and Stratford, Vega, Dalhart, and Channing in Texas, where crop production provided the primary livelihood. When the Hereford project, which included 31,728 acres in Deaf Smith, Castro, and Parmer counties, began in September 1935, approximately 40 percent of the wheat and sorghum growing area had suffered wind damage. Hummocking had occurred in fields, and drifts had built up along fencerows. In some areas from one to four inches of soil covered the grass. On the essentially flat terrain moisture ran off following heavy rains. With two-thirds of the tract in cultivated acreage, the conservationists started a program for the preservation of moisture by contour listing 3,930 acres and terracing 10,313 acres. Instead of annually planting wheat, cooperating farmers also followed better cropping practices by growing grain and forage sorghums, Sudan grass, and broom corn. On pasture land the technical specialists ran contour furrows and restored the native grass sod. Tree windbreaks were located at strategic points. Within three years after the Hereford project began, most of the soil blowing had ended, wheat yields jumped from 2 bushels to 15 bushels per acre, and choice land that had sold for $8 per acre in 1935 went for $35 per acre in 1938.

Three demonstration projects in Colorado emphasized the restoration of grazing areas. At the Smoky Hill River demonstration area in Cheyenne County, which adjoins the Kansas border, more than four-fifths of the 160,000-acre tract was open range, owned primarily by non-residents who had taken no measures to protect the vegetative cover. In formulating a plan for the project, the Soil Conservation Service specialists sought to achieve controlled grazing as well as to restore the grasses. After erecting fences around 67,815 acres as a means of keeping livestock off the pasture, they constructed contour furrows on 33,493 acres by 1937 to aid in the preservation of moisture for the grass. Two other projects, Cherry Creek and Black Squirrel, which were located at the foothills of the Rocky Mountains near Colorado Springs, included extensive range land where flood waters from the upland slopes had destroyed vegetation. In order to restore the grassland farmers permitted the building of contour furrows and ridges and the planting of 1.5 million trees and shrubs to control gullies, protect dams and ditches, and provide windbreaks.[22]

The presence of enormous sand dunes in the southern Great Plains prompted the Soil Conservation Service to initiate a special research project. Though found in all the Dust Bowl states, the most extensive number of dunes appeared in a line between Curry County, New Mexico, and Seward County, Kansas. Their heavy concentration in Dallam County, Texas, in particular, resulted in the establishment of the Dalhart Substation to the Amarillo Experiment Station in 1936. At that site three separate dunes which had developed as a result of the destruction of surface cover by cultivation or overgrazing ranged from 50 to 880 yards in length, 30 yards in width, and as much as 26 feet in height. Using the wind as the power for reducing the size of the accumulations, scientists installed three types of wind intensifiers—signboards, sandbags, and wind channels. Then they ran dragpoles, disk harrows, and tractor blades over the deposits as a means of loosening the sand to make for easier blowing. After successfully leveling of the largest dunes within two years, the primary work at the substation shifted to the planting of grasses to establish a permanent vegetative cover.[23]

The Soil Conservation Service's efforts in the southern Great Plains were enhanced by the Emergency Conservation Work division of the Civilian Conservation Corps. Assigned to programs formulated and directed by the bureau, CCC camps of approximately 150 men each supplied a significant labor force. Beginning with five camps in Texas in 1935 and nine camps in Colorado two years later, twenty-three CCC units were operating in those two states and in Kansas by 1941.[24]

ECW Camp SCS-14-T at Memphis, Texas, typified the activities of the CCC operations. Opened on July 1, 1935, to serve a 25-mile radius in portions of Hall, Collingsworth, Donley, and Childress counties, the camp assumed the responsibility for controlling damage from both wind and water erosion in an area where cotton was the dominant crop. On cultivated acreage the camp workers aided cooperating farmers by surveying contour lines and laying terraces. They also supplied the labor for running contour furrows, seeding range land, and building stock tanks and dams. In the first year of the Memphis camp's existence, the young men constructed 130 miles of terraces, 1,500 check or silt dams, and 16 stock tanks. They also furrowed 1,500 acres of pasture land and planted twenty miles of trees and shrubs.

Despite the extensive efforts of the Soil Conservation Service and the Civilian Conservation Corps in the Dust Bowl area, President Roosevelt's promotion of the Shelterbelt Project attracted greater attention nationally. Conceived as a method for limiting the force of the wind, the plan called for the planting of strips of tree windbreaks 100 miles in width along the 99th meridian from northern Texas to the Canadian border. With each belt an average of 1/2 mile in length, 132 feet in width, containing from 17 to 21 rows of trees, the program began operation on the H. E. Curtis farm near Mangum in Greer County, Oklahoma, on March 18, 1935.[25]

While under the supervision of the United States Forest Service through the Prairie States Forestry Project headquartered at Lincoln, Nebraska, the Shelterbelt Program depended upon the cooperation of federal and state governmental agencies as well as individual farmers for its implementation. Since Congress refused to appropriate adequate money, the Federal Emergency Relief Administration supplied both direct funding and WPA labor crews. The state extension services oversaw the work and certified the individual landowner's compliance in each county, while the Soil Conservation Service provided technical aid and helped in the selection of suitable locations for the shelterbelt. With landowners expected to furnish the land, fencing materials, and maintenance of the trees, the Farm Credit Administration offered loans to those property holders in need of financial assistance.

With the exception of the eastern Texas Panhandle counties of Childress, Hall, Collingsworth, Wheeler, and Gray, the shelterbelt plantings were located outside Region 6 of the Soil Conservation Service. However, after encouragement from the bureau's officials the Texas director of the Shelterbelt Project in the late 1930s deviated from the original plan and launched an experiment in tree planting on the Texas high plains in the area from Hale County southward to Dawson County.

The cooperative arrangements with the Civilian Conservation Corps and the Forest Service represented only one phase of similar relationships that the Soil Conservation Service maintained with other federal, state, and local agencies. Following the Supreme Court's invalidation of the Agricultural Adjustment Act of 1933, Congress enacted the Soil Conservation and Domestic Allotment Act in February 1936, an amendment to the Soil Conservation Act of 1935. Though designed primarily to distribute funds to farmers, under the guise of encouraging conservation practices by making payments for substituting soil-conserving crops for soil-depleting crops, one portion of the legislation, the Agricultural Conservation Program, did provide for subsidies to landowners who engaged in soil-building practices. Under the plan the federal government paid a maximum of $1 per acre for fallowing, strip cropping, contour listing and furrowing, planting sorghum that would not be harvested, seeding alfalfa, sweet clover, or cowpeas, terracing, and establishing permanent pasture. Since in most states the director of extension served as the chairman of the AAA committee and the county agent acted as the local administrator of the program, the Soil Conservation Service played a secondary role to the extension service by offering technical assistance and aiding farmers in formulating conservation plans so that they might obtain more financial aid.[26]

Of immediate interest to frustrated farmers on the windswept plains in 1936 was the $2 million appropriation for emergency wind erosion control included in the Soil Conservation and Domestic Allotment Act. Conceived and pushed by the Regional Agricultural Council for the southern Great Plains, a body of representatives from federal and state agencies, the scheme paid farmers who furnished their own equipment 20¢ per acre for listing their cultivated land or following other prescribed practices. Where the work had to be hired, 40¢ per acre was paid. Although the plan was administered by the state extension service through the county agents and local farmer committees, the Soil Conservation Service supplied survey personnel, particularly in Texas and New Mexico, where state regulations required listing on the contour. Begun between March 20 and 28, 1936, in all the five states, the project enlisted agricultural operators in 112 counties who protected 15,828,456 acres within 2 years.[27]

While such emergency wind erosion control programs offered temporary relief to farmers in distress, their necessity indicated the lack of a comprehensive effort not only to deal with the immediate problems but also to institute long-range regional plans. Too often the federal and state agencies' efforts were limited in their scope and influence. The demonstration and experiment programs of the Soil Conservation Service as well as the Emergency Conservation Work of the Civilian Conservation Corps and the Shelterbelt Project too frequently affected only those landowners and tenants living within the immediate vicinity of their operation. The assistance offered by the Agricultural Adjustment Administration, the Federal Emergency Relief Administration, and the Farm Credit Administration was geared primarily to the distribution of funds as quickly as possible without much concern for the permanent effects. The state extension services were overwhelmed by administering the large number of federal farm relief measures under their jurisdiction. Consequently, this piecemeal approach offered temporary remedies to combat erosion but practically no planning on an individual basis for the maintenance of a long-term conservation program.

Yet even in the midst of these emergency and temporary efforts wide-range plans evolved. A new dimension was added to the federal and state participation in soil erosion control when the Texas legislature enacted a law in 1935 creating wind erosion control conservation districts. Based on the belief that local citizens could more effectively identify and take action upon their own problems, the legislation authorized residents in nine Panhandle counties to establish districts, with the commissioners' court in each entity acting as the governing body. Powers were granted not only to inaugurate programs to halt blowing dust but also to enter onto any property to correct any erosion problem with or without the consent of owners. To finance the operations of the districts each participating county was permitted to retain 20 percent of the automobile registration fees, any road or bridge taxes, and a portion of its state ad valorem taxes. The significance of this development lay in the ability of the local governing entity to formulate both temporary and long-range plans, to deal directly with every landowner in the district and to make agreements with federal and state agencies.[28]

Almost immediately after the wind erosion districts began operation, their governing boards sought federal assistance. Moore County officials led by Judge Noel McDade went to Washington to request funds to pay impoverished farmers $1.50 per acre for listing and seeding crops. When Department of Agriculture personnel referred the delegation to Finnell in Amarillo, the regional conservator vetoed the proposal because of lack of financial resources. However, Finnell agreed to cooperate with the Moore County board as well as those in other districts in formulating and implementing conservation plans.

Finnell kept his commitment in the spring of 1936 when each county wind erosion conservation district, the Texas Extension Service, and the Soil Conservation Service signed a memorandum of understanding. In the arrangement the Extension Service assigned an assistant county agent to each district and a supervising assistant district extension agent to educate farmers in wind erosion control practices. Besides contributing to the payments of the agents' salaries, the Soil Conservation Service offered such aid as conducting erosion surveys, training the assistant county agents, and providing broad supervision of the work in exchange for approving the personnel and programs. The erosion districts supplied funds for the projects and administered the regulations.[29]

The work needed in the Texas wind erosion districts was enormous. A reconnaissance survey by the Soil Conservation Service in eight of the counties indicated that 2 million acres of wheatland required terracing and that grazing control practices should be instituted on 3.7 million acres. Furthermore, extensive efforts for leveling hummocks and fencerow accumulations, retaining permanent vegetation, seeding grass, and building row crop terraces were also required.

Though much of this suggested work proceeded satisfactorily, tension arose between the Texas Extension Service and the Soil Conservation Service. In December of 1936 Finnell complained to H. H. Bennett that by ordering its personnel not to cooperate with the Soil Conservation Service, the administration of the Texas Extension Service was undermining not only the efforts in the erosion control districts but on other projects as well. A few months later the regional conservator declared that the assistant county agents had failed to support the prescribed programs and indeed had encouraged farmers not to participate. Instead, the agents promoted what Finnell considered to be piecemeal plans, "dissociated entirely from our efforts." Consequently, he recommended that the memorandum of understanding with the districts not be renewed but be replaced with an agreement with the erosion districts whereby Soil Conservation Service staff members would supplant the assistant county agents.[30]

Finnell's irritation and suggested remedy reflected a controversy that had been developing between the Soil Conservation Service and the state extension services not only in Texas but throughout the nation. The trouble began when Congress included in the Soil Conservation Act of 1935 a proposal that soil conservation districts, similar to the Texas wind erosion conservation districts, be established in communities, counties, watershed areas, and similar entities. Since most state extension services had signed memoranda of understanding with the United States Department of Agriculture in 1914 which gave them administrative control of federal farm programs within their borders, the suspicion grew that the Soil Conservation Service was trying to usurp control over conservation work. This appeared even more clearly with the suggestion that the district boundaries not necessarily be contiguous with county lines, which limited the influence of the county extension agents. Jealous of the threat to their power, the state extension service directors organized in opposition to the standard act for the creation of soil conservation districts that Secretary Wallace sent to each state legislature.

Though often bitter fights ensued, the legislatures in the five Dust Bowl states enacted laws similar to the standard act between 1937 and 1939. While only minimal opposition developed in Colorado and Oklahoma, the New Mexico law passed only after Department of Agriculture officials appealed directly to Governor Clyde Tingley. In Kansas the standard act was originally rejected in favor of the creation of soil conservation associations under the control of county farm bureaus. The Texas legislature approved the law after Secretary Wallace threatened not to extend technical assistance to the state.[31]

The organization of the soil conservation districts in most states followed a basic pattern. Twenty-five landowners in a proposed district could petition a state conservation committee consisting of the directors of the state extension service and the experiment station, a representative from the state planning board, the state commissioner of agriculture, and an appointee of the secretary of agriculture to permit a hearing and to call an election. If a majority of the landowners and operators approved, a district committee of two supervisors appointed by the state conservation committee and three supervisors elected locally acted as the governing board. The board had the authority to prepare a general plan to deal with the particular problems of the district and as a governmental entity could more effectively coordinate requests for assistance from state and federal agencies.[32]

In most areas of the Dust Bowl farmers and ranchers readily accepted the soil conservation district idea. For those seriously interested in attempting to control erosion permanently, the concept offered the opportunity for them to make their own decisions and to call upon governmental agencies for aid. The Soil Conservation Service in Region 6 supplied technical assistance and equipment upon the request of the landowners. In some districts the governing boards obtained help from the Civilian Conservation Corps. With thirty-seven Dust Bowl soil conservation districts in operation by 1940, the first major steps toward long-term erosion control had been taken.[33]

While the soil conservation district concept offered the opportunity for every landowner to engage in long-term erosion control, modifications in the Agricultural Adjustment Administration programs encouraged participation. Unlike the Soil Conservation and Domestic Allotment Act, which provided a $1-per-acre incentive for engaging in conservation practices, the Agricultural Adjustment Act of 1938 imposed a penalty of $1 per acre on any cooperator who permitted his soil to blow temporarily and complete withdrawal of all assistance if no attempt was made to correct the condition. Furthermore, the Agricultural Adjustment Administration made an effort to adapt its program to the southern Great Plains by introducing an experimental plan in Sherman County, Texas, and Greeley County, Kansas, in 1939 which placed drought-resistant sorghums in the same category as wheat for making payments. With the adoption of this special arrangement throughout the region the next year, the Agricultural Adjustment Administration strengthened the soil conservation effort.[34]

Further attempts to correct regional erosion on a long-term basis began in 1934, when the federal government instituted a program providing for the acquisition and retirement of submarginal land. Originally administered by the Agricultural Adjustment Administration and the Federal Emergency Relief Administration, the project became the responsibility of the Division of Land Utilization of the Resettlement Administration in 1935. However, with the enactment of the Bankhead-Jones Farm Tenancy Act in 1937, the Bureau of Agricultural Economics, and later the Soil Conservation Service, assumed control of the program.[35]

With several million acres of cultivated and pasture land severely eroded and unproductive, causing farmers and ranchers to face extreme poverty, the southern Great Plains received considerable attention from all the agencies. The plight of rural residents in Morton, Stevens, Meade, and Seward counties, where from 60 to 90 percent of the population depended upon federal relief payments for survival, typified conditions in several portions of the region. In response to the situation the Resettlement Administration established in 1935 the Southwestern Kansas Land Use Adjustment Projects in the four counties, the Southern Otero County Land Adjustment Project in Otero and Las Animas counties in Colorado, and the Mills Land Use Adjustment Project in Harding County, New

Mexico. By 1941 the agencies had acquired 3,592,844 acres in fifteen projects in Region 6.[36]

Upon purchasing the land the federal agencies took steps to restore it to a productive condition. First, families were removed from the farms and ranches and resettled elsewhere. Then work began in revegetating the grassland, returning a portion of the cultivated acreage to pasture, and planting cover crops on the remaining cropland. Once restoration had succeeded and no further threat of erosion remained, the government leased the property to private individuals.

The Bankhead-Jones Farm Tenancy Act through the Farm Security Administration offered even more assistance in the fight to alleviate conditions in the Dust Bowl area permanently. Since by 1938 the Agricultural Adjustment Administration offered aid only to those farmers who attempted to prevent erosion, the Farm Security Administration agreed to make loans for carrying out such control practices as contour tilling and the planting of cover crops, using future AAA payments as collateral.[37]

Officials of the Soil Conservation Service in Region 6 and the Farm Security Administration in Region 12 worked together closely in erosion control efforts. The Soil Conservation Service provided technical assistance for such Farm Security Administration projects as the tenant purchase program and the Ropesville Resettlement Project in Hockley County, Texas. The Farm Security Administration, in turn, required the submission of conservation plans before any operator received a loan. However, of all the cooperative ventures, the implementation of plans for the reorganization of farm units probably had the most significant impact. This was first begun when the Soil Conservation Service specialists in Cheyenne County, Colorado, reached the conclusion that the small size of many farms and ranches inhibited the success of many operators. Arrangements were made so that individuals who already controlled from 320 to 640 acres could obtain long-term leases on an additional one or two sections of land. With the Farm Security Administration financing livestock purchases, improvement expenses, and lease payments, 392 farm and ranch units in western Kansas, eastern Colorado, New Mexico, and Oklahoma were reorganized between 1936 and 1941.[38]

The two agencies, along with the Bureau of Agricultural Economics, also worked together to implement the Pope-Jones Water Facilities Act of 1937. This law, which provided federal assistance for the development of stock ponds, irrigation systems, and wells to permit better land use on farms, called for the Soil Conservation Service to supply general supervision, technical direction, and construction work, while the Farm Security Administration offered financial services. By 1941 there were twenty-one water facility projects benefiting 41,400,630 acres in the five-state area.[39]

By the time the United States entered World War II in 1941, agricultural conditions in the southern Great Plains had improved. Rainfall had returned to normal, and dust storms had declined in frequency. The programs of the federal, state, and local agencies had all made contributions to the control of the most serious erosion and the restoration of prosperity. When Finnell closed the Region 6 headquarters of the Soil Conservation Service at Amarillo on July 1, 1942, he could already observe the long-range impact of his and many others' work. Though several million acres of land that had once faced destruction were again productive and soil conservation districts, which kept a surveillance of potential problem areas, were functioning, the most significant result of the efforts was the widespread adoption of conservation practices by individual farmers and ranchers. Stubble burning and overgrazing declined. Contour listing, strip cropping, and the maintenance of vegetative cover became standard procedures. While residents of the five states of the Dust Bowl would face periodic droughts and dust storms in later years, remembrance of the situation in the 1930s tended to make them more conscious of the need to protect their soil.

C. ROGER LAMBERT

3.

SOUTHWESTERN CATTLEMEN, THE FEDERAL GOVERNMENT, AND THE DEPRESSION

American cattlemen, perhaps more than any other group in twentieth-century America, have prided themselves upon their independence, their ability to stand on their own feet, and their role as the "backbone" of American society. Their way of life, cattlemen insisted, was the last refuge of the old Jeffersonian agrarian virtues; they alone remained pure from the taint of government and governmental supervision. This purity, that independence were never total and suffered their greatest challenge between 1929 and 1939. The Great Depression presented a threat to all of agriculture; cattlemen were not immune. As the New Deal developed financial aid programs, cattle raisers found their independence challenged by their own greed as government programs began putting money into the pockets of other farm groups but not cattlemen. Instead, federal projects for other agricultural commodities raised the prices cattlemen paid for feed and other commodities. The final and perhaps greatest challenge to the cattle industry came from the most disastrous drought in modern American history. Confronted with depression, government activism, and drought, in addition to the traditional survival problems of cattle raising in the arid Southwest, cattlemen experienced a traumatic decade.

And yet, as a seeming contradiction to this independence, the cattlemen depended on government assistance—free or cheap range, help against disease, financial aid—almost as much as most other economic groups in American society.

When speaking of the "cattlemen," the folklore imagery—movie-and television-induced—immediately takes over. We automatically envision the romantic cowboy, lean and white-hatted, riding the open range, chasing half-wild and lean cattle while riding an equally wild but beautiful horse and, perhaps, fighting wild Indians or even more dangerous rustlers. In this concept, the cattle raiser existed on the edge of civilization, immune from the effete East and dependent on government only for occasional police support via the local sheriff or marshall. In reality, as John T. Schelebecker has clearly shown, the basic transition to ranch farming and/or pasture farming was already nearing completion in the 1920s.[1]

Nature and economics with a push from government forced the move to ranch or pasture farming, just as they forced the replacement of the swashbuckling adventurer in the urban business arena. In the more intensive raising operation as it was developing in the twenties, smaller land units were typical as were production of feed crops, emphasis upon better quality livestock, better care of land and cattle, earlier marketing, and more attention to the influence of the rest of society upon the cattle industry. Evidence seemed to prove that the combination of cattle raising and farming brought a higher return on investment and assisted the producer in surviving the ravages of nature and economic difficulties. By the late 1920s old style cattlemen derided the "white-faced bulls and hornless milk cows," the garages "filled with all kinds of cars," the cowboys wearing "bib overalls," and the bungalow "that's got electric lights an' hot and cold water."[2] These changes were symbolic of the transformation, as was the humorous experience of the Texas banker who had always wanted to meet and talk to a real rather than a Hollywood cowboy. In June 1940 he finally saw two in a small hotel in a small town in "remote West Texas. They were just in from the round-up, hankering for a semi-annual haircut, a monthly bath, and a squint at the bright lights." He considered them as authentic as the "smell of a sweating cow pony." He overheard: " 'But you can't desert me Tuesday night, Bill,' " in perfectly good English, " 'that is our regular bridge night—and we are four rubbers down in the tournament.' 'Can't help it,' replied the other, 'I must hear Lily Pons in *Lakme* and Larry Tibbets in *La Traviata*—so I'm flying to Dallas that afternoon—sorry!' "[3] The depression and drought of the 1930s helped complete the transformation of the cattle industry, though it had nothing to do with the interest of cowboys in opera.

Cattlemen experienced most of the same economic stress in the 1920s as other farm operators. Wartime expansion and wartime prices (a peak of $14.50 a hundredweight in 1918) resulted in collapse. By 1922 prices hovered around $6.00, with New Mexico the lowest at $5.00. Added to the prices and the usual problems with nature, cattlemen in the early twenties suffered a drop in their export market and extreme credit difficulties. The mid-twenties proved kinder to the cattle industry, as rain was usually plentiful, prices gradually improved, and the growing urban market increased its demand for beef. More, perhaps, than any other major agricultural commodity, beef had regained prosperity by 1928. Indeed, prices were sufficiently good ($10.95 per hundredweight) and demand sufficiently great that cattlemen tended to clear their herds, even culling their breeding stock.[4]

The favorable situation for livestock growers ended with the coming of the depression. Although livestock prices did not drop as precipitously with the depression as did those of some other farm commodities, they declined steadily and disastrously after 1929. By 1932 the farm price of beef cattle had fallen 50 percent below the 1929 level and continued to drop through 1933. More than the decrease in prices, the disparity between costs and prices exerted a disastrous influence on cattle producers. The disparity was not so great for beef cattle producers as for others, with beef in 1932 maintaining 75 percent of the pre-war purchasing power while pork retained only 42 percent of its exchange value and a bushel of wheat held only 37 percent. This somewhat stronger position permitted the cattlemen to take a more independent stand than other producers as the New Deal farm programs were developed in the winter of 1933-34.

As the New Deal price-raising programs improved the price of feed grains, the cost-price disparity for beef increased. When this was added to the other major problems, the cattle rancher found himself in serious trouble. Reluctant to accept the fact of an urban depression and resistant to falling prices, cattlemen began to hold their cattle as early as 1929 for a market recovery. In the following four years they disposed of steers but retained their female animals, which brought a continued increase in total numbers. By April 1934 cattle numbers reached some 20 percent over 1929, or an increase of 10,650,000 head. The number of breeding cows was the highest on record, and farms and ranges had become heavily overstocked. The increased numbers became increasingly important as drought began to influence range conditions after 1930.[5] Drought not only affected the conditions of the range and the cattle but also brought forced sale of livestock.

A Texas Drought Committee reported in August 1930 that some of the state was experiencing a third year of drought. The Texas drought victims, the committee insisted, "are not mendicants, but are the bone and sinew of the country. They are hardy, resolute and determined. They have withstood the hardships of the last three years with a spirit undaunted." After emphasizing the traditional independent qualities, the committee warned, "Their backs are to the wall. They survived two years of dreadful drought without a murmur, hoping and expecting that the next year would be a fruitful one, and that they might be relieved." That expectation that "next year would be a fruitful one" was not only a typical but almost a universal feeling throughout the drought region. Similar reports on the effects of the drought came from throughout the Southwest in the early thirties.[6] The committee requested mortgage assistance, loans, transportation relief, feed, and work. The drought conditions would build and spread until in early 1933 lack of moisture presented serious problems in the Texas Panhandle, eastern New Mexico, Colorado, and the northern Great Plains. Limited feed and transportation assistance came through the Hoover administration and the Red Cross after 1930. But President Hoover opposed extensive direct federal involvement in drought assistance. He preferred the self-help type of programs and urged that producers help themselves. His administration did urge that the great surplus of wheat (much of it held by the Federal Farm Board) be fed to starving livestock.[7]

Clearly, the Texas Drought Committee, with Hoover, was interested essentially in what was called self-help types of assistance. Among the various self-help measures was the attempt to assist nature to return to normal. The traditional prayer for rain days was common, and some experimented with efforts to make it rain. One Arkansas farm family, remembering the legend that it always rained during battles and perhaps the rainmaking efforts of earlier droughts, attempted their own rainmaking. Apparently in hope that it was the smoke rather than the sound of battle that brought rain, they set fire to the brush and grass. The fire got out of control and burned down the house and barn. It did not rain.

Others sought more limited if not more practical drought assistance. One man sent President Franklin D. Roosevelt $1 and urged that Roosevelt establish a drought aid fund and solicit $1 contributions from all Americans. Others dreamed of canals from the Great Lakes or the Mississippi River to water the drought-plagued plains. Others thought that the new technology might be put to use by having airplanes sprinkle the drought areas. Such starry-eyed dreaming was preferable to the doom sayers, who warned that the drought was punishment from God for one or more of the sins of society.[8] It was not until the Agricultural Adjustment Administration in 1933 and its major farm programs that significant government involvement in drought assistance to the livestock industry developed.

When Congress prepared the Agricultural Adjustment Act, cattlemen, partly because they were still more solvent than many other major farm commodity groups and partly because the spokesman organizations were under the influence of the larger producers, succeeded in keeping livestock off the basic commodity list. This meant that the government possessed limited ability to aid the industry and no real power to exert control over production. Agricultural planners in the Roosevelt administration intended to develop a joint control of production program involving both beef and pork. With beef excluded from the AAA and pork prices reaching disastrous levels, AAA officials developed an Emergency Hog Purchase Program in August 1933. The AAA intended to buy pregnant sows and young pigs to restrict future market supplies and also to provide a form of relief to hog producers. Although hog growers gave limited cooperation to the limitation aspect of the program, they were eager to receive the relief that came with the sale of the young pigs. Immediately cattlemen, especially in the drought-affected state of Texas, demanded similar relief.

Even before the hog purchases began, some Texas ranchers, including Dolph Briscoe, president of the Texas and Southwestern Cattle Raisers' Association, pleaded with Washington that they must now have assistance and admitted that they should have come under the AAA when it was formed. By mid-summer 1933 cattlemen, faced with declining prices, worsening drought, surpluses, and feed problems, began to regret their exclusion from government aid. They were not sure what form the assistance should take, but after the hog buying started cattlemen immediately decided that this was the answer to their surplus problem. With cattle prices continuing to fall—average prices fell from $3.97 per hundredweight in July to $3.61 in September—and feed prices on the rise, Texas cattlemen were ready to forgo some of their independence.[9]

The Northeast Oklahoma Cattlemen's Association joined the Texas ranchers when it complained that cattle prices were $2.00 per hundredweight less than at the same time in 1932 and urged that it was "imperative that something be done at once." The association insisted that federal authorities "devise means of rescuing the industry from the disaster with which it is threatened." To all such pleas the AAA responded with sympathy but reminded the cattlemen that "cattle were eliminated [from the AAA] at the request of livestock men in various parts of the country."[10] Until cattle became a basic commodity, agricultural authorities insisted that they could do little to assist the ranchers with either drought or surplus-price problems.

Drought, falling prices, the lure of what the AAA might be able to do for them, and a few tantalizing bits of aid completed the conversion of cattlemen to acceptance of federal assistance. In the fall and winter of 1933-34 the Federal Surplus Relief Corporation purchased some live cattle and more beef cuts for relief use. The FSRC was a joint creation of the AAA and the Federal Emergency Relief Administration to handle the pork derived from the Emergency Hog Purchase Program. It had power and money from the two parent organizations to buy surplus agricultural commodities for distribution to relief recipients. This beginning of the federal food programs provided a most sensible unity for the problems of surplus farm commodities and hungry unemployed Americans. Ranchers wanted the FSRC to spend all its money on beef. In October the FSRC announced that it would begin buying large numbers of lower grade cattle for relief distribution. This would relieve the overburdened cattle market, and officials anticipated that "heavy purchases largely of she-stock" would reduce the breeding capacity and reduce future market supplies. Some cattle and beef products were purchased, but never in the quantity or at a price to give any major satisfaction to the livestock industry. Complaints and demands for increased assistance continued throughout the fall. Cattle organizations met and insisted that federal action was vital to save the industry.

In November the FSRC developed an experimental project in cooperation with the Texas Rehabilitation and Relief Commission to buy and slaughter live cattle. With half a million dollars Lawrence Westbrook, director of Texas relief, was to purchase cattle and create canning facilities to prepare the beef for relief distribution. Authorized to pay a minimum price of $1.75 per hundredweight, Westbrook bought and canned a little over 22,000 cattle. Texas considered the project a tremendous success; it combined work for the unemployed in the canning plants, food for the hungry, and relief for the cattlemen. The purchases apparently raised prices on cutter cattle as much as $1.25 per hundredweight over the previous price. It gave jobs to over seven thousand out-of-work Texans. The nineteen canning plants provided much valuable experience for the much larger canning operation of 1934. Texas relief officials immediately requested $1 million to continue the operation. Spokesmen for the cattle industry urged that millions be set aside to buy several million surplus cattle. FSRC officials worked on the development of similar operations in a number of other surplus beef states, but funds were not available and this project was not continued.[11]

The Texas purchases were well designed to fulfill the twin objectives of the FSRC—relieving farmers of price-depressing surpluses and providing needed food to the hungry unemployed. Since Roosevelt was determined to give needed assistance to both farmers and the unemployed, the purchase project combined both objectives in a unique and valuable way. This was the immediate conclusion of a number of spokesmen for the Texas cattle industry. While they objected to almost every other agricultural program in operation, cattlemen found no complaint about the Texas experiment. Cynics might assume that this was only because of the direct benefit to their industry, and cattlemen did express a certain selfishness in their demands for federal assistance. Most of them, however, emphasized the more positive and multi-benefit character of the program. While the Texas experiment was not continued, the FSRC continued to purchase livestock and beef products through April 1934. But if these purchases were helpful, they were too low in price and limited in quantity to provide significant relief to the cattle industry. As the cattlemen insisted that they must have real help or their industry would be destroyed, the AAA officials continued to emphasize that "real help" could only come after cattle were made a basic commodity under the Agricultural Adjustment Administration.[12]

There existed fundamental differences between AAA leadership and cattlemen as to the character of assistance needed by the industry. AAA planners were convinced that the livestock industry just like other major commodities was in a serious surplus condition which required significant reduction and then restriction of production. Cattlemen believed that the problems of the industry were only the normal and temporary ones caused by climate disturbances, low prices, and high feed costs. They continued to deny surplus production and blamed processors and the distribution system for their distressed situation.[13]

In the winter of 1933 hundreds of cattlemen met in West Texas gatherings to demand federal action. They suggested massive purchase programs, the spaying of heifers to limit future output, restrictions on imports, and greater credit facilities. Most still preferred some form of relief rather than AAA production control, but in December the Panhandle Livestock Association declared that cattle should become a basic commodity. In January the American National Livestock Association met in Albuquerque, New Mexico, and, while the Texas representatives (forty out of forty-five) wanted cattle to come under the AAA, the delegates did not take a position on the issue. The convention did agree to permit a Committee of Five to work with Washington and take the action necessary to "secure to the industry the relief desired." The cattlemen wanted relief without a processing tax and with minimum controls. With the drought increasing its influence, the committee agreed to support making cattle a basic commodity. Representative Marvin Jones and Senator Tom Connally, both from Texas, led the movement to make cattle a basic commodity; they came under the AAA in the Jones-Connally Act of early April 1934.

Although that step was taken, the disagreement on the character of a federal program continued. The Jones-Connally Act had provided $50 million to purchase diseased cattle and for relief purchases. The major sum provided in the act, $200 million, required cooperation in production control and repayment through the processing tax. After prolonged and often less than harmonious discussions, the cattlemen and the AAA planners reached near agreement on a production control-relief plan for the livestock industry. Before any program could be implemented, the drought forced development of a vast emergency relief assistance program.

The AAA leadership expected that the emergency project could be used as the first step in a control of surplus program.[14] Before the year ended, the drought would eliminate more cattle than either the AAA or the producers had wanted, and it would also give victory to the livestock industry over the AAA planners.

The 1934 drought was the most devastating in American history. Building for five years, it struck in the late spring of 1934 with unprecedented fury. With exceptionally high temperatures added to precipitation as much as 50 percent below normal for Texas from June through August, the cattlemen faced disaster. Throughout the Southwest streams and ponds went dry, wells had to be redug, fish were reported dying in the overheated low water, and the water table fell by as much as seven feet in the Texas Panhandle. Low production of feed crops over the previous year or two meant that cattlemen had virtually no access to supplies of feed. Soon stockmen were feeding Russian thistle, prickly pear, and then soap weed. Before fall two-thirds of the country in twenty-four states, virtually the whole area west of the Mississippi River, suffered sufficiently from the drought to be classed as emergency and receive federal drought aid.

Drought relief involved a vast array of measures designed to give immediate relief, to preserve basic foundation herds for the future, and to bring long-term reformation of land use in the semiarid region. The most impressive and, for the time, most important of the immediate relief measures was the purchase of cattle suffering from the effects of drought. Although leaders had anticipated some form of surplus removal of cattle for months, and the brief experimental program in Texas served as precedent, putting together the machinery to buy and handle some 8.3 million cattle plus lesser numbers of sheep and goats was a monumental task. The first public mention of a drought purchase came in early May; by the end of May the Drought Relief Service was in operation and had started buying cattle.

As the emergency buying started, AAA officials anticipated that it would constitute the surplus removal phase of the livestock control program. They talked of buying around 3 million cattle, and the seller was required to sign an agreement which required his participation in the future production control program. Officials seemed to anticipate difficulty in getting cattle owners to participate in either the purchase or the control program. As the drought area expanded and as owners proved eager instead of reluctant to sell their stock, it became necessary to revise the earlier projections.[15]

One of the most controversial elements in the original purchase was the Emergency Cattle Agreement, which required the seller to participate in future adjustment programs. Although the administration defended the contract on the basis that it permitted the guarantee of some money going to the debtor cattlemen, many cattlemen saw it as coercion or "usurpation of authority." Payment for the drought cattle was divided into two parts, benefit payment and purchase payment, with a benefit portion reserved for the raiser, and with the creditor able to take the purchase portion. Officials argued a benefit payment was the only way to guarantee the grower some money and it could only be made with the signing of the agreement. After the controversy they found ways in the sheep and goat purchases to reserve part of the cash for the producer. In reality, officials required the agreement as a way to ensure future cooperation in a control program. They could not be sure how many surplus cattle would be removed by the emergency purchase, and they felt certain that a production control measure would be required. Faced with charges of "duress" and with far greater than expected purchases, AAA leaders began to retreat in July by reducing the pledge to two years and early in 1935 pledging that no control program would ever be put into effect without producers giving their approval to it.[16]

When buying started, the AAA saw it as a helpful method of surplus removal; this attitude changed quickly. At the beginning of June officials anticipated buying at the rate of 50,000 cattle a week for a total of around 3 to 5 million. The last week in June saw the purchase of 262,009 head, and mid-August purchases were close to 600,000 head per week. In late June E. W. Sheets, head of the Drought Relief Service, which was responsible for the buying, privately suggested the possibility of the government buying up to 8 million cattle. Although the Federal Surplus Relief Corporation officials, responsible for handling the cattle, felt Sheets was trying to frighten and hurry the FSRC processing, other leaders feared by August that the government might be forced to buy 14 million cattle.[17] The whole emphasis of the publicity on the purchases changed.

Spokesmen were instructed to drop all discussion of surplus removal and to emphasize that the purchases were designed to provide relief to cattlemen and to save the industry from total disaster. AAA officials now talked about saving the foundation herds, adjusting cattle numbers to available feed supplies, and preserving food for the needy. As protests about the purchases grew, agricultural leaders began to emphasize that the purchases were also designed to preserve the total amount of beef.[18] Although the AAA would later seek to develop an adjustment program for the livestock industry, officials found it vital to divorce the purchases from the adjustment efforts.

The Drought Relief Service established a rather complex organization to handle the purchase program. At the national level the DRS, headed until August by Sheets, supervised the buying. State directors in each drought state handled the project. As buying was begun in a county, local committees working with inspectors from the Bureau of Animal Industries handled the actual buying on the farm. The local committee determined price, which was based on condition and age and ranged from $1 to $14 for purchase and from $3 to $6 as benefit payment. The BAI inspector determined whether the animals were fit for human consumption. Those cattle found edible were turned over to the FSRC, which operated a variety of programs to provide the livestock for relief use. The animals condemned as unfit for use were disposed of on the farm—usually shot and buried. Even these animals—diseased and emaciated as they were—could be used by the owners and in some localities relievers for food purposes.[19]

Over 6,200,000 cattle were preserved for food purposes; without the purchase many of these would have died and most of the others would have gone on the regular market, thus further depressing prices. Three and one-half million were processed for relief use by private processors under contract from the FSRC. Some 2,700,000 head were turned over to the state relief agencies, which contracted with private processors to handle some of the cattle and used relief canneries to preserve the rest. In Texas, which had a head start because of the late 1933 program, the relief canneries handled some 420,000 cattle. The canneries employed some 30,000 unemployed Texans and produced around 50 million cans of beef for relief use. As the purchase program developed, neighboring states came to Texas to learn how to operate their own canneries. The FSRC hoped to use some of the cattle it received in a rehabilitation type of program supplying improved stock to some of the low income farmers of the South in particular. Ranchers and agricultural officials opposed this form of relief on the basis that it would create competition and that the AAA had promised that the cattle purchased would not reenter normal trade channels. Thus, the redistribution of the emergency cattle was very limited.[20] Without question, the relief use of the drought livestock was of tremendous value.

For southwestern cattlemen the most important element in the purchase program was the removal of weak and all but worthless livestock at a price equal to or better than the prevailing market price. Although some Texans insisted that it violated their principles to accept this kind of government aid and some apparently refused to sell to the DRS, the response from throughout the Southwest proved that in time of crisis most southwesterners were willing to forgo some of their independence.[21] Although the five southwestern states had only 13.4 million of the 67 million cattle total in the country, they sold more than 3.5 million out of the 8.3 million purchased by the government. A major reason for this, of course, was the extent of the drought in the area, as over a major part of the region less than one-fourth of the normal feed supplies was produced in 1934. Too, the purchase program was in full operation as the drought exerted its worst effects in the Southwest. Some of the other areas had been hit earlier and had already weeded out their herds.

In spite of the major assistance given to the Southwest, its people protested violently when the DRS sought to restrict and then end federal purchases. In August, as buying reached a frantic pace and some federal officials grew alarmed with predictions of 14 million cattle or more to be bought, the AAA changed focus in a major way. A total restructuring of the relief program came, with the major emphasis shifted to preservation of foundation herds, provision of feed, and long-term reformation of agriculture in the plains states. As federal officials announced that buying would be curtailed and then ended, producers quickly protested that they must be permitted to sell their stock. The protests came from throughout the Southwest and the mountain states, but Texans predominated. In August the AAA created the Federal Livestock Feed Agency in Kansas City to coordinate feed supplies throughout the drought area at "equitable prices." At the same time a Drought Plans Committee was created to supervise and limit drought purchases. Emphasis was now placed on preservation of foundation herds through the provision of feed loans to stock owners. Ranchers argued that cattle were not worth the feed it would take to keep them alive. Jay Taylor, president of the Panhandle Livestock Association, warned that as many as 3 to 4 million cattle would die if purchases were ended. While many of the protests came from individual stock owners, the most effective action came through the larger owners and the livestock associations. Taylor and Grover B. Hill, officer of the Panhandle Association and AAA director of cattle purchases for that area, led in organizing cattlemen in the West Texas and New Mexico region. The cattlemen sent a delegation made up of Hill, Taylor, and others to Washington. After recruiting Texas representative Marvin Jones, chairman of the House Agriculture Committee, they warned the AAA that federal refusal to continue purchases could doom the livestock industry to the loss of millions of cattle. The AAA was sympathetic but insisted that money was all but exhausted and buying would have to end. The cattlemen then went to Secretary of Agriculture Henry Wallace, who was also sympathetic but refused to commit the government to continue buying and pointed out that Texans had received more than their share of relief money. The decision now became political, and the government agreed to continue buying. Purchasing was extended for three months, but owners did not sell.[22]

The demand for continued buying was essentially the determination of the cattlemen to have the government to fall back on in case of need.

The relationship had been somewhat reversed by the late summer of 1934. Now the AAA, which had sought to get cattlemen under the wing, was insisting that cattlemen should stand on their own feet. The Livestock Feed Committee warned that stockmen would depend on the government as long as the DRS continued to buy. The one-time independent cattlemen now pleaded and even demanded that the government continue to protect them. When it started to rain over some of the drought region and cattle prices improved, cattlemen either decided not to sell or sold their cattle to speculators rather than to the government.[23] This standoff continued until the AAA sought to develop a control program and the cattlemen felt they no longer needed the government.

Early in 1935 the AAA developed a production control program which involved beef, pork, and feed grains. It would require a processing tax on both beef and pork to finance a reduction in the production of grain. This was essentially what the AAA had wanted to do in the spring of 1933 when the beef producers refused to come into the AAA. Now that cattlemen were on the basic commodity list, the opportunity for a joint program had come. Beef producers responded immediately. A cattleman delegation, with Grover B. Hill, the Panhandle leader, on it, met with the AAA. They were united in their opposition to the grain reduction plan and to the processing tax. Texas opponents to the program insisted that there was no longer a beef surplus and that cattlemen should not be penalized for the problems of the pork producers. In March Congressman Jones insisted that the grain control program would violate the promise made to cattlemen that they would not be hit with a processing tax without their approval. Cattlemen insisted that the government could help them with tariff protection, easier credit, and similar supports. When the Southwestern Cattle Raisers Association held its annual convention in mid-March, it expressed strong approval of the Emergency Cattle Purchase Program but strongly opposed participation in the control program. By the fall of 1935 the AAA was ready to admit defeat. Gerald B. Thorne, head of the AAA Livestock Division, admitted that enough cattlemen were opposed to the program to prevent adequate participation. Although cattlemen had promised to participate in some control program, the government was not willing to attempt to force their cooperation. Having received the desired relief for their industry, cattlemen now thought they were ready to return to their vaunted independence. The reality of that independence would be somewhat tarnished, as the government participated in assistance programs more actively than ever.

Cattlemen seemed to have escaped dependence on government and even took pride in their ability to take advantage of federal relief without having to pay for it. Officials were somewhat surprised that some southwestern counties sold more cattle under the purchase program than the census said existed in the county. Some Texas ranchers apparently used the purchase to rid themselves of their low grade stock, and then purchased better breeding stock to reestablish their foundation herds.[24] In reality, federal assistance continued throughout the depression thirties and later.

Even before the entry of cattle into the AAA, the Department of Agriculture had expanded some of its traditional activities such as the anti-tick program. With the alarm about excessive buying and the reorganization of the livestock structure in August 1934, great emphasis was placed upon conservation of feed and reformation of the agricultural use of the Plains. With the extreme shortage of feed supplies agriculture officials took a number of steps during the summer and fall of 1934 to increase supplies for the winter. In addition to movement of cattle to pasturage in non-drought states, AAA officials quickly moved to open curtailed acreage to production of feed crops. It was estimated that almost 2½ million tons of hay and forage were produced on contracted acreage. AAA officials also contracted with corn belt states to harvest and bale over 76 million tons of corn fodder and corn stover which normally would not have been preserved. On the same basis some 30,000 tons of soy bean hay was contracted in Illinois. Surplus sugar cane from Puerto Rico and the Philippines were used for molasses. Agricultural officials encouraged drought area producers to substitute molasses for the scarce feed grains, and they estimated that some 10 million gallons went into the drought region.[25] Without a doubt, the feed loans and the special efforts to preserve and produce more livestock feed certainly enhanced the chances of survival for those cattle left in the Southwest.

Drought continued to influence the Southwest through the thirties as the wind began to raise the great dust storms on the denuded southern Plains in 1935. A major feeding effort was again required, and there was even consideration of another cattle purchase. In 1936 dust continued to swirl, and the government did engage in a very small and unpublicized purchase program. These activities remained much in the nature of emergency, as was true of the Civilian Conservation Corps, Works Progress Administration, and other work projects. The various work relief agencies put their people to work digging wells, building farm ponds, and helping farmers with conservation activities as well as road building and the normal relief projects. There was a major effort starting in 1934 to supply work relief in the rural areas as a partial answer to the drought.[26]

The idea of providing some kind of long-term remedy for agriculture in the semiarid plains of the Southwest developed early in the drought. The major effort here would be in the area of conservation, but there was also a movement to regional planning. The Soil Erosion Service—which in 1935 became the Soil Conservation Service of the Department of Agriculture—received $5 million dollars from emergency funds in August 1933 to develop conservation programs. It used the money to establish demonstration projects—the first just east of Dalhart, Texas. By October 1934 some 30,000 acres were in the demonstration project, and quickly similar projects were established in all the southwestern states, with several projects operating in the Texas Panhandle. Too, the conservation people were concerned with reseeding the bare soil and began in the mid-thirties collecting grass seeds, particularly of some of the native grasses which had successfully held the soil in place before the farmers and ranchers destroyed the native sod. In July 1936 the conservation people reported that they had collected almost "800,000 pounds of the native grass seeds" and that they had developed a "vacuum cleaner type of stripper" for the collection.[27] These efforts were admirable, but their success was somewhat limited, and the Russian thistle may have been more valuable for holding the worst blown of the soil.

From cattlemen the conservation people wanted the obvious. Cattlemen had contributed to the Dust Bowl through overgrazing. While they wanted less farming and more cattle raising, conservation leaders wanted ranchers to rotate pastures and to restrict the number of cattle carried on each unit of land. They also urged terracing and wind-breaking activities. President Roosevelt led in the shelterbelt idea. He also contributed to the idea of water on every farm. In a memorandum he listed five things that the drought and dust-stricken state of Oklahoma needed and suggested that it might be a good idea "for our people to start the slogan: 'A Pond for Every Farmer.'"[28] Throughout the last half of the decade and into the late 1970s, the government would sponsor cattlemen in reseeding their bare lands, building ponds or tanks, terracing, clearing mesquite or cedar lands, rotating pasture, reducing the stock carried per section, and many other similar conservation works.

Closely connected to the conservation movement but with an even broader objective was the establishment of the Great Plains Committee. After several devastating years of drought Roosevelt created in July 1936 this committee to study and recommend a master plan for the semiarid region. He made it clear that he did not want, as many people feared he did, to make the region into an essentially government-owned, semi-depopulated region. In August the committee met in Amarillo and then in other regions of the Dust Bowl. In its report the group made the expectable conclusions. Much of the region should never have been plowed—this was particularly true in the sandy soil of the Southwest. Much of the farmland should be turned back to grazing land. The states should establish soil conservation legislation, which Texas had already done. Local areas should create soil conservation districts which would have some power to supervise land use. The committee suggested that depopulation had already started and would almost certainly continue. While much that the conservationists and the Great Plains Committee recommended was only haphazardly implemented, their projects have continued to serve as a lure to cattlemen in obtaining federal funding without losing much of their independence. Perhaps, like many other groups in American society, cattlemen have been able to convince themselves that these forms of aid are only the due of the industry that is the "backbone and sinew" of the nation.[29]

The continued desire and need for federal assistance would be expressed through the thirties. At the Presidential Drought Conference for Oklahoma on September 3, 1936, Governor E. W. Marland pointed out that after the "longest and hottest spell we ever experienced" Oklahoma farmers "have no feed for their cattle or stock and nothing for their families." Malcolm Miller, relief representative, reported that temperatures had ranged between 100 and 120 in July. The state received only a quarter of normal rain in July and about one-tenth in August. The Governor estimated that up to 100,000 farm families needed to go on relief. Congressman Wesley Disney insisted that "immediate supplies of food for people and livestock [are] imperative."[30] A similar request for assistance came in 1939 from Representative Richard M. Kleberg, Texas congressman of the King Ranch, who had opposed the Jones-Connally Act. A spokesman for the White House pointed out that the Division of Feed and Seed Loans of the Farm Credit Administration was making crop and feed loans. The Federal Surplus Commodities Corporation, which had replaced the FSRC, supplied food. The Works Projects Administration was ready to expand its relief workforce, and the Farm Security Administration had its rehabilitation loans available.[31]

In the next great drought of the Southwest, in the 1950s, a similar attitude can be found. After paying some attention to the advice of the conservationists in the late thirties, the semiarid area farmers and ranchers threw it all aside in the 1940s. In World War 2 the region experienced an unfortunate combination like that of the first World War—a tremendous demand for all that could be produced and relatively high precipitation rate. To meet the wartime needs ranchers and farmers expanded to the limit of their productivity. By 1945 the Soil Conservation Service warned about the bad effects of the war. But farmers and ranchers ceased the conservation efforts. As a consequence, there were again signs of a renewal of the dust storms. At a West Texas water conference in 1948 it was emphasized that water was the great issue for West Texas. The 2½ million people of West Texas and the 5 million head of livestock once again faced drought and water shortages. By 1952 a major drought covered virtually all the Southwest. Ranchers demanded the same kinds of assistance they had received in the thirties. They wanted massive purchase programs with loans, feed, and transportation aid.[32]

Depression, drought, and government activism changed cattle raising in the Southwest. The depression seemed most seriously to effect, in rare cases even destroy, both the smaller and the larger producers. Those with medium sized operations who combined feed production with cattle raising seemed to survive best. Although there was an increase in the average size of cattle farms, the drought brought a significant reduction of cattle. The cattle population in 1940 was down across the nation by some 1½ million, but in the states of the Southwest by some 2 million. Non-drought states had increased their numbers of stocker cattle, which meant that they had less dependence on the Southwest for their feeder calves. Drought also brought an increase in the production of feed crops such as sorghum, and, influenced by conservationists, it brought better pasture management. Government activism saved the cattle industry, but it also created a continuing relationship between cattlemen and government. While the cattlemen escaped from the adjustment programs, they received subsidies through the conservation programs which helped to maintain the dependence of cattlemen. After 1940 cattlemen still talked about their independence and their serving as the "bone and sinew" of the traditional values, but it was a tainted independence. Some still expressed their preference that cattlemen would not take subsidies from the government, but it was with the knowledge that their numbers were fewer than ever before.[33]

BILL C. MALONE

4.

COUNTRY MUSIC
IN THE DEPRESSION SOUTHWEST

When hard times descended upon the nation in 1930, hillbilly music had completed about ten years of commercial evolution. Despite the all-encompassing and pejorative nature of the term "hillbilly"[1] —a term coined and applied by outsiders—the music contained many styles and was a product of the rural folk South. The emergence of the radio and recording industries in the early twenties had permitted rural balladeers, fiddlers, banjoists, and string bands to present what had been local art forms to an ever widening audience. Most performers had never succeeded sufficiently to free themselves totally from farming or wage labor, but the success, or wide reputation, of a few entertainers such as the Carter Family, Vernon Dalhart, and Jimmie Rodgers inspired thousands of people to try their hands at professional music.

From the very beginning of its commercial development in the early twenties, southwestern musicians had made vital contributions to the genre. The first documented recordings by a white folk performer were those of Eck Robertson, a fiddler from Amarillo in 1922. Carl Sprague, from Alvin, Texas, recorded the first cowboy songs in 1925; and Vernon Dalhart (Marion T. Slaughter), from Jefferson, Texas, recorded the first hillbilly "hit," "The Prisoner's Song," in 1924.[2] During the thirties, as the music business underwent profound transformations, the percentage of Southwestern musicians on radio and recordings increased significantly.[3] The thirties were a transitional decade for country music, a time of innovation and change marked by growing dissemination when the music began to move away from its rural moorings. Although southwestern musicians played crucial roles in both the popularization and modification of country music, the music of the region still showed evidence of its folk origins and of its rural past.

No region of the United States was more strategically situated than the Southwest to demonstrate the interplay between tradition and modernity. Southerners, both black and white, had comprised the bulk of original migrants into the region from the older states, and the Southwest in the thirties still demonstrated the legacy of its Confederate past. A few old ex-soldiers could still evoke memories of the Lost Cause, and politicians in Texas and Oklahoma generally aligned themselves with their brethren in the southern states. The music of the region was heavily indebted to the folklore of the eastern states. Many of the venerable British ballads and lovesongs survived the westward migration, and the camp meetings and the religious singing schools, where the shape-note teachers held sway, were as strongly cherished in the Southwest as in the Southeast. The fiddle was the king of folk instruments, and everywhere the house party—a neighborhood dance held in a private home—prevailed as the most important social diversion in villages and farm communities. While the white rural music of the Southwest was basically "British"-derived, it had borrowed heavily from the music of southern blacks, and it would continue to draw sustenance from other ethnic groups with whom "Anglos" came in contact. By 1930 white rural musicians in Texas had had ample opportunities to hear the music of Cajun performers as they moved with their compatriots into the southeastern part of the state in the triangle defined by Beaumont, Port Arthur, and Houston. In the region below Austin little enclaves of German, Polish, and Czech settlers, along with a much larger contingent of Mexican residents, contributed songs, dance tunes, and instrumental styles which often moved into the music of the surrounding Anglo groups.

The Southwest was a region, significantly, where the culture of the South came in contact with the ethos of the cowboy, and where Anglos mixed their music with that of the ethnic groups who lived near them. And in the thirties, when the oil boom marked Louisiana, Oklahoma, and Texas off from their sister southern states, pointing the way toward their future industrial progress, the region still clung tightly to its rural and agricultural ways. Tenantry still enthralled thousands of its farmers,[4] and agricultural habits remained close to what they had been one hundred years before.

Many rural southwesterners grew up reading and clipping old songs printed on the "Young People's Page" of the *Dallas Semi-Weekly Farm News*,[5] and radio listeners during the thirties could still hear echoes of the South's oldest ballad and string band music. There has been such a resurgence of interest today in Western Swing, and such a cult surrounding Bob Wills and his music, that it is often forgotten that Texans knew and loved many other forms of folk music which could be heard frequently during the thirties. Walter "Peg" Moreland, a one-legged balladeer who was called the "king of the ditty singers," knew thousands of songs (such as "Stay in the Wagon Yard" and "Abdul Abulbul Amir") which he sang for years over WFAA in Dallas. Cecil Gill, the "Yodeling Country Boy," made almost no recordings but was a regular fixture for twenty years on such Fort Worth radio stations as WBAP, KFJZ, and KXOL (a total of 6,448 live fifteen-minute broadcasts).[6] Day after day, accompanied only by his guitar, Gill sang and yodeled Jimmie Rodgers's songs and old-time sentimental songs such as "Picture on the Wall." The Herrington Trio, from Wichita Falls, Texas, also specialized in the sentimental parlor songs of the nineteenth century, and could often be heard on late night radio shows singing such songs as "Give My Love to Nellie, Jack" and "The East Bound Train." Cowboy singers abounded on radio stations all over the Southwest during the thirties, and listeners could hear singers such as Cowboy Slim Rinehart, Texas Jim Robertson, Red River Dave McEnery, Jules Verne Allen, Marc Williams, Gene Autry, and Tex Ritter who sang both the old-time cowboy songs and newer ones emanating from the Silver Screen. Gospel singers were also plentiful throughout the region, but the two most important groups were the Chuck Wagon Gang in Forth Worth (D. P. Carter with his children Ernest, Anna, and Rose) and the Stamps Quartet in Dallas. Singing to the accompaniment of a guitar, the Chuck Wagon Gang, who originated in Lubbock, represented the country tradition of gospel singing, while the Stamps Quartet, founded by Virgil O. Stamps from Gilmer, was a product of the shape-note publishing house experience.

Southwestern country music fans were particularly fortunate in that Jimmie Rodgers, the legendary Blue Yodeler from Mississippi, and acknowledged now as the "father of country music," lived in Texas from 1929 to 1933.[7] In May 1929 he moved into a $50,000 home in Kerrville called Blue Yodeler's Paradise, but was living in a much more modest home in San Antonio at the time of his death from tuberculosis on May 26, 1933. Rodgers appeared on vaudeville bills in towns and cities throughout the region, and was the headliner on such tent repertoire shows as those headed by Paul English, Leslie Kell, and J. Doug Morgan.[8] Rodgers definitely identified with Texas, and he recorded several songs, such as "The Yodeling Ranger" and "Land of My Boyhood Dreams," which illustrated his romantic fascination with his adopted homeland. Southwesterners had closer first-hand acquaintance with the Singing Brakeman (as Rodgers was also called because of his former occupation as a railroad man) than people in any other part of the country, and several people who later became professional musicians, such as Floyd Tillman,[9] actually saw him in concert. Several prominent southwestern singers—like Ernest Tubb, Tommy Duncan, Jim Reeves, and Lefty Frizzell—have acknowledged the direct influence of Rodgers on their own careers, while others, such as Gene Autry and Jimmie Davis, clearly profited professionally because of their ability to sing Rodger's songs and yodel in a fashion similar to his. Most people knew Jimmie Rodgers only through his recordings, and he was, in fact, one of the few recording artists of twenties origin who survived and prospered during the hard times of the thirties.

While the recording industry was forced to make serious adjustments in order to survive the depression, radio was entering its heyday. Even the most humble family could generally afford to buy a battery-powered radio, and sitting around the family parlor listening to radio broadcasts was, along with the movies, one of the few inexpensive social diversions available to Americans. President Roosevelt demonstrated the political utility of the medium with his fireside chats, and many people clung to his messages and to the news reports and market dispatches for hopeful signs that the economy was improving. Beyond its usefulness as a source of rapid information, the radio was a constant companion and the least expensive form of entertainment available. Millions of Americans found escape in the soap operas, variety shows, comedies and dramas, and musical shows. People were introduced to music they had never heard before, and in fact could not have heard under any other circumstances. The big bands were popularized through radio broadcasts, and popular crooners found the radio microphone to be an effective and intimate device for circulating their art.[10]

Country music made its first penetration into a national market through the medium of radio broadcasts. Southwestern listeners could easily hear the broadcasts of the major hillbilly barn dances over the 50,000-watt stations WLS in Chicago and WSM in Nashville, and the program popularized over the latter station, the Grand Ole Opry, became a fixture in national entertainment after 1939 when it gained network status on NBC.[11] Closer to home, southwestern listeners could hear local barn dances, or continuing radio series with a rural flavor, on their own stations or ones in contiguous areas. Typical of such shows was the Saddle Mountain Roundup, broadcast over KVOO in Tulsa in the late thirties. The program never gained the status of the Grand Ole Opry, but it was regionally popular and it provided an attractive format for many performers who had already attained popularity elsewhere, or who would soon achieve national reputations. "Cousin" Herald Goodman, one of the mainstays of the show, had earlier been a member of the Grand Ole Opry, and part of a smooth-singing trio called the Vagabonds (best known for "Lamp Lighting Time in the Valley"). KWKH in Shreveport, like most radio stations with wide coverage, periodically attracted singers and musicians from other areas, such as the Shelton Brothers (Bob and Joe) from Texas, and fiddling Curley Fox from Tennessee.[12]

Hillbilly entertainers in the thirties were a migratory breed who moved from radio station to radio station, often in widely scattered sections of the country. This movement gives testimony to the pervasive influence of the radio as a formative device in the shaping and development of country music. Musicians, in fact, generally felt that radio exposure was more important for their careers than was recording. Consequently, a singer or musician sought a regular spot (often without pay) and then tried to establish himself as a favorite in the territory blanketed by the radio station. Personal appearances were usually arranged by the singer himself and were determined by the amount and origin of correspondence received from listeners. Performers usually posted their own placards or distributed their own handbills, traveled by automobile with their bass fiddle strapped on the top, gave a show in a schoolhouse or movie theatre ("the kerosene circuit") often without benefit of an amplification system, hawked their pictures and songbooks, and then left hurriedly at the end of the show in order to make it back to the station in time for their early morning radio program. It was a dangerous, unglamorous life, and usually economically unrewarding except for a few performers who sold large quantities of picture-song books.

The leading promoter of country music in the Southwest during the thirties was Gus Foster ("Uncle Gus"). Foster was unusual in that he promoted talent, accompanied it to new locations, and then served as announcer and master-of-ceremonies for personal appearances. He moved with a group of entertainers from North Carolina to Tulsa, and then down to KRLD in Dallas right at the end of the thirties. Uncle Gus was a dapper, dark-haired man with a mustache who, according to his musical contemporaries, "could sell anything." Like so many of the colorful radio personalities of his era, Foster was as popular with the listeners as the musicians were, and his photograph appeared prominently in the brochures and songbooks. He also introduced a large number of southeastern entertainers to the southwestern public. A North Carolina duo, Homer and Walter Callahan (better known as Bill and Joe),[13] came to KRLD with a group called the Blue Ridge Mountain Folk, which included two former members of the Coon Creek Girls, Daisy Lange and Violet Koehler, and eventually some of the finest musicians in the entire field of country music, fiddlers Georgia Slim Rutland and Howard "Howdy" Forrester, and mandolinist Paul Buskirk.

As important as KRLD, KVOO, KWKH, and other southwestern stations may have been, none of them could equal the power of that possessed by the Mexican border stations, popularly called X-stations because of their call letters. Located in cities near the Texas border, and with their transmitters aimed at the United States, these stations were Mexican-owned but were often leased to American businessmen who used them to hawk their products in the United States. In 1932 Dr. J. R. Brinkley, the goat gland man, became the first of the X-station entrepreneurs when he leased station XER (later XERA) in Villa Acuna across from Del Rio. Brinkley had earlier owned a station in Milford, Kansas, where he promoted his hospital and his pet nostrum, the transplantation of goat glands in order to restore male sexual potency. Brinkley became a real power in Kansas, almost winning the governorship in 1930, but his medical and radio licenses were revoked and he transferred his operations to Texas. With a power sometimes exceeding 100,000 watts XERA transmitted its broadcasts all over the United States and Canada. Brinkley gave his medical spiel and sold his books; evangelists preached their sermons; businessmen hawked their merchandise; politicians made their exhortations; and gospel and hillbilly musicians circulated their southern-derived music to all corners of the United States. Beginning in the late thirties, XERA (which became XERF) and similar stations such as XEPN, XELO, and XEG ("the Voice of North America") featured a steady stream of folk musicians whose programs were carried primarily by transcription. The Carter Family (A. P., his wife Sara, and sister-in-law Maybelle) came down from the Clinch Mountains of Virginia with their old-time style of music to XERA, where they performed from 1938 to 1941. Each evening at about 9:30 listeners could hear the familiar opening strains of Maybelle Carter's thumb-style guitar playing and the Carter theme, "Keep on the Sunny Side."[14] On various evenings listeners could also hear such performers as Cowboy Slim Rinehart, J. R. Hall (the Utah Cowboy), Jesse Rodgers (Jimmie's cousin), the Pickard Family, the Stamps Quartet, or the Callahan Brothers. The interminable advertising (for patent medicines, baby chicks, prayer cloths, "autographed pictures of Jesus Christ," etc.) was almost too much to bear, but the patient listener could be sure of hearing much of the best in traditional country and gospel music.

Annoying or not, advertising was something the hillbilly fan had to get accustomed to, for the art had become firmly associated with country music during the thirties. Homespun humor and music were everywhere employed to promote business interests, and a Texas product, Crazy Water Crystals, was in the forefront of this fusion between commerce and music. The Crazy Water Crystals Company of Mineral Wells, Texas, began sponsoring radio shows in 1934 on a local basis but soon expanded into markets throughout the nation. Crazy Water Crystals were sold in packages, and when dissolved in water and consumed, would cure, according to the makers, almost every ailment known to man. Actually, the product was nothing more than a laxative, but it made its way into homes throughout the United States by means of radio advertising. Crazy Water Crystals became associated with all types of popular music programming, but it was most closely identified with country music. In the two Carolinas and Georgia Crazy Water Crystals sponsored a large number of hillbilly acts, several of whom carried the word "crazy" in their titles (J. E. Mainer and the Crazy Mountaineers, for example). And in Charlotte, North Carolina, Crazy Water Crystals sponsored, with very lucrative results, the Crazy Barn Dance each Saturday night.[15]

Radio may have been the most important disseminator of country music during the thirties, but another medium, the movies, probably did most to fasten upon the music an image which has remained: the cowboy myth. The cowboy image actually asserted itself in country music from the beginning of the music's commercial history, and southwesterners had earlier done their part to blend the images of the hillbilly and the cowboy. Eck Robertson, in fact, wore a cowboy costume to New York in 1922 when he made his (and country music's) first recording.[16] As noted earlier, Jimmie Rodgers recorded several romantic cowboy songs and posed in chaps and sombrero for publicity photos. Cowboy singers, such as Carl Sprague, Jules Verne Allen, and Marc Williams, were plentiful on radio and recordings during the twenties and early thirties, but the western mystique did not become firmly identified with country music until after 1934, when Gene Autry took his music to Hollywood.

Orven Gene Autry was born in Tioga, Texas, on September 28, 1907, but he moved to Oklahoma with his parents about 1925. Autry learned the trade of telegraphy and was working for the St. Louis and Frisco Railroad in Chelsea when, coincidentally, Will Rogers heard him singing one day in the telegraph office and suggested that he try his hand at professional music. The recordings that Autry made between 1929 and 1934 were squarely within the hillbilly tradition, and marked by a close similarity to the sound of Jimmie Rodgers.[17] Autry, though, was already calling himself "Oklahoma's Singing Cowboy" by the time he went to Chicago in 1931 to become part of the WLS National Barn Dance. On the strength of his popularity on radio in Chicago, and because of hit recordings such as "Silver Haired Daddy of Mine" (one of the most popular hillbilly songs of the thirties), Autry was signed to a movie contract in 1934. He appeared briefly in a Ken Maynard film, "In Old Santa Fe," and then was given a feature role in a cowboy-science-fiction serial called "The Phantom Empire." His long tenure as America's number one singing cowboy began in 1935 with his first feature film, "Tumbling Tumbleweeds," and by 1937 he was also winning polls as the most popular western film star of any variety. Through his popular films, recordings, personal appearances, rodeos, and, after 1939, his long-running CBS radio feature "Melody Ranch," Autry took country music to a large and impressionable audience that otherwise might not have listened to it. He had the widest exposure of any country singer in the thirties, and with his depiction of the cowboy he provided country music with an image that was much more appealing than that of the allegedly backward hillbilly. There is no way to document the number of people who may have been inspired by Autry to learn the guitar or attempt a career in music, but the Hollywood singing cowboys who followed in his wake are easily detailed. Such singers as Tex Ritter and Roy Rogers built careers as leading men in grade B westerns,[18] while many others, such as Ernest Tubb, Jimmie Davis, and Bob Wills, made periodic appearances as supporting actors. The cowboy identification inspired by Autry was both lasting and pervasive. Until at least the mid-fifties virtually all country singers garbed themselves in cowboy attire, and many of them—whether they came from the hills of West Virginia or from the Maritime Provinces of Canada—gave themselves and their bands cowboy names like Hank, Slim, Tex, the Ranch Boys, the Riders of the Purple Sage, or the Drifting Cowboys.

The cowboy singers were not the only entertainers in the thirties who contributed to the popularization of the term "western" as applied to country music. By the end of the decade southwestern listeners had become aware of several local string bands on radio stations throughout Texas, Oklahoma, and Louisiana who combined jazz and popular idioms with country music, and even *Time* magazine took notice of the "hot dance rhythms" coming out of the region. This music would come to be known after World War 2 as Western Swing. The style was a direct outgrowth of the rural string band music of the South, but it was made unique by the work of innovative musicians in the Southwest. Texas fiddlers and their rural cousins in the Southeast knew the same music, but Texans very early became recognized for their eclecticism, improvisation, and experimentation. The fusion of cultures in the Southwest may have contributed to instrumental variation, but it has also been noted that the provenance of fiddle contests in the Southwest also encouraged fiddlers to improvise in order to win over their competitors. Eck Robertson, for example, who was a frequent winner in these contests, performed "Sally Goodin"—a basically simple tune—in seemingly endless variations.[19] Fiddle and guitar bands were everywhere, and several of them, such as Oscar and Doc Harper (Terrell, Texas), Jess and Cecil Humphries (Burnet, Texas), and the East Texas Serenaders (Lindale), recorded during the twenties and early thirties. But the evolution of Western Swing really began in the summer of 1929, when another fiddle and guitar band, Bob Wills and Herman Arnspiger, started playing for house parties in the area around Fort Worth.

Wills was born in Limestone County, Texas, on March 6, 1905, but grew up in West Texas near the community of Turkey.[20] He could scarcely avoid hearing fiddle music, because relatives on both sides of his family (the Willses and the Foleys) played the instrument, and his father—John Wills—often played for country dances. Although Wills absorbed a tremendous number of country dance tunes from his forebears, he also loved and listened to the blues and popular music of his youth, and testified to a particular liking for the music of Bessie Smith. Wills was highly representative, therefore, of that rural generation which came of age in the twenties and after, in that he learned as much music from the media as he did from folk sources. Much of the music he performed as a professional musician came directly from recordings, or was inspired by the western movies in which he sometimes appeared.

Wills and Arnspiger were joined by singer Milton Brown in 1930, and they began performing on Fort Worth radio stations as the Aladdin Laddies (sponsored by Aladdin mantle lamps). In January 1931 they gained the sponsorship of the Burrus Mill and Elevator Company and created one of the seminal bands of Western Swing, the Light Crust Doughboys. The popularity they won on KFJZ prompted the active support and encouragement of Burrus Mills's general manager, W. Lee O'Daniel, who became their announcer and master of ceremonies. O'Daniel had at first been indifferent about the group, and he had had no prior experience with country music. But he astutely recognized the band's commercial potential, and his own rise to fame was largely a consequence of his association with the Doughboys. O'Daniel's warm, genial personality and his folksy chatter endeared him to millions of Texans, and he gradually built a constituency based on his radio audience which elected him to the Texas governorship and the United States Senate. His pseudo-populism and down-home charm may have won him a large statewide following, but O'Daniel seems to have had difficulty in maintaining good relationships with his musicians, and few of them speak of him with much affection today. By the summer of 1933 both Milton Brown and Bob Wills had left the Doughboys, and each formed his own band, the Musical Brownies and the Texas Playboys (first called the Playboys). The Light Crust Doughboys have endured to our own day, but O'Daniel severed his connections with Burrus Mills, began selling his own product, Hillbilly Flour, formed his own group called the Hillbilly Boys (which featured the great singing of Leon Huff), and made his plunge into politics.

Between 1933 and 1936 Milton Brown and his Musical Brownies made their headquarters in Fort Worth and did much to give that city its reputation as "the cradle of Western Swing." Broadcasting on KTAT and playing for dances at the Crystal Ballroom, the Brownies made frequent forays into Texas and Oklahoma, where they built a large and loyal audience. Brown's blues-tinged singing—his specialty was "St. Louis Blues"—influenced a generation of southwestern country singers, and his musicians made innovations that still affect the sound and styles of virtually all types of country music: Cliff Bruner and his jazzlike fiddling, Jeff "Papa" Calhoun and his honky tonk piano, and Bob Dunn and his electric steel guitar (probably the first electrified instrument in country music). Before his death in April 1936 Brown had made the Musical Brownies the most popular string band in the Southwest, and after that date several of his musicians went on to create other bands that would take the Texas swing sound all over the region.[21]

Meanwhile Bob Wills recruited a band and went first to Waco and then to Oklahoma City and Tulsa. The stint in Tulsa from 1934 to 1942 has been called their "glory years." The Texas Playboys, as they were now called, disseminated their art through numerous personal appearances, recordings, and movies, but most southwesterners knew them through their radio broadcasts. Listening to Bob Wills and the Texas Playboys each noon on KVOO was a ritual that many people shared and still remember with deep affection.[22] Listeners thought of Wills and his musicians as part of the family, and they showered them with letters, food, and gifts. By the time Wills arrived in Tulsa, the Texas Playboys were no longer simply a string band, but had added drums, piano, and horns, and were capable of playing everything from the latest pop hits to the oldest hoedowns. They may very well have been the most versatile dance band in the United States, and in the person of the much imitated Tommy Duncan they had a skilled vocalist who, while preserving a rural flavor, could compete favorably with most big band singers.

Despite the excellence of his musicians, the driving force of the Texas Playboys, and the member who gave the band its distinctiveness, was Wills himself. Wills did not play the hot, jazzy style featured by such Playboy fiddlers as Jesse Ashlock, but his blues-tinged fiddling still attracts the attention of imitators today (country superstar Merle Haggard spends most of his free time trying to learn the Wills fiddle style). Wills's unusual tenor voice also dealt effectively with songs like "Mexicali Rose," but it was his personality which made the most compelling imprint on his audiences. Wills always exuded an air of supreme self-confidence and ebullience as he strutted around the stage shouting his ceaseless commentary and "ah ha's" and calling out to his musicians by name as they took their instrumental breaks. There were numerous sad songs in the Playboy repertory, such as "I Wonder If You Feel the Way I Do," but the whole tone of the music was one of joyous escapism, and thousands of depression-dwelling Americans found comfort in the sounds of songs like

"San Antonio Rose" and "Take Me Back to Tulsa."[23]

By the middle of the thirties bands derivative from the Musical Brownies and the Texas Playboys, or imitative of them, could be heard all over the Southwest. Adolph Hofner and His Boys in San Antonio, the Bar-X Cowboys and Leon Selph and the Blue Ridge Playboys in Houston, Bill Boyd and the Cowboy Ramblers in Dallas, the Tune Wranglers in San Antonio, and even former Cajun bands in Louisiana, such as Leo Soileau and the Four Aces, were only a few of the musical groups who played the developing Western Swing style.[24] Western Swing musicians contributed songs and instrumental patterns to the larger field of country music which have endured, and they pioneered in the use of drums, piano, and electric instruments. Few people could afford to have a band as large as that led by Bob Wills in 1938, but even the smallest of southwestern bands generally exhibited some influence drawn from Wills or other Western Swing musicians.

Although its identity was not clearly established at the end of the thirties—and its descriptive label was not yet being used[25]—the style now known as "honky tonk" was taking shape during the decade. Honky tonk country music did not really mature until after World War 2 (as in the music of the Alabama Hank Williams and the Texan Ray Price), when it virtually became the sound of mainstream country music, but a large number of southwestern musicians during the mid and late thirties laid the groundwork for its future development. As its name suggests, honky tonk music developed in bars and dance halls of the post-Prohibition Southwest, especially in the oil towns of East Texas, where a relatively prosperous clientele provided an audience eager for musical diversion. The oil boom of the late twenties and early thirties created alternative occupations for many rural Texans, provided a new source of money during depression days, and thereby increased the demand for recreation and amusement. Itinerant musicians roamed through the almost frontier-like boom towns of East Texas, and professional groups generally found eager audiences there with money to spend. Even before prohibition repeal made many of these towns wet, musicians often found root beer stands to be convenient sites for entertainment gigs.[26]

Of all the styles of country music which developed in the Southwest, honky tonk music was the closest organic reflection of a people and society in transition. It appealed to an increasingly urban, working class audience— but an audience with rural roots and values. People's adjustments to city life and industrial occupations ran the gamut from easy assimilation to stubborn rejection. Many clung to past habits and associations and, in their quest for cultural diversion, many gravitated to honky tonk music as the best expression of the dynamics of the old way of life meeting the new.

The music was heard on the radio, records, and concert appearances, but its natural habitat was the honky tonk, the locale that did so much to change the form and content of country music.

The honky tonk drew a diversely motivated audience. Some customers were pensive types who cried in their beer; some merely wanted a few moments of respite before going home; many wanted to dance, find a companion, or socialize with their friends. In any case, music under such conditions had to be amplified in order to be heard. A strong dance beat was emphasized; drums and bass were introduced; and instruments were electrified. Once introduced in a dance hall setting, such changes were next incorporated into radio and recording sessions.

Honky tonk lyrics rarely embodied the nostalgia or pastoral sentimentalism of older country music, and gospel music certainly did not intrude into the honky tonk setting. Honky tonk lyrics were the inevitable products of people who were southern-rural in origin, fundamentalist in religious morality, and who were being thrust inexorably into an urban-industrial milieu and confronted with problems that could not easily be resolved. Low pay, job insecurity, city pressures, marital problems, and family fragility could be perceived only in terms of what people already knew. If frustration turned to protest, the protest was expressed in personal terms and aimed often at imagined evils. Often disappointment evoked only self-pity, or was worked out in terms of getting drunk or raising hell.

The themes of honky tonk music were often "new" but were couched in terms of the traditional morality. Much self-pity, as in Ted Daffan's "Born to Lose," Rex Griffin's "The Last Letter," and Floyd Tillman's "It Makes No Difference Now," and strong slices of guilt, as in Jerry Irby's "Driving Nails in My Coffin" or Daffan's "Heading Down the Wrong Highway," accompanied such themes as illicit love, divorce, and drinking. Almost always the consciousness of the punishment for sin colored the lyrics of the songs. The honky tonk world spawned its own myths and realities as well as the body of songs to describe them. Many songs emerged to describe the musicians' problems in the "fighting-and-dancing" clubs (as Glen Campbell would later term them),[27] or the typical temptations, such as the honky tonk angels, awaiting anyone who frequented beer joints. Al Dexter, from Troup, Texas, appears to have recorded the first song to have "honky tonk" in its title: "Honky Tonk Blues." And he later recorded one of the giant country hits of World War 2, "Pistol Packin' Mama," which was based on his memories of the violent world of East Texas oil town honky tonks during the thirties.[28]

By the end of the decade, after Prohibition repeal had spawned scores of out-of-the-way watering holes, there was an untold number of singers and musicians playing in "night spots" throughout the region. Many of them followed the age-old practice of "busking," i.e., playing only for what customers were willing to donate to them. The luckier ones played for a regular nightly salary, or for a percentage of the gate or beer sales. Some, of course, were house bands who enjoyed a measure of security. A few were able to branch out from tavern gigs to radio shows and maybe even to phonograph recordings. A very few might even graduate to superstardom. Most, however, enjoyed only local recognition and held down other jobs while singing at night or on weekends.

Southwestern-born singers and styles began to make themselves heard nationally in country music by the end of the thirties. In fact, despite the overall success of mountain singer Roy Acuff during the war years, country music was actually dominated by the music of the Southwest (especially Texas) at least down to the mid-fifties. Such musicians and singers as Ted Daffan, Al Dexter, Floyd Tillman, Cliff Bruner, Jimmie Davis, Dick Reinhardt, Moon Mullican, and Ernest Tubb made the nation conscious of what its southwestern honky tonk clientele had been aware of for years. With such recording men as Decca's Jack and Dave Kapp and Okeh's Art Satherley leading the way, talent scouts for the major phonograph companies began combing the byways and backwaters of Texas, Louisiana, and Oklahoma looking for talent. When Ernest Tubb went to the Grand Ole Opry in December 1942 on the strength of his hit Decca recording of "Walking the Floor over You," he took the honky tonk style to Nashville and probably did most to popularize that music throughout the nation. Although Tubb began his career in 1936 as a yodeling disciple of Jimmie Rodgers, and in fact was actively encouraged by Rodgers's widow, his sound and style were shaped and honed in the dance halls of Texas.[29]

Although honky tonk music addressed itself to many of the personal needs of the people who listened to it, it did not touch as many lives as did gospel music. In fact, the honky tonk fan, and singer, were usually persons who grew up attending a fundamentalist Protestant church and listening to religious music. Rural southwesterners were heirs of the Great Revivals of the early nineteenth century which had spread the power of Methodism and other evangelical groups across the southern frontier. They often received their first musical training in church, or from the itinerant teachers who taught the shape-note method in numerous singing schools throughout the South. By 1920 the paperback shape-note hymnals had made their way into millions of southern homes from Virginia to Texas, and were being issued on an average of twice a year by numerous gospel publishing houses. Southwesterners had ample exposure to the hymnals through two very important publishing houses, the Stamps-

Baxter Company in Dallas, and the Hartford Company in Hartford, Arkansas, each of which employed touring quartets to advertise their books. No quartet had a larger following than the Dallas-based Stamps Quartet, and no writer was more beloved, nor more influential, than the Oklahoma-born Albert E. Brumley.

Brumley, who was born on a tenant farm near Spiro, Oklahoma, in 1905, began writing songs soon after he attended a singing school near his community in 1922. He worked as a teacher, singer and staff writer for E. M. Bartlett's Hartford Music Company, a company Brumley now owns in Powell, Missouri. His first successful composition in 1931, and one of the most popular and most recorded gospel songs of all time, was "I'll Fly Away," with a spirited melody and structure reminiscent of the nineteenth-century camp meeting songs. Brumley songs thereafter entered the repertoires of all the gospel quartets, moved into most of the country churches via the shape-note hymnals, and from there into the permanent possession of the southern folk. His compositions,[30] memorable because of their simplicity and melodic beauty, were quintessentially southern in tone and theme, and his highly sentimentalized choice of imagery posited a conception of Heaven, with its placid rivers, perennially blooming flowers, and reunited family circles, that was immensely satisfying to depression-era southerners. The Brumley songs generally fell into two categories: nostalgic songs, such as "Nobody Answered Me," "Rank Stranger," and "Dreaming of a Little Cabin,"[31] which breathed with a consciousness of life's evanescence as they affectionately described an abandoned and decaying rural world held together only by the steadfast love of mother and father; and conventional religious songs, such as "I'll Meet You in the Morning" and "If We Never Meet Again," which speak of a reconciliation in Heaven amidst scenes of pastoral bliss. Heaven, in short, contains those desired qualities so sadly lacking in temporal life: stability, abundance, and permanence (a land "where the charming roses bloom forever, and where separations come no more").[32]

The otherworldly message of the religious songs was certainly consoling to millions of southerners, but to many people who wanted social justice in this world such songs were, at best, fatalistic and, at worst, oppressive. Potentially, music has always been a disturber of the social peace, but it was employed in the thirties, as never before, as a vehicle of social protest and as a weapon in the class struggle to raise the consciousness of American workers. Workers in the textile communities of the piedmont South, the plantations of the Arkansas and Mississippi deltas, and the coal camps of eastern Kentucky produced a large body of songs which chronicled their grievances and called for a united and militant response. Northern radical labor organizers took many of these songs back home,[33] and such southern balladeers as North Carolina's Ella May Wiggins and Kentucky's Aunt Molly Jackson were admitted to the pantheon of American working class radical heroes and heroines.

Commercial country singers rarely sang songs of overt protest. Most of their music was frankly escapist, if not downright defeatist, and even the honky tonk singers, who often concerned themselves with social problems, merely complained of personal or private grievances. Country music, however, has always been an extraordinarily topical music, and the songs of the thirties commented frequently on hard times and New Deal legislation.[34] Although most of the depression songs were written or performed by southeasterners—e.g., Billy Cox's "NRA Blues" and "Franklin D. Roosevelt's Back Again;" Slim Smith's "Breadline Blues;" Blind Alfred Reed's "How Can a Poor Man Stand Such Times and Live;" the Carter Family's "No Depression in Heaven;" and Roy Acuff's "Old Age Pension Check"—some southwestern-based entertainers did comment on the depression. Gene Autry even did a song about a radical labor leader, "The Death of Mother Jones." [35] Goebel Reeves, from Sherman, Texas, sang about hoboes (as in "Hobo's Lullaby" and "The Hobo and the Cop") as did ex-brakeman Jimmie Rodgers (e.g., "Hobo Bill's Last Ride" and "Hobo's Meditation"), who had been well acquainted with the knights of the road long before the Great Depression set so many homeless men afoot throughout the nation. The mood of the depression songs was by no means exclusively gloomy, however, and singers often conveyed confidence about their abilities to survive, as in Jimmie Rodger's "No Mo' Hard Times Blues." But very few of the songs exuded the easy optimism of "My Million Dollar Smile" (written by W. Lee O'Daniel and recorded by the Light Crust Doughboys), which advocated smiling the depression away.

While the singers of the Southwest made only occasional musical references to the depression, and even fewer statements about social injustice, the region was the birthplace of America's most famous protest singer, Woodrow Wilson "Woody" Guthrie. Born in Okemah, Oklahoma, in 1912,[36] Guthrie was heir to the rural music traditions of the South, and his long list of compositions shows an indebtedness to older folk melodies ("So Long, It's Been Good to Know You" is set to the melody of "Billy the Kid"; "Philadelphia Lawyer" to that of "The Jealous Lover"; "This Land Is Your Land" to "Little Darling Pal of Mine"; "The Good Reuben James" to "Wildwood Flower"; "Pastures of Plenty" to "Pretty Polly"; etc.), and his guitar style was a rather rough approximation of that of Maybelle Carter.

Although his melodic sense was obviously derivative of older forms, his use of lyrics was original, and his social consciousness was rare among country singers. It is difficult to know the extent to which Guthrie's experiences in the Southwest shaped his political awareness, because comparatively little is known about his ideas before he moved to California in 1937. He had begun his rambles in 1926 when he was fourteen years old, traveling through Texas and particularly in the towns along the Gulf Coast. Then he moved to Pampa, Texas, where he worked in a liquor store and at other odd jobs while also playing at country dances along with his Uncle Jeff. Guthrie had certainly rubbed shoulders with the working class before 1937, and had felt the rigors of the great dust storms which ravaged the area around Pampa, but his preoccupation with the Okie migrants did not come until he began living and singing among them in California.[37] In Los Angeles he teamed first with his cousin, Jack and later with a girl from Missouri called "Lefty Lou" to sing hillbilly songs over station KFVD. Guthrie soon engrossed himself in the problems of the migrants, singing and composing songs for strikes and unemployment rallies, and his sympathies were pronouncedly radical when he moved to New York in February 1940 in the company of actor Will Geer (the late Grandpa on television's "The Waltons"). In New York he was immediately seized upon as "the new Joe Hill," [38] and he became a part of a small left wing circle that was active on behalf of labor causes and vigorously anti-fascist. In 1940 Guthrie went to Washington, D.C., and recorded his dust bowl ballads for the Library of Congress (including "Do Re Mi," "Talking Dust Bowl Blues," "Blowin' Down This Road").[39] Guthrie's compassion for his fellow Okies was profound, but after his move to New York and his immersion in radical politics, he spoke for them but not to them. Although a few of Guthrie's songs, such as "Philadelphia Lawyer" and "Oklahoma Hills" (the latter co-composed with his cousin Jack Guthrie),[40] eventually became popular with the southern folk, most of his songs were known only to a small coterie of radical intellectuals in New York. But Guthrie became the godfather of what is now called the urban folk music movement, and he has remained the chief inspiration for scores of singers, most notably Pete Seeger, Jack Elliott, and Bob Dylan, who have contributed mightily to the awakening of the American people to a consciousness of social injustice.

The decade of the thirties, therefore, was a time of expansion and transition for country music, when the genre moved dramatically away from its folk roots and became increasingly known to the public-at-large through the vehicles of radio, recording, movies, and personal appearances. The music everywhere exhibited the marks of change, but the Southwest was a crucial arena for the interplay of tradition and innovation. Here was the site of the Mexican border stations, and the headquarters of the Crazy Water Crystals Company, two phenomena which played powerful roles in the mass national dissemination of southern-derived rural and gospel music forms. Here also was the locus of the cowboy, whose romantic image became so firmly attached to country music during the thirties. Southwestern musicians contributed to the general popularization of country music and pioneered in the development of styles and genres that have had enduring effects on American popular culture: Gene Autry and his "made-for-movies"[41] cowboy songs, Ernest Tubb and his honky tonk sound, Bob Wills and Western Swing, Albert Brumley and sentimental gospel music, and Woody Guthrie and the protest song. Although the Great Depression was an era of economic scarcity and human deprivation, it was a period rich in musical wealth, the self-affirming product of a people caught up in a chaotic decade of economic and social transformation.

DONALD W. WHISENHUNT

5.

THE SEARCH FOR A VILLAIN

With the exception of the Civil War, the Great Depression of the thirties affected American morale as much as any event in American history. As economic conditions worsened from the stock market crash in 1929 until the inauguration of Franklin D. Roosevelt in 1933, American faith and optimism in the future were seriously challenged. Public reaction to the depression at both the national and state levels followed fairly definite patterns. Virtually everyone, at one time or another, attempted to find a cause—perhaps "the" cause—for the crisis. In some respects the search for the culprit became almost a witch hunt.

Americans were not the kind of people who readily accepted this new state of affairs; neither were they willing to take the blame for it themselves. From almost the beginning of American history we had been very willing to place the blame for our misfortunes on others. As Richard Hofstadter stated, "There was something about the Populist imagination that loved the secret plot and the conspiratorial meeting. There was in fact a widespread populist idea that all American history since the Civil War could be understood as a sustained conspiracy of the international money power."[1] This so-called conspiracy theory not only manifests itself in the belief that there is a large, organized plot against the American way of life; it is also reflected in the attitude that events are beyond the control of the individual—that someone else is the cause of the crisis. Hofstadter was also correct, at least for the thirties, when he explained, "Indeed, what makes conspiracy theories so widely acceptable is that they usually contain a germ of truth."[2]

From the time that Americans realized that an economic crisis was truly upon them, they began to seek the cause—the villain. Especially during the period of the Hoover administration was this quest active. Since Texas was a large state with a diverse population and a mixed—though still largely agricultural—economic base, it serves well as a microcosm of America at large.

Texans found the cause or causes of the depression almost everywhere they looked. In fact, a man from Crockett in East Texas named almost everything when he listed the following causes of the depression: war debts, failure to join the League of Nations, a conflict between agricultural and industrial America, the Federal Reserve System, speculation, the protective tariff, poor agricultural profits, and increased taxation.[3] Most Texans who expressed themselves were not as inclusive. Usually the individual was moved to speak out in one form or another when he was particularly angered or upset by one or two issues. By analyzing the opinions expressed in various forms, a picture of Texas thought begins to emerge.

The major cause of the depression in the minds of most Texans related to the policies—or lack of them—of President Herbert Hoover and the Republican Party. The administration in office always runs the risk of being blamed for trouble; Republicans were doubly vulnerable in the early thirties since they had been in power since 1921. Having taken credit for prosperity, they were unwilling to accept the consequences of their business policy. Texans, however, were quick to remind them of their responsibility.

Since it is easier and simpler to personify evil, Hoover was most often directly blamed for the depression or for doing nothing to end it. The South, perhaps more than any other area, blamed Hoover for its troubles, particularly since some of these states, Texas included, bolted the traditional Democratic Party in 1928 to help elect him; now they had been betrayed.

Hoover refused to take action that was against his own personal philosophy of government, even though it might have been popular. His prestige suffered when Arthur Woods, the big businessman chairman of the Committee on Unemployment, advocated that everyone buy two of everything—automobiles, telephones, radios—to end unemployment. When the well-known financial empire of Samuel Insull collapsed shortly before the nominating conventions in 1932, Hoover was further weakened.[4]

Hoover received many personal insults from Texans since it was much easier to put the blame on him personally. Hobo jungles became "Hoover Hotels," a jalopy was the "Republican Prosperity Model," and jackrabbits were now "Hoover Hogs" or "Hoover Ham."[5] One Texan told Governor Franklin D. Roosevelt of New York soon after the election of 1932 that "Hoover Hogs" had been praying for his election since they had suffered so much and their numbers had decreased during the Hoover administration. The *Big Spring News* declared that Hoover hated poor people; one man called him a "jellyfish"; and another paper was insulting about the extravagance evident in Hoover's secretarial staff.[6] A rural editor warned Texans to beware of electing Ross Sterling as governor in 1930 because his promises of prosperity might be just as disastrous as Hoover's had been in 1928. Since "we are reduced to 'lasses and corn bread with Hoover," the editor did not wish to "forgo the 'lasses" with Sterling. After the election a farmer asked Sterling how the nation would survive "while Hoover and you may suck your thumbs." Another Texan declared, "Truly, I have been hit hard, but I deserve no sympathy, I voted for Hoover."[7]

Hoover did have his defenders in Texas, although they were neither so numerous nor so vocal as his detractors. They believed that if anyone could bring the nation out of the depression it would be Hoover; others who did not believe that the depression was Hoover's fault thought he had done all he or any man could do.[8]

Of those who refused to attack the President personally, many were willing to blame the Republican Party and its administrations for the trouble. Most of the Texas congressional delegation, including Senator Morris Sheppard, believed that the nation was "so sick and tired of Republican misrule" that it would gladly turn to the Democrats in 1932. Congressman Wright Patman was convinced that Republican policies favoring the wealthy were responsible for the stock market crash and subsequent developments; Thomas L. Blanton blamed ten years of Republican extravagance.[9] Martin Dies declared that "the Republican Party has sowed the wind and now is reaping the whirlwind." Despite their attempt to avoid the responsibility, he believed Republicans would be judged by history for causing the depression.[10] A number of private citizens believed that the Republican Party, acting in an un-American way, had brought dishonor upon itself and distrust for those in power. They were possibly driving the state into the hands of communism, pauperism, or autocratic socialism.[11]

Although only a few of the state newspapers blamed Republicans, those that did were usually rather vehement about it.[12] One of the most striking attacks came from a South Texas editor who claimed that, despite the good character of many Republicans, their system of government was wrong.

It is based on the principle of prosperity for the upper lords who are supposed to let some of the prosperity percolate down to the underlings.

Such a policy is fallacious and erroneous . . . . Traced back to its original it is seen to be founded on the old theory of the divine right of kings—the right for the great and the mighty to have their place in the sun while the toiling masses sweat and labor, starve and shiver to uphold a civic structure built on a foundation of shifting sand.[13]

The election of 1932 prompted many individuals to speak out against Republicans. For example, one person updated the Lord's Prayer and ended by beseeching God to "lead us not into Republican Presidency, for Hoover has all the power, Mellon all the money, Rockefeller all the oil, and we have patched pants for ever and ever."[14]

A serious criticism that Republicans had difficulty refuting was that their promises of continued prosperity proved to be untrue almost as soon as Hoover took office. To some Texans the whole period of Republican rule was merely a reign of economic terror designed to impoverish the "little man" for the benefit of the rich.[15] One citizen declared, "The efforts of the Republican bunk dealers has only served to accentuate the belief of us farmers that the Lord gave and the Republicans have taken away."[16]

Governor Roosevelt received numerous letters from Texans telling him that the Democratic opportunity had arrived; that the Democratic Party could win only as long as it was the party of the people as Bryan had said it was; that defenders of the Republican Party could no longer be found in the South; that he could win if he did not step into the shoes of old guard Republicans.[17] One of the many Texans addicted to poetry, some good and some very bad, was able by using Negro dialect to express his feelings toward the Republican Party in very simple terms.

> When de war quit, in nineteen eighteen,
>   Our Country was prosperous, serene.
> De Republicans grabbed it,
>   and since they Crabbed it,
> She's as shakey as a Hula Queen.
>
> Republicans have had their chance,
>   And failed at the art of finance,
> They've failed to hit,
>   And will have to admit,
> That wid us, they've tore their pants.
>
> If we had what we haven't got,
>   We certainly would have a lot,
> The Republican stroke,
>   Has got us all broke,
> So let us try to change the plot.[18]

Even one physician, a member of a profession long considered conservative, succumbed to the hatred for Republicans. In his letter the Republican Party appeared to be the devil incarnate.

The life of the Republican Party is one of plunder. It has no principles and is ruled by policy, the cornerstone of which is the doctrine of protection, under which the rich are privileged to rob the masses. From protection they have never wavered but as occasion had seemed to demand, they have espoused in every instance the cause of the mighty against the weak. They are entrenched in power behind a breastwork of riches and maintain their position by bribery, subterfuge, falsehood and misrepresentation. Their appeal is to avarice, passion, prejudice and bigotry. Under the Republican rule we have seen the rich grow richer and the poor grow poorer. They have reduced the richest and happiest people in the world to beggary and misery.[19]

Hoover and the Republican Party were the first to be attacked, but the other deities of the twenties—particularly banks and business in general—also came in for their share of the blame. The major argument was that, accidentally or through design, money had been removed from circulation, resulting in deflation that caused the dollar to be worth more than normal. The people, therefore, simply did not have enough money to buy the necessities, pay their debts, and keep the economy running smoothly.[20] When banks continued to fail as the depression deepened, the press tried to stop deteriorating confidence in the banking system; individuals became concerned that the runs might continue; many businesses were crippled by the further restriction of money in circulation.[21] Many Texans, convinced that the bankers were deliberately restricting circulation because of fear or because they were deliberately trying to bankrupt the country, continued to lose respect for the banking system. A man from Brownsville, hoping to get a true picture of the public sentiment, asked over forty people if they would deposit $10,000 (if they had it) in a bank; in each case the answer was negative, and many responded with violent criticism of both national and state banks.[22]

Only a few people believed Hoover's charge that the Federal Reserve System was responsible for the depression, but among them were Congressmen Wright Patman and Martin Dies and former Governor Jim Ferguson, who believed that stricter federal regulation should be established over the Federal Reserve System to forestall such a calamity in the future.[23] An attorney from the town of Comanche almost lost his composure when writing to Congressman Sam Rayburn about the damage caused by both the Federal Reserve System and the local banks.

And it is damn strange to me that you fellows up there in Washington cannot understand what has been done to the public! The truth about it is, we have no money to do a damn thing. . . .

If every damn bank was sunk into the ocean, and every railroad was torn up and moved away, and every God-derned public building was blown away by a cyclone, the people of this country could go right on and do business, but when you have stopped the currency from going to the people, who grow and manufacture the products which we eat and wear, and paint our faces with, as well as manicure our nails, by God, you have stopped the thing![24]

Anti-bank sentiment was also expressed by the labor press and by the official publication of the League of United Latin American Citizens. The latter group was so distressed by usurious rates charged by banks that it asked why the federal government should not abolish all privately owned banks and establish a government-owned system that would be fair to the average citizen.[25]

Texans also became more resentful of business after giving praise—perhaps only lip service—to the business philosophy of the twenties. Although most of the criticism came from individuals, the commercial press—and occasionally business journals—joined the chorus. An individual, a newspaper, or even a business organ that praised business might have to face public displeasure.

On the rare occasions when the commercial press blamed business for the depression, the criticism usually was barbed. The *Austin Statesman* challenged business spokesmen who said that the solution was to leave the country in the hands of business. The editor remarked that businessmen had their opportunity in 1930 when Congress refused to take action; however, business had done nothing to ease conditions. Another daily newspaper opposed the demand of the United States Chamber of Commerce that government be turned over to business, because when it was done in the twenties the result had been to concentrate wealth further into the hands of the few, with little attendant public responsibility.[26] One South Texas editor expressed the sentiment of many when he declared, "The culprit in the case is not General D. Pression, . . . but . . . Mr. Capitalist, who is putting out nothing but holding fast to that which he has." Anti-business sentiment, reflected by Congressmen Hatton Sumners and Marvin Jones, was also an issue in the gubernatorial election of 1932.[27]

Organized labor in the state demanded that instead of the people trying to find other causes, the blame should be placed squarely on industry where it belonged. Business disregard for the welfare of the workers and public at large should be dealt with in a firm manner. The Dallas Chamber of Commerce, for example, should not be allowed to advertise outside the state about how good Texas conditions were when, in reality, there were no jobs at all.

Various segments of the public in Texas expressed anti-business sentiment. Charges that great businesses were untaxed and that commercial interests were in control of the government were quite common.[28] As a bank employee from Roxton explained, "Our Captains of Industry, our 'head hunters' have lost their rabbit's foot and are 'all wet.'"[29]

Significantly, as criticism of industry continued class consciousness became more pronounced among individuals. A Latin American journal declared that we were governed only for the benefit of the wealthy; others, when speaking of "our people," did not include the rich. Some believed that the wealth of the nation was created not by the few rich people but by the "masses"; that the average citizen had no voice in governmental affairs; that the wealthy were willing to use the poor for cannon fodder in wartime, but were unwilling to help them in time of trouble.[30] One gentleman asked Congressman Rayburn, "How can your conscience allow you to squander the people's tax money on such women as Mrs. Longworth, many times a millionaire, who so far as the majority of the people are concerned is not worth ten cents?"[31]

Although not all religious groups in Texas were willing to challenge business leadership as was being done by numerous national religious figures, many, including one Catholic newspaper and some fundamentalist Baptist leaders, did become critical of it.[32]

The few defenders of business were mostly the small town weekly newspapers. During the entire period under discussion many of them continued to speak of business as if the depression had never occurred. They declared that a depression was not an argument against modern corporate finance; since the government was dependent upon industry the only way government could correct its problems was to adopt business methods. As late as the spring and summer of 1932, papers were still declaring that if let alone business could end the depression; one paper, believing businessmen to be greater heroes than any military leader or political official, advocated the establishment of a business hall of fame.[33]

On the rare occasions when individuals defended business, they were more concerned about small businesses that were being destroyed by the giants. A San Antonio resident declared: "Business has become the forgotten man. Let our Party espouse his cause, and want will vanish, the depression be forgotten and prosperity again be the normal state of all our people."[34]

Few business publications came to their own defense, but most of those that did believed the reason for the depression to be the upsetting of natural law by government interference with business. The West Texas Chamber of Commerce wondered if perhaps the rights of the dollar were not being destroyed by the overemphasis on human rights; it was very happy, however, when Governor Sterling, himself a businessman, selected the regional chambers of commerce to help distribute funds, because "in each case the personnel of the committees reveals that the foremost business and professional men and women of West Texas have been selected."[35]

Perhaps the resentment against business and Republican leadership can best be illustrated by the actions taken by freshman Congressman Wright Patman against Secretary of the Treasury Andrew Mellon. Mellon, long considered the best secretary of the treasury since Alexander Hamilton, increasingly came in for virulent attacks as the depression deepened.[36] On January 6, 1932, Patman astonished his colleagues and the nation when he stated on the floor of the House of Representatives, "Mr. Speaker, I rise to a question of constitutional privilege. On my own responsibility as a member of this House, I impeach Andrew William Mellon . . . for high crimes and misdeameanors." He based the charges on a law of 1789 that forbade any person directly or indirectly involved in trade or commerce from holding the office of secretary of the treasury.[37] Although the action received little public attention, Hoover, according to one student of the period, was so frightened by it that he appointed Mellon to the vacant post of ambassador to the Court of St. James. One of Hoover's personal aides, without mention of the Patman incident, said that Mellon was appointed to the London post because his financial abilities would be helpful in the war debts controversy.[38] Whatever the reasons, the event did not receive much attention in Texas. The few papers commenting editorially were astounded that such an unqualified man as Mellon should be appointed to a very sensitive diplomatic post. As for Patman's role, Texans were not certain that he had been instrumental; however, since he might have been, they were willing to let him take the credit.[39]

Obviously, the most highly respected people in the twenties—the Republican Party and big business—were the most criticized for having brought on the depression, but they were not the only causes that Texans found. Some of the other beliefs were quite serious and were widely held, while others were much less significant.

Overproduction was considered a cause of the depression by such groups as a Senate subcommittee of which Morris Sheppard was a member, the daily, weekly, and special interest press, and professional economists.[40] A rather meaningless distinction was made by a number of citizens, including Congressman Wright Patman, who declared that underconsumption rather than overproduction was the cause. A few even argued that neither overproduction nor underconsumption could be blamed since the real cause was underdistribution. Conditions were such that food and goods produced in one area were not available to those in other areas that desperately needed them.[41]

Another cause of the depression to many Texans was the hoarding of money by individuals. Since such a development had not been encountered in previous depressions, President Hoover did not know what, if anything, he could or should do about it. He therefore continued his unimaginative and unoriginal approach by trying to convince the hoarders to spend their money or deposit it in banks. Although a number of Texas newspaper editors believed he was partially correct, a few individuals disagreed with him.[42] Since most people recognized the problem to be one of confidence more than anything else, the solutions proposed included taxing hoarded money, guaranteeing bank deposits to restore confidence, and lowering the salaries of hoarders until all their reserves were spent.[43]

Although President Hoover, during the campaign of 1928, envisioned a nation where the wealth was spread evenly among the people, many Americans, by the 1930s, complained of its concentration in a few hands. For some this was a major cause of the depression. Most Texans agreed that the wealth was not evenly distributed; estimates of twenty, fifty, or one hundred men controlling 75 or 80 percent of the wealth, and thus the nation, were common.[44] Even though a number of people believed that the holders of great wealth had a responsibility to the public to use it wisely, one Dallas citizen disagreed when he wrote to the *Hebbronville News*. "One who has accumulated wealth owes nothing to his fellow man other than to attend strictly to his own business and vote to set up equal rights for all to use the earth. He served his fellow man when he accumulated his wealth, and his accumulation is nothing more than his reward for service rendered."[45] The editor was undoubtedly correct when he replied that this attitude was responsible for much of the disrespect for the wealthy.

Such thoughts . . . are in harmony with the thoughts and beliefs held by the high-jacker, the gangster, the highway man and all those who believe they have the right to take whatever they can by might, or strategy, or duplicity, or chicanery. It is this thought . . . that is rushing to destruction the present capitalistic system and is going to create such antagonism to wealthy men that they will become victims of an enraged and outraged populace.[46]

Solutions for this problem included limiting the amount a person or business might own, higher progressive taxation, and inheritance taxes to limit the passing of huge fortunes to others.[47]

The protective tariff, long an issue in American history, came in for much criticism during the depression. Although many Texans believed that Republican high tariff policies were the root of all economic problems, there were others who were a bit more sophisticated about the matter. They believed that the tariff was just as harmful in the long run to business interests as it was to the farmer and consumer because it tended to stifle international trade.[48] This attitude was best expressed by a dentist from Dublin, Texas. "The 'rich' and factory operators have acted very foolish in having a tariff that operates to their advantage & against the common people & thereby killing their buying power & now they have no buyers for what they make."[49]

By and large, the farming interests in Texas were most opposed to the tariff policy of the previous ten years. Some newspapers demanded a reduction or even the elimination of the tariff to ease the farmer's condition. Texas political leaders were quite vocal in charging that the tariff was the cause of the depression and of the farmer's serious plight. Governor Sterling told a mass meeting of farmers in 1931 that the tariff was the main cause of low prices, and state Senator Pink L. Parrish of Lubbock made it an issue in his campaign for congressman-at-large in 1932. Congressmen Jones and Garner both declared that the return of prosperity could come only when the price of their purchases was reduced.[50] Congressmen Box, Dies, and Lanham believed that the tariff which had restricted international trade hurt agricultural products the most. These gentlemen believed we had been so favorable to special business interests that we had legislated ourselves into a depression.[51] Congressman Sumners, in a statement very reminiscent of Bryan's Cross of Gold speech, spoke the feeling of many Texans.

If somebody looks wise and proposes . . . an absurd thing for these farmers he is classed as a profound economist. Yet we know that these producers of exportable surpluses have no share in the tariff system. I am not speaking in prejudice here. I come from no mean city myself, but we city people have to recognize that if we would put our idle men to work, we have to give these farmers a chance to buy. That is all there is to it. The city people who manufacture do not seem to realize that they are living off the bounty which this Government forces these farmers and others to pay. What is the tariff but a bounty; and what is the tariff boost in the sale price but a sales tax which people have to pay.[52]

A number of farm journals and businesses directly dependent upon agriculture were constant attackers of the high tariff policies that benefited only industrial groups.[53]

A sampling of opinion among individuals indicates that Texans were opposed to the tariff mainly because the farmer was not protected. They therefore advocated the passage of tariff bills that would protect agricultural products, in some cases to the exclusion of all others.[54] One man told Franklin D. Roosevelt that he could be elected if only he would: "Put on a Number 9 pair of brass toed shoes and kick down that damnable wall of high tariff, that was built on a rotten foundation—built especially for the rich—and place a tariff on what the farmer raises on the farm and garden and nothing else. . . ."[55]

A sampling of other public opinion including newspapers, congressmen, cattle raisers, and the Texas Bar Association, shows that they agreed with the idea of placing tariffs on imported agricultural products.

Another cause in the eyes of many was excessive taxation; if not the cause, it was at least prolonging the depression. Since high taxes stifled industrial development, no improvement could be made in the general economic situation until they were reduced. Therefore, high taxes were responsible for unemployment and the other evils of the depression. Since so few people were heavily taxed, something had to be done to prevent the chaos that would result when they could no longer pay.[56] One man very clearly stated the problem when he replied to a creditor's demand for payment, "You dont no how hard I live. Had to sell my milk goat to pay my Tax & done with out my coffee & many other things."[57] At least one woman was concerned that Franklin Roosevelt might not win the presidency because poor people in Texas could not pay the poll tax. Even A. S. Burleson, postmaster-general under Woodrow Wilson, spoke out from his retirement home in Austin against oppressive taxes.[58]

One solution attempted by the Hoover administration was the passage of a national sales tax to balance the budget and equalize the tax burden. Senator Connally, believing it to be designed for the benefit of the wealthy at the expense of lower income groups, fought the tax along with liberal senators from other parts of the country. Texas businessmen implied that they would support it if it meant also a reduction in corporate income taxes, but those upon whom the tax would fall most heavily vociferously opposed it.[59] One man from Texarkana best expressed this disgust with Congress and proposed a way of alleviating the problem in a poem to Franklin Roosevelt.

> We wait upon dear Congress,
> On them all eyes are set;
> But taxes and more taxes
> Are all that we seem to get;
> But we still have the ballot,
> And take it as a bet
> That yet, somehow—it won't be long now—
> Dear Congress will be "wet."[60]

Another manifestation of the discontent was shown by the growing number of people advocating "tax strikes" or "tax holidays." This revolt, led by the State Taxpayers Association of Texas, was an attempt to organize sections of the state to support reduction. If reduced taxes were not forthcoming, the next step was to refuse to pay them altogether. There were those, however, who believed American taxation not to be oppressive when compared with other countries. Some Texans believed a danger to the government was inherent in indiscriminate reduction; particularly education would be hurt.[61]

Since the United States was predominantly Protestant and, to a degree, fundamentalist, many of the people believed the depression to be merely the fulfillment of the scriptural prophecy of seven good and seven bad years. This attitude was particularly strong in the rural areas where fundamentalism flourished. Quite a large number of Texans concurred in this theory. Others thought depression had occurred because of the lack of honesty, the competitive economic system that caused people to be immoral, or the abdication of spiritual leadership by ministers in the twenties. Regardless of the truth of the charges against religious leadership, churches tried quickly to take moral leadership during the depression. The Catholic press did not attribute the cause solely to immorality, but it did believe the only real solution to the problem was a return to a more moral life.[62] Protestant groups, much more outspoken, thought that the depression could be ended only by a religious revival. It was not unusual for them to require unfortunate transients to endure sermons about how their evil ways had caused the depression, before they were fed. The most outspoken of the group, J. Frank Norris, preached that the depression was a sign of the end of the world and that the "New Deal" of Franklin Roosevelt was a sure indication that Christ would soon return. He believed the depression had come because the nation had turned away from fundamentalism to the "social gospel" which had little to do with man's salvation.[63]

Many Americans agreed with Hoover and the Republican Party that the real cause of the depression was international. This involved the restriction of international trade caused by world tariffs, heavy international indebtedness, and the collapse of European credit institutions. Texas newspapers that concurred tried to persuade Texans that American prosperity was dependent on world conditions, that all the world must prosper or none would, and that international commerce was the key to world prosperity.[64]

The most serious question of a foreign nature involved the cancellation, reduction, or postponement of war debts and reparation payments. In keeping with his desire to restore confidence, Hoover began in the summer of 1931 to suggest a one-year moratorium on war debts payments. Emphasizing that this did not in any way imply cancellation, he did believe, however, that it would be the stimulation the world needed. Immediate world and national reaction was generally favorable.

Texas press reaction to Hoover's action was generally favorable. War debts, a hindrance to world trade since the end of the war, would probably never be collected anyway. Therefore, Hoover's action would show our good faith to the rest of the world and might help to restore confidence. A few papers, moreover, believed that the partial or complete cancellation of the uncollectable debts would be a greater stimulant to world prosperity than merely a one-year moratorium.[65]

Strangely enough, Texas political leadership did not agree with public opinion. Those congressmen who commented on the moratorium—Blanton, Patman, Lanham, Garner—were all opposed to it because it would probably lead to cancellation. The two Texas senators disagreed; Sheppard supported the bill in the Senate while Connally voted against it.[66] Individual Texans, believing Hoover's actions were correct, were willing to reduce the debts or to cancel them altogether.[67]

One of the most serious issues during the depression was national Prohibition. During the twenties Prohibition had caused an increase in crime and a health problem; the economic conditions of the thirties made some people believe that it caused the depression. Prominent individuals, including former Governors Jim Ferguson and Will Hobby, were convinced that repeal would eliminate many social problems, would decrease government expenditure for police protection, and would help end the depression because of the number of people who would be employed and the increased governmental revenue available from taxation of liquor. There were those, however, who opposed repeal both on moral grounds and with the argument that it would not really help the economic situation because it would create more problems than it would solve.[68]

Antagonism toward foreign groups, particularly Mexicans, increased in Texas as rising unemployment caused the depression to worsen. Most editorial comment made during 1930 before the depression became very severe stated that the number of aliens in Texas exactly equaled the number of people unemployed. The fact that Mexicans would work for less wages and would accept lower living standards was responsible for much of the trouble. Texas political leadership was also concerned about the number of jobs taken by Mexican aliens. The unemployment commission called by Governor Sterling in 1931 recommended that immigration be restricted and that American workers be given preference wherever possible.[69]

Congressman Blanton, long an advocate of restriction, continued his demands on the floor of Congress and by the introduction of immigration bills. Congressman Dies, from the beginning of his service, hoped for a seat on the Committee on Immigration and Naturalization. Through the years his bills restricting immigration were usually for a complete five-year restriction and a time limitation for becoming naturalized.[70]

The most serious attempt to limit the number of aliens was made by John Box of Texas, who wanted to apply the quota laws to all countries of Latin America. To support his bill he placed numerous letters in the *Congressional Record.* Most Texans agreed that Mexicans were displacing Texas workers; that they accepted lower wages and living standards; that they might become a majority in the state; and that they were mongrelizing the population. Generally, organized labor, both in the nation and in Texas, and a number of individuals supported the Box bill. There were farmers, however, who opposed the measure on the grounds that it would limit the number of workers available for agriculture, since most native Americans would not perform menial tasks.[71]

Quite a number of Texans believed the cause, or at least the continuation, of the depression was the number of married women who worked outside the home. This caused unemployment to be more severe and brought suffering to many families whose fathers and husbands could not work because some married women were holding jobs they should have. Most of the defense for working wives came from the big city dailies who argued that in most cases wives were working because they were forced to do so to feed their families. They did not condone women being employed when no need existed, but employers should be careful not to discharge a worker just because she was a woman.[72]

Texans found many other causes of the depression. Because we had become fat, lazy, stupid, and selfish we had overindulged in too much installment buying that caused too much indebtedness. Increased automation—the "machine"—was blamed by many for the trouble; the automobile was the most vicious machine because it was designed to cost more money to operate than the average citizen could afford. Other causes included price cutting forced by the proliferation of chain stores and government interference with private business.[73]

No one cause identified by Texans could be considered the only reason for the depression. Even so, many of the villains discovered by Texans were contributing factors to the economic distress. Texans revealed that very seldom were they willing to accept personal responsibility for the depression; instead, they searched for the outside cause—the villain. In so doing they exhibited a common American characteristic widely expressed in the thirties.

LIONEL V. PATENAUDE

6.

TEXAS AND THE NEW DEAL

By 1932 the depression had fastened its grip on the United States. As factories closed, savings dissipated, and bread lines grew, optimism, once endemic in the American character, faded. It was replaced by despair, reflected in the faces and worn clothes of men who began to lose hope of ever working again. As conditions continued to deteriorate, people, especially heads of families, lost their self-respect. For millions of Americans the future, if indeed there was one, seemed bleak. But this grim outlook was about to change, for the election of Franklin D. Roosevelt gave hope to a nation that desperately needed confidence.

Texans were similarly affected. The return of the Democratic Party to power, with its charismatic leader, engendered popular support for the New Deal. The enthusiasm was more than political and traditional, however, as economics was a potent factor. The new bureaucrats' preoccupation with agricultural problems and the resultant influx of federal money were indeed a boon to the largely agrarian state. Because of these factors Texans forged close ties with the new political order.

It would be misleading to say, however, that Texas was in the same condition as states in the Northeast. Certainly, by the early thirties Texans knew something was wrong with the economy. Falling prices, people out of work, and economic projections made for uneasiness among the populace and the business community.[1] Nevertheless, evidence indicates that the depression, overall, was less devasting to the state than to industrial or poorer areas of the South. Of course, Texans were already poor, and to many assessing one's degree of poverty was a futile exercise. Farmers especially, used to a hardscrabble existence, tightened their belts and continued to scratch a marginal living from the soil. Yet in spite of the suffering of many Texans, large amounts of federal monies and an economy less dependent on industry, with resultant lower unemployment, combined to soften the economic hardships endured by other areas of the United States.[2]

In spite of these factors, hard times were real for much of the state's population. Miserable cotton prices and drought spelled disaster for thousands. Yet diversification of crops helped to blunt the blow for others. Also, the East Texas oil boom, while causing instability in the petroleum industry, helped the economy at a critical time.[3] As a result, even though the average person probably was not aware of it, the Texas economy rebounded faster than the industrialized part of the nation. Nevertheless, Texans had to wait for the deficit spending of World War II before the depression could be laid to rest.

While favorable statistics may have been comforting to college professors and chamber of commerce employees, average Texans undoubtedly suffered, some more and some less. So much depended on where one was geographically, or what occupation one pursued. Obviously, a government or oil field worker was better off than a dirt farmer or pecan sheller. But regardless of the economic or social niche an individual occupied the New Deal softened the economic and psychological impact of the depression. In the process, political, economic, and social institutions were affected and, indeed, in some cases, dramatically changed. Big government would have a lasting imprint on what had been up to this point a conservative society.

In analyzing the effect of the New Deal on Texas, one cannot overlook the impact which Texans had on its political structure. Thus, many of the events that influenced residents occurred outside of the state, notably in Washington.

One of the first significant political events emerged during the Democratic convention of 1932 in Chicago. There is little doubt that the negotiations between Sam Rayburn and Jim Farley laid the groundwork for an intimate relationship between Texans and the New Deal. Rayburn and Garner had discussed their strategy prior to the latter's departure from Washington. Rayburn agreed to support Garner's candidacy for president as long as he had a reasonable chance of victory. Under no circumstance did Garner want to deadlock the convention and force a repetition of the disaster of 1924. When Rayburn told him over the telephone that a deadlock was a strong possibility, he agreed to release both the Texas and California delegations. Thus, when Garner decided to switch his votes to Roosevelt on the crucial fourth ballot, this move, in effect, made the New York governor president of the United States. But it was not without a struggle, as the Texas delegation became involved in a fierce factional controversy and the voting members approved the Garner-Rayburn decision reluctantly. Even though a straight-out "deal," as most people understand the term, was not made, Roosevelt, Farley, et al. were in debt to Rayburn and Garner.[4] Neither side ever forgot, even when Roosevelt's programs became increasingly unpopular both among Texans in Washington and the politicians at home. And over the years of this political experiment Texans in both positive and negative ways were identified with the Roosevelt regime. This factor must be understood if one is to comprehend the resultant impact of the New Deal on the conservative establishment in Texas.

Texans played a more important part in guiding the course of the administration in Washington than men from any other state. Roosevelt's victory in 1932 gave Texans power, prestige, and influence unparalleled in modern times. From March 4, 1933, to the end of the New Deal in 1938, key positions were staffed by men from Texas. The New Deal was enhanced, modified and, in some cases, appreciably slowed by their actions. Already well known for its geography, Texas now became even more important in national politics. The reverberations of this power were felt in the remotest corners of the Lone Star State.

There were four basics of Texas strength: the vice presidency as conducted by John Nance Garner; the power and prestige of Sam Rayburn in his roles as chairman of the Committee on Interstate and Foreign Commerce and majority leader, and in his relationship to the Vice President; the Texas congressional delegation and the influence of certain nonelective Texans in Washington.

The importance of John Nance Garner to the New Deal and his impact on the conservative Texas establishment has been generally ignored by most professional historians. But how can one disregard a man who undoubtedly was our most powerful Vice President? As a legislative tactician for Roosevelt and later as a bitter opponent, he wielded a vast undercover influence such as few men have had.[5] Knowing virtually everyone in Congress and having tremendous pull with the Texas congressional delegation, he could work wonders or obstruct the legislative process. Since he in many ways represented the conservative element, most Texans in Washington and many politicians at home followed his lead.[6]

While Garner's influence was normally felt in Washington as indirectly affecting Texas, there were times when he directly intervened in both appropriations and politics concerning the Lone Star State. Certainly, no one who was wise would make a federal appointment without first consulting him. And it affected the state insiders who, comprised of men who scorned federal meddling, could not overlook the largess of dollars gushing out of Washington. Texas became one of the leading clients of the federal government, from the moment it received the first unmatched FERA grant to the end of the New Deal, by which time $1,457,320,759 had been poured into the state. Garner's generous hand helped to open, and keep open, the federal cornucopia during his years as vice president.

Sam Rayburn, although more liberal than Garner, could accurately be described as a member of the Texas conservative establishment. This did not prevent him from supporting the New Deal, however, and his influence was felt in both Texas and Washington politics. Rayburn's contributions were not confined to influence, for he was basically responsible for key legislation, especially in the first New Deal. He played a major role in the passage of the Securities and Exchange Act, the Truth in Securities Act, the Federal Communications Act, the Rural Electrification Act, and most important, the Public Utilities Holding Company Act. According to Garner, this legislation became the foundation of the New Deal.[7] While his legislative achievements greatly added to his stature, his connection with Roosevelt was even more important as he and the President became partners in the New Deal. He became even more indispensable after his selection as majority leader. Already indebted to Rayburn, Roosevelt considered him his key man in Congress, especially when New Deal programs were in trouble.[8] As Rayburn's prestige rose in Washington, so too did his influence in Texas, especially on local politicians, as well as on the ranching, farming, and business interests.

But most important to the impact of Texans on the New Deal was the personal friendship and working relationship of Garner and Rayburn. Both had become extremely valuable to Roosevelt; for the most part, they operated as a team.[9] An important aspect of this affinity was their connection with what was undoubtedly the most powerful congressional delegation that ever sat in Congress. Texas had, according to Jim Farley, "immense power, nothing up there [Washington] could compare to it." Roosevelt once said that he thought Texas was "running the government of the United States more largely than any other state." Both Garner and Rayburn had enormous influence on Texas congressmen. While Garner dealt directly with them in the Senate, a great deal of his power was exercised in the House through Rayburn.[10]

Most of the Texas delegation was comprised of men from small towns, many of whom had studied law. Also, they were a mature group, averaging 50.5 years in age. Because of their age, professional backgrounds, and the geographical areas they represented, most tended to be conservative in their outlook. Yet, because they had been exposed to populist ideas in their youth, their positions on money and banking issues seemed radical to the eastern establishment. Indeed, some of Garner's statements during the campaign had been upsetting enough to Roosevelt that he, in effect, assigned a New York newsman to "baby-sit" the vice presidential candidate to ensure that he did not make any more rash statements.[11]

Committee chairmanships were the key to the delegation's clout since seniority made nine Texans chairmen of permanent committees. Of this number, five were considered major positions. Moreover, a Texan headed the powerful Un-American Activities Committee. In addition, several held high ranking posts on other committees. With their conception of New Deal programs tempered by their background, these men were in a position to manipulate them or, in some instances, to kill or severely modify the original intent. Assuming that representatives and senators normally represent the wishes of a substantial number of their constituents, one can readily see the conservative nineteenth-century mores of Texas society exerting an influence in Washington all out of proportion to the state's importance.[12]

Elective officials, however, were not the only important Texans in the Capitol, as several appointees were scattered in key positions in the administration. One in particular was better known and more powerful than anyone except Garner, and in some ways his power exceeded the latter's. He was, of course, Jesse Jones of Houston, chairman of the Reconstruction Finance Corporation. During the New Deal Jones's stature increased to where he was not just a Washington personality but an institution. Taciturn, profane, and with no discernible ideology, Jones was another of the Texas brand of conservatives. Never a New Dealer, he was certainly an unusual character to be operating among the liberal entourage of the President.[13] Ironically, that was probably the source of his strength in Washington political circles.

One of the most successful administrators in the nation's history, he was in absolute control of the RFC and commanded the respect of his colleagues, Congress, and business. Self-supporting in day-to-day operations, the RFC gave Jones the power to be referred to as the emperor of the economic system of the United States.[14]

Like Garner, Jones had a tremendous amount of undercover influence, and his effectiveness was enhanced by his friendship with the Vice President. Considering the fact that they were the second and third (which was third is open to debate) most powerful men in Washington, they could be a formidable combination when they focused their political influence on an issue.[15]

Throughout the New Deal these two Texans worked together. Their old style loyalty to the Democratic Party and their essential conservatism, reflecting the feelings of most of their fellow Texans, often resulted in modifying the demands of their more liberal colleagues, and their consultations sometimes resulted in advice to the President that slowed some ill-conceived plans.

As a group Texans in Washington initially supported Roosevelt. This was especially true of the Vice President, who played an important part in the legislation of the One Hundred Days, a part that is still not recognized by most writers. Congressmen generally went along as Democrats, not because of ideological conviction, with the principles of the New Deal.[16] These were happy times for conservative Texans in Washington, as eastern bankers were being punished, latent southern populist views were being expressed, and money was pouring into Texas.

But Texans in the Capitol were not a part of the social movement that accompanied the New Deal. Since the first New Deal's primary aim was relief and recovery, not social reform, there was little resistance from the Texas group. Thus, Garner, Rayburn, et al. and a majority of the congressmen approved most of the early administration programs.[17]

This support began to change with the inauguration of the second New Deal. Old Cactus Jack began to have doubts early in the game, especially about spending policies. But Garner's fanatic loyalty to the Democratic Party transcended his doubts. As an incipient welfare state began to emerge, however, he indicated disagreement.[18] So too did the congressional delegation, as most of them were not sympathetic to the reform phase of Roosevelt policies. Attacking Wall Street and advocating financial reform was something they understood, but except for Maury Maverick or W. D. McFarlane, the only true liberals, most were out of step with proposed social reforms.[19] Essentially, Garner, Jesse Jones, and most Texas congressmen were too conservative for the second New Deal. Moreover, many incipient welfare state programs were alien to the ideology of congressmen whose rural clients constituted the bulk of the constituents. It was upsetting to them, and their reluctance to go along began to surface in various ways.[20]

The relationship between Roosevelt and the Texas dynasty began to go sour in the fall of 1936. Jesse Jones was not in sympathy with Roosevelt's handling of the sitdown strikes, while Garner was simply furious. Moreover, the Vice President had his first and, according to him, last knockdown, dragout argument with the President over this issue. Things were never quite the same between them after this hostile encounter.[21] But the court struggle of 1937 proved to be the catalyst that caused the Texas bunch to stampede. Even loyal Sam Rayburn had his doubts. Garner, Tom Connally and Hatton Sumners, in particular, by their actions, both public and private, in effect killed the court bill. To further complicate matters, Roosevelt commissioned Garner to obtain the best possible compromise, and when it resulted in an agreement not to his liking, he accused the Vice President of a sellout for which he never forgave him. From this point on, with Garner leading the way, Roosevelt had difficulty in getting anything through Congress if the

Vice President, especially, and key Texas congressmen, did not approve. Garner became the real power in Congress, and politicians and bureaucrats of all persuasions consulted him, mostly in private, on the prospects of their pet projects getting approval. Indeed, he became so powerful at this juncture that there were times when he told the President what he could or could not have relative to legislative proposals.[22]

There is no doubt that the New Deal affected the conservative Texas establishment in Washington. Men who found many federal programs contrary to their political and social philosophy modified their views enough at first to accommodate the President and the party. Moreover, there was little objection, indeed there was a scramble, for federal monies. But essentially these agrarian Democrats with some latent populist heritage could only support the New Deal insofar as it did not clash with their basic conservative beliefs. Concepts of welfare states, collectivism, and other ideologies were alien to their way of life, and as a result most of them were never true New Dealers. Moreover, their views were well known in their districts, which helped influence their constituents. Nevertheless, the Roosevelt regime had a strong impact on the home front.

In Texas the New Deal had to contend with entrenched frontier mores. Recently associated with the frontier and primarily agricultural, the people of Texas were, in theory, wedded to the classic concepts of individualism. But the combination of depression and the influx of federal money had a powerful and, in some cases, shattering impact on the institutions of the people.

The immediate effect of Washington on Texas came in the form of relief funds. In a state where acceptance of any form of charity carried a stigma to be avoided at all costs, it was indeed amazing to see the alacrity with which Texans not only accepted it but, in a short time, demanded more. Hunger and relief money proved too much for vestigial frontier institutions.[23]

Federal relief payments produced some surprising social changes. Large numbers of people, especially Negroes and Mexican Americans, received more money and fringe benefits on relief than they had in their normal occupations before the depression. In some cases, New Deal relief programs were a pure bonanza. This disturbed Lorena Hickock, an investigator and personal friend of Harry Hopkins, who commented in a letter to him that while relief was not so good for whites it was an economic plus for many Negroes and "Mexicans." Elaborating on this theme, she mentioned that government aid to this group was enormously popular and that they were coming on relief as fast as they could.[24]

Relief money also had an impact on the work ethic. As early as 1934 recipients declined to work out of their trade, avoiding jobs which paid less than relief wages. This was particularly true in farming. Moreover, relief money and crop reduction programs instituted demographic change as large numbers of rural people moved to cities to get on relief rolls.[25]

New Deal programs helped to establish a permanent relief system in Texas, which was recognized when the State Department of Public Welfare was established in 1939. Edward J. Webster, in writing to Harry Hopkins, relayed the remarks of a Dallasite which, in effect, said it all. Commenting about the influence of relief on children, this man stated that while relief in any form had been considered a social stigma a few years ago, now people and, most important, children were not only accepting it but becoming accustomed to the system. One of his greatest concerns was the fact that these young people, after being conditioned in this manner, would be voting some day and, ipso facto, helping to make the laws of Texas.[26]

But if the average relief recipient was happy to get help, there was a segment of the population that was not so pleased with the system—the business structure. In general, businessmen and over 90 percent of the bankers backed the New Deal at the start. Amon Carter, Fort Worth's principal booster, perhaps expressed the feelings of many when he said the President had performed in a marvelous manner. But by the second year there were signs of discontent that indicated the honeymoon was over. In this transition period between the first and second New Deals, Texas businessmen were cautious about new economic experiments originating in Washington. Government agricultural policy, the growth of unions, and unbalanced budgets served to disenchant the chamber of commerce mentality.[27]

Federal relief policies also caused anxiety. From the start there was a persistent fear that relief monies would compete with industrial wages. Moreover, there was concern that relief, by itself, dulled initiative. By late 1934 businessmen had generally developed a hostile attitude toward federal welfare programs. In ensuing years some even opposed the concept.[28]

By the advent of the second New Deal, the swing to the left also caused disapproval by Texas business. Taxation and labor policies were especially unpopular. Particularly shocking was the President's court proposal in 1937. Many considered Roosevelt's plan as tampering with a sancrosanct institution; some even felt it would open the door to dictatorship. Lawyers and bankers, especially, were articulate in denouncing the concept. For many businessmen this was the final excuse to break away from the New Deal.[29]

But regardless of this latent hostility Texas entrepreneurs did not hesitate to avail themselves of benefits derived from federal spending in

Texas and adjacent areas. Even the reviled relief payments proved to be a boon, especially to the Dallas wholesale market. This helped business to recover faster in Texas than in the country as a whole. Indeed, by 1937 the editors of the *Dallas Morning News* characterized the depression as more psychological than real.[30]

Initially greeted with enthusiasm, governmental programs saw their support deteriorate as prosperity returned, taxes increased, and labor appeared to rise in favor as opposed to business. Support for Roosevelt policies began to decline in 1934 and continued to weaken during the course of the New Deal. Businessmen had had high hopes that the President would solve the depression, but this feeling faded as the New Deal seemed to drift leftward. One major concern was the fear of the growing power of federal bureaucracy. Above all, this crystallized the opposition to new programs. Belief in residual frontier mores and the lack of responsibility normally associated with affluence caused large numbers of businessmen to become inordinately suspicious of Roosevelt's policies. Thus, by 1938, regardless of relative prosperity, the New Deal was no longer popular in the Texas business community.[31]

Labor, however, had a different viewpoint. From the start Texas labor was behind the New Deal. Even though unemployment was lower than in eastern and midwestern states, it still was substantial enough to be a problem in urban areas. Workingmen needed help and they looked to the President for guidance. The right to organize, as exemplified by Section 7 (a) of the National Recovery Act, boosted workers' morale. Moreover, many felt recovery would follow. Yet, in spite of urging by the labor press, there was no rush to comply. The concept of organizing free of coercion from employers was a new experience, and the average worker was not prepared for the opportunity. The recent emergence from the frontier, the relative newness of unions, and the slow impact of the growth of urban areas combined to slow the drive for unionization. Even though there was an increase in union activity, workingmen, worried over losing their jobs, remained cautious.[32]

And well they might, for the initial impact of recovery was more disappointing to labor than to any other group. Businessmen and farmers had both experienced some degree of benefit in the form of price rises for their products. But the labor movement was still harrassed by low wages and high unemployment. To Texas workingmen it seemed that Roosevelt was interested in placating business more than labor. Also, throughout the New Deal labor legislation and various social programs did not seem to have much immediate material effect on the working class.[33]

Yet, in spite of these disappointments, the New Deal over the long run changed the workers' outlook. Most held a high opinion of the President and his programs. Also, their experience with the depression and the new order loosened ties to a frontier heritage. The beginning of class consciousness infiltrated the labor movement as the President came to be regarded as a hero who was leading the laborer in a fight against an insensitive capitalist class. And the workers of Texas backed Roosevelt with their votes.[34]

The loyalty of organized labor to the President resulted in widespread gains in the years following 1938. Greater unionization, higher pay, elimination of many substandard working conditions, and improved job security were rewards received by the workingmen of Texas for their support of the New Deal.[35]

Farmers, however, did not have to wait; indeed, many could not. Hopelessly in debt, and familiar with residual populist ideology, they were among the first to reevaluate frontier mores. For tenants, especially, there was no choice, as thousands were forced from the land by crop reduction programs. Indeed, from 1930 to 1940 sharecroppers and tenants declined by almost 60 percent. Thus, a system arising from the ruins of Reconstruction began to disintegrate. It was never to be quite the same again.[36]

Rural Texans, once the embodiment of self-reliance, went on relief in huge numbers, providing 50 percent of the cases. Moreover, in turn, over 80 percent of these were farm laborers and tenants. Many moved to the city because of easier access to relief. In the process significant social and demographic changes ensued, for large numbers of the impoverished were Negroes and Mexican Americans. Moreover, this situation, combined with crop reduction programs, helped to speed the growth of urbanization.[37]

With the introduction of government crop reduction programs, farmers were supportive, while ranchers, reluctant at first, soon joined in pleading for handouts. By 1935, in spite of complaints relating to government methods, there was no doubt that farmers not only backed, but indeed demanded, government price supports. Ranchers, albeit accepting aid, were never so enthusiastic. But the dirt farmer of Texas, caught up in an economic maelstrom which he could not handle, did not hesitate to accept money from Washington.[38]

There can be little doubt that the New Deal had a powerful impact on the Texas farmer. During the worst part of the depression, for example, government payments substantially altered his income and living standards. This resulted in a twofold effect for most, i.e., upward economic mobility and improved morale. And he expressed his thanks to the political party that he perceived had rescued him from disaster by backing the

New Deal and Democratic programs for the next two decades. But this was not all, for despite his initial caution and his continuing lip service to the ethic of individualism, the Texas farmer accepted federal control over his crop production instead of depressed prices. No longer would the Texas farmer face the future alone with his plow. With prosperity theoretically guaranteed by Washington, he willingly modified his mores to adjust to the demands of the twentieth century.[39]

Readily discernible was the New Deal impact on the state's conservative politics. At the start most Texas politicians were extremely happy to join the parade. Both Miriam "Ma" Ferguson and James V. Allred, as governors, supported the New Deal. Indeed, Jimmy, although basically not a true New Dealer, utilized it as a springboard for his political aspirations.[40]

Both governors during the New Deal, plus the bulk of the state's politicians, understood the new relationship between the federal government and Austin. Texan officials soon learned that cooperation meant money, and they frantically sought ways to obtain the maximum. Democrats, as a rule, supported the New Deal, but on occasion with reservations. Most Texans were Democrats first and New Dealers second. At all times there was an undercurrent of hostility to the concept of federal dominance of the states. And they felt strongly about any potential encroachment upon the state's right to control its own resources.[41]

By the mid-thirties the rapport between the New Deal intellectuals in Washington and Texan politicians began to wear thin. As long as money had been pumped into the state and eastern bankers were punished according to neo-populist ideology, Texans could approve of the Roosevelt experiment. Most people had faith in Roosevelt, and that seemingly was the important thing. But as soon as social reforms that threatened established institutions were suggested, Texan ardor for the New Deal cooled.[42]

Dissent was not confined to professional politicians, for there was discontent among certain business and professional groups. The New Deal was altogether too radical for some Texans, and they began to oppose the administration in the hope that the government could be returned to the people, a code word for control by themselves. Subdued at first, the latent hostility to big government broke into the open in 1936 when a small group of Democrats and other malcontents formed the Liberty League. In Texas its offshoot, the Jeffersonian Democrats, waged one of the most vicious, if ineffective, campaigns in the state's history.

The membership of this group did not have a broad popular foundation in the state, as it appealed primarily to lawyers and big businessmen, with farmers and ranchers comprising a third group. Probably never involving more than five thousand members, this organization nevertheless numbered H. R. Cullen and Mars McLean, of the oil fraternity, plus Will Clayton and Lamar Fleming, of the cotton firm Anderson, Clayton, and Fleming, among its members. These men and others felt the New Deal was leading America to chaos.[43]

In spite of crude emotional appeals, plus adequate financing, the Jeffersonians made little headway during the campaign. Even J. Evetts Haley, chairman of the group, admitted that their opposition was ineffective.[44] But real trouble was just over the horizon, for when Roosevelt tried to restructure the federal court system Texans, as well as their representatives in Washington, were caught up in the bitter party-splitting struggle which followed.

Within a few days after the President made his plan known, the Texas Senate came out against it, while the House tabled a resolution to commend the proposal. These actions attracted nationwide attention and were interpreted as a blow to Roosevelt and the New Deal. At the same time opposition was evident among many members of the legal profession, as several groups voiced concern. Moreover, the Texas Bar Association polled its members and revealed that they were approximately four to one against the court proposal.[45]

Texas businessmen were also among the strongest opponents of the plan. Local affiliates of the National Association of Manufacturers, United States Chamber of Commerce, and the American Bankers Association all opposed the President on this issue.[46]

Others reacted differently. Labor groups supported Roosevelt. Dirt farmers generally did also, while ranchers were not so enthusiastic. Texas politicians were also divided on the question. While some prominent men supported the plan, others, including Governor Allred, ostensibly an ardent New Dealer, were not wildly enthusiastic. Available evidence, however, indicates the majority of Texans favored the court reorganization.[47]

The court struggle had some momentous effects in Texas. Significantly, business and professional groups, substantial numbers of newspaper editors, lawyers, and politicians now openly opposed the New Deal. This occurred in spite of the knowledge that the average Texan supported Roosevelt. But the opposition, even though small, was articulate and had access to the communications media. Ex-Governor James V. Allred put it succinctly when he said that the court plan helped to mobilize opinion against a regime that was already losing favor. With the passage of time opposition to the President and his policies became more open, vocal, and caustic. No longer did one worry, at least among the Texas establishment, about antagonizing friends or acquaintances by criticizing Mr. Roosevelt.[48]

The court plan proved to be the turning point for the New Deal, polarizing Texans along socioeconomic lines, with upper class groups normally against and lower level ones for reform. But even though many voters now regarded administration proposals with suspicion, the New Deal was far from over in Texas. Although, one cannot disregard the evidence that its initial momentum had slowed considerably, the average Texan still held President Roosevelt in high esteem, a feeling that Democrats could exploit for political advantage for years to come.[49]

In evaluating the New Deal in Texas one must understand the recent emergence of the state from a frontier environment. Many residents still adhered to the ethic generated in this milieu toward work and the laissez-faire functions of government. Now, however, they were confronted with a new problem that demanded some sort of positive action. But laissez-faire philosophy did not seem capable of alleviating the hardships engendered by the severest depression known to Americans. People were desperate for help. When it was forthcoming from the federal government, Texans were simply not up to the task of maintaining their frontier institutions.

Yet, there was resistance exemplified in a modest way by continuing lip service to the idea of rugged individualism. This concept was especially alive in rural areas, where vestigial frontier psychology still remains today. In practical terms, however, the resistance to big government encountered in business and political circles was never fully eradicated. At times during the New Deal this opposition assumed serious proportions, especially prevalent in the political arena. Indeed, the Roosevelt regime laid the foundations for struggles which surfaced in the next and following decades over the essential political and philosophical roles of government.

It is apparent that the New Deal affected every segment of Texas society. Ranging from increased material benefits, better economic opportunity, more security, to changes in basic philosophy, the New Deal left its mark on the state in a manner not envisioned by the most perspicacious Texan at its start. For Texans, whether residing in Washington, the Panhandle, or the shores of the Rio Grande, life would never be the same. Conservative Texas had been introduced to the twentieth century.

STEPHEN F. STRAUSBERG

7.

THE EFFECTIVENESS
OF THE NEW DEAL IN ARKANSAS

Today historians are involved in a reassessment of the New Deal on the state level. Reexamination of government policies have led to new appraisals as to the efficiency of the Roosevelt administration in grappling with America's most profound economic crisis.

An analysis of Arkansas in the thirties will illustrate how the federal government attempted to revive the economy without disturbing its underlying social structure. Prior to the onset of the depression Arkansas had major economic problems. In 1929 the state's per capita income was only $305, almost 50 percent below the national average. Sharecroppers often received substantially less. Moreover, the prices of the three major economic exports—cotton, timber, and coal—were depressed. Residents in low lying areas of the state had barely recovered from the disastrous 1927 Mississippi flood. Inhabitants of the Ozark mountain area in northwestern Arkansas lived on the meager yields of eroded hillside farms. Except for cutting and selling of crossties, they were not in the cash economy.[1]

State finances in the twenties had been largely committed to the building of farm-to-market roads. After municipalities and counties experienced difficulties in floating bonds, Governor John Martineau in 1927 committed the state's limited financial resources to funding the ambitious highway construction program. As a consequence of the assumption of locally incurred debts, the state's revenues went to pay the interest on bonds that eventually totaled over $160,000,000. By 1929 Arkansas had the heaviest per capita state debt in the nation; it was approximately nine times greater than the $14 million average state gross revenue. All other state services were starved in order to service the securities.[2]

Arkansas's banking infrastructure was weak. The state's chief bank, the American Exchange Trust Bank headed by A. B. Banks, with forty-five branches throughout the state, had become interlocked with the speculative empire of Rogers Caldwell of Nashville, Tennessee. The financial connection was to force the closing of the bank in November 1930.[3]

The final catastrophe eventually to befall Arkansas was a drastic shift in weather patterns. Beginning in 1930 the state suffered from periodic droughts. Since most industrial workers also farmed, the weather's effect reduced an essential source of food. To add to the cup of misery the Arkansas and the Mississippi rivers continued their pattern of periodic flooding in the low areas. Nature appeared to be in league with man in creating almost unbearable conditions.

Almost unwavering in their conservative views, Arkansas's political leaders had few ideas on how to deal with the crisis. Harvey Parnell, who had become governor in 1928 upon the resignation of John Martineau to take a federal judgeship, chiefly concerned himself with the highway question. The revelations of corruption in the highway administration and the trial of A. B. Banks, president of the American Exchange Trust Bank, for financial malfeasance smeared Governor Parnell's administration. In the wake of the drought of 1930 the only solution to the state's troubles was to appeal to Washington for assistance. In 1931 farmers received a modest seed loan as a response to their overwhelming needs.[4]

As the highway debt mounted, the state legislature initiated a searching examination of the allocation of road construction contracts. The investigation revealed a pattern of favoritism and corruption. In the wake of the revelations Junius Marion Futrell of Paragould was elected governor in 1932. An ultraconservative, Futrell was convinced that technology was the root cause of Arkansas's problems. Only by repudiation of machines and a return to hand labor could society provide both full employment and self-sufficiency. The Governor was fearful that federal assistance had the potential for social disruption by upsetting the existing wage rate. Finally, as was the case with most Arkansans, he did not trust "foreigners," as out-of-staters were labeled.[5]

By 1932 the state's economy appeared to be barely functioning. Not a single county was paying its obligations in cash. The state could no longer service its heavy debt. Feelings of helplessness were pervasive. Voluntary agencies could not handle the enormity of the problems. The politically indifferent people of the Ozark mountain region of Arkansas began to talk of revolution as their plight worsened. In order to qualify for assistance staunchly independent farmers had to declare themselves paupers. Modest work projects funded by the Reconstruction

Finance Corporation could employ only a small proportion of the affected population. Black sharecroppers were told to depend upon their landlords for help. "Live at home" was the most commonly given advice. Unemployed workers' councils were formed in Russellville, Fort Smith, and Little Rock to demand greater federal assistance. By July 1932 payrolls in Arkansas had fallen 45.5 percent from the 1929 level, and bank deposits had decreased from $137 million in 1929 to $62 million. An estimated 95,000 men were unemployed. The worth of the state's cotton crop had fallen from $120,000,000 in 1929 to $42.8 million in 1932. Overall agricultural values had declined more than 50 percent down to $100 million.[6]

State expenditures reflected the economic decline. The educational system barely functioned, since teachers were paid with scrip, the value of which was determined by individual merchants. All state employees received only a fraction of their authorized salaries. In his inaugural address Governor Futrell advocated reduction of state expenditures by 50 percent. Moreover, he proposed that the state spend only $2.5 million a year. To accomplish this objective all state salaries would have to be reduced and the state debt renegotiated. Although these goals were not met entirely, the state experienced austerity, with expenditures being reduced by $1.4 million.[7] Arkansans in need of assistance had no hope of aid from the state government.

The inauguration of Franklin D. Roosevelt in March 1933 marked an important turning point in Arkansas's fortunes. With no initiatives forthcoming from state officials, only the national government could provide the leadership so necessary for recovery. The first impact of the New Deal came from the bank holiday designed to prevent panic runs on banks. The state banking structure had barely limped along since 1931. Now the federal government forced weak financial institutions to merge. After the reopening of banks the long series of bank failures ended. Nevertheless, potential borrowers found it difficult to secure loans.[8]

The single most difficult problem faced by the average Arkansan was public relief. Traditionally, assistance for the indigent was a church and community responsibility. Since acceptance of aid was often considered demeaning, few confessed to being in dire circumstances. Many counties maintained work farms for the poor. In the face of natural disasters the American Red Cross augmented local efforts.

The first attempt at state-supported relief resulted from a grant from the Reconstruction Finance Corporation (RFC) in 1932. These funds were to be used to hire the unemployed to work on road and levee construction projects. Each county was to be responsible for the allocation of funds, and prospective clients were screened by three-man county boards. Given the enormity of the economic problems, many of the applications were rejected. Disappointed applicants claimed discrimination, Criteria as to eligibility included queries as to the applicants' standing in the community. Those individuals labeled lazy or shiftless found it difficult to secure assistance. Usually well-established white farmers were the most favored relief recipients.[9]

In May 1933 Congress created the Federal Emergency Relief Administration (FERA) to take over RFC work projects. The FERA, administered by Harry Hopkins, offered a far greater range of relief programs as well as direct financial aid to individuals. States were required to create separate relief agencies to deal with the expanded programs. Hopkins sent Aubrey Williams, a social worker from Alabama, to Arkansas to organize the relief program. Williams clashed immediately with conservative Governor Futrell, who demanded direct control over any relief operations.[10] Williams wanted social workers to staff the new agency. Upon his arrival in Little Rock, Williams witnessed a riot outside the old post office. Relief applicants demanding admission to the office had been refused admittance. Upon investigating relief operations, Williams concluded that the officials were clearly incompetent to deal with the magnitude of the problem. Edward McKinley, the state commissioner of labor, had allowed political patronage to permeate the system. Upon returning to Washington Williams discovered that Futrell had complained bitterly to Senator Joseph T. Robinson about Williams's visit. The Governor warned the senator that social workers or outsiders would undermine the Negroes' willingness to work in the cotton fields.[11]

A compromise was achieved in August 1933 with the appointment of William R. Dyess, a planter from Osceola, Arkansas. Dyess, a native born Mississippian, had moved to Arkansas in 1926 and in 1932 had worked for Futrell's election in politically important Mississippi County. Although not trained in social work, Dyess had the administrative ability to work with the new bureaucracy. As chief administrator of the ERC Dyess won the support of both Williams and Hopkins. Williams, on his return visit in August 1933, was pleased by the progress Dyess had made in the reorganization of relief. Dyess depended heavily upon Floyd Sharp, his executive secretary, and William Rooksberry, the reemployment director, for guidance in the administration of relief.[12] Nevertheless, the paucity of professionally trained people on the county level was to impede the efficient functioning of county relief agencies.

In the fall of 1933 Congress created the Civil Works Administration (CWA) to deal with the expected increase in unemployment during the winter months. The CWA in Arkansas, headed by R. C. Limerick, former chief engineer of the Arkansas Highway Department, employed almost

60,000 people on road projects. Nevertheless, of the 270,000 people registered for relief less than 100,000 were able to find employment. In April 1934 the CWA was terminated and the FERA work projects, including small vegetable gardens, road construction, transient camps, and direct food relief, took its place. Despite the expenditure of more than $61 million, FERA work projects provided the barest subsistence for individuals.[13] To alleviate agricultural dislocation the Rural Rehabilitation Agency gave modest loans for seed and fertilizer.

Although Hopkins did not intend it to do so, the FERA also supported education. By February 1932 725 schools had closed and more than 1,200 had shortened terms. Many schools were forced to depend upon subscription or to charge fees. The state's 3,193 school districts supported only 12,953 school teachers, at an average salary of $540 paid in either cash or scrip.[14] Governor Futrell believed that only primary education merited state support. By September 1933 the state's Emergency Relief Commission was requesting federal assistance. In the school year 1933-34 the FERA reluctantly spent $696,000 to support the public school system. Reluctantly, because Hopkins opposed permanent dependence upon federal largess. Particularly troubling to Hopkins was the decision of the Arkansas General Assembly to forgive property taxes that were unpaid in 1934. Both Hopkins and Williams believed that Arkansas should exhaust its own financial resources for education before asking for additional assistance. In the fall of 1934 Hopkins threatened to freeze money for education unless the state levied additional taxes. Pressure from the Arkansas congressional delegation caused Hopkins to relent, and the state received $1 million for the school year 1935. Finally, in March 1935, the state passed a 2 percent sales tax, a portion of which would go to support education.

Complaints about the administration of welfare continued to plague Arkansas. The state had never confronted the specter of long-term unemployment. Hopkins feared that prolonged unemployment would lead to permanent dependence. In March 1934 Mrs. Gertrude Gates, a native Kentuckian who held a graduate degree in social work from the University of Chicago, was sent to assist Dyess in the FERA work projects. Gates wanted instructors in social work to be sent to Arkansas in order to work with her staff. Immediately staffers complained that Mrs. Gates was going to replace Arkansans with "foreigners" as county social service supervisors. Senator Hattie Caraway asked that Mrs. Gates be removed. Despite Williams's support Mrs. Gates left Arkansas on July 1, 1934, for Wisconsin.[15] Her removal demonstrated that the New Deal in Arkansas was not to change existing social relations.

A report of the Bureau of Agricultural Economics indicated that the acceptance rates for clients for rural rehabilitation loans reflected a pattern of discrimination. Across the state white clients were granted loans at a rate three times higher than blacks. In addition, since loans of less than $10 were not granted, small farmers often received nothing. Finally, since county committees were concerned with possibilities of repayment, applicants who had been on relief for more than four months were virtually eliminated. Consequently, much of the money allocated to the state in 1934 went to farmers affected by the drought rather than to the hard-core unemployed.[16] Such decisions were not unpopular in a state where poverty was considered one of God's afflictions. Ironically, the philosophy of self-sufficiency or "live at home" that underlay most of the hopes for permanent recovery were continually undone by the periodic droughts that wiped out the vegetable gardens.

In view of the inequities that had come to be associated with relief programs it is not surprising that the summer of 1934 saw the formation of protest groups demanding better treatment. The most important of these organizations was the Workingmen's Union of the World located in Fort Smith. The two founders, Ben F. Vick and John Eakins, former followers of Robert LaFollette's Progressive Party, established locals throughout the Arkansas River valley to try to get relief payments raised to the level of neighboring Oklahoma. The union drew its strength from unemployed coal miners. In the fall of 1934 the Workingmen's Union called a strike to demand that the $7 a-week pay scale be increased, as well as to denounce the humiliating treatment clients received at the Forth Smith relief office.[17] In February 1935 the union, spurred on by radical students from Commonwealth College, a socialist labor commune located in Mena, Arkansas, went on strike to try to block a proposed salary reduction for relief workers. In response to appeals of public officials, Dyess suspended all federal assistance in Sebastian County. With no source of supporting funds, the strikers gave up their efforts. However, in an attempt to dramatize their grievances, they staged a hunger march in Fort Smith. The union leaders and some students from Commonwealth College were arrested and charged as revolutionaries. Claude Williams, an activist Presbyterian minister, and Horace Bryan, a young firebrand from Commonwealth College, were sentenced to short jail terms.[18]

In February 1935 the Democratic administration decided to channel relief in two directions. Those able to work would be given employment in an expanded version of the FERA to be called the Works Progress Administration (WPA). Those individuals who were infirm or unable to be placed in the labor force would be supported by the state. Hopkins informed Arkansas that the state would have to create a Bureau of Public Welfare. Still burdened by the heavy highway debt and dependent upon federal assistance to keep the educational system afloat, the legislature balked at the passage of any additional taxes. To impress upon the state the seriousness of the situation, Hopkins withdrew all relief funds from Arkansas until new revenues were raised. Futrell warned the legislature that people's lives were held in the balance.[19]

The suspension of federal relief was a painful blow to Arkansas. The FERA was spending thousands of dollars and supporting almost 400,000 people. Hopkins promised that the aid would be resumed if the legislature allocated revenues to support the estimated 41,000 people ineligible for WPA jobs. In the meantime Dyess authorized the issuance of surplus commodities from relief commissaries. In view of the threat, on March 13 the House passed by 51 to 49 a sales tax bill that levied a 2 percent tax on all commodities except for specified food and medicine. The state estimated that the revenue of approximately half a million dollars was necessary for the Public Welfare Commission. The bill also provided that the Commission must distribute unemployment relief funds in the county on the basis of population. Hopkins rejected the state's proposed allocation plan and instead demanded that the money be spent on the basis of need. Eventually Arkansas spent an average of $6 per month for the aged and infirm. On March 17 Hopkins released $1,528,415 to assist the state until the first of August.[20] Arkansas was the only state to receive such transition funds.

The concept of assistance to the indigent was still violently opposed by many middle class persons. On April 4, 1935, a suit was filed in Pulaski Chancery Court to contest the constitutionality of the sales tax. For two months the tax was not collected in the state's most populous county. On June 3rd the Arkansas Supreme Court ruled the tax constitutional. Nevertheless, the situation remained confused. Attorney General Carl Bailey informed Roy Prewitt, head of the Welfare Commission, that only $150,000 were available for relief expenditures. Although the state had agreed to match federal grants, revenues derived from the new tax were inadequate. Merchants in Stuttgart and Malvern refused to collect the tax.[21]

A group called the Arkansas Sales Tax Repeal Association met in Little Rock to lobby the legislature. In the midst of the growing controversy Attorney General Bailey reversed himself and declared that the expected $1.5 million could come from the general welfare fund. Governor Futrell designated 35 percent of the sales tax revenues for unemployables and the remaining 65 percent to the common school fund. When Roy Prewitt publicly complained of the paucity of the allocated funds, he was forced to resign.[22]

In April 1935 Congress authorized $4.8 billion to finance the WPA.

Hopkins decided to retain Dyess as state director and Floyd Sharp as deputy director. Dyess had tried to get the counties to deal with the relief question rather than to get additional federal support. Consequently, he was not popular among county judges. But Dyess had also been instrumental in establishing an agricultural colony in Mississippi County. This model plantation built and run by welfare recipients became a showplace of the New Deal's agricultural policy.[23] Dyess had gained considerable political strength as a result of the allocation of relief funds and was mentioned as a possible gubernatorial nominee in 1936.

In the fall of 1935 Arkansas started to operate under the new dual system. Unemployables found it difficult to make ends meet on the allotment. Education also suffered from the loss of federal money. By January 3, 1936, Pulaski County schools closed. Several counties exhausted their cash reserves by November. Craighead County closed its jails to save money. Finally Arkansas received a special grant of $300,000 to assist its Public Welfare Commission. The plea to continue federal assistance was personally carried to Washington by Dyess and his finance director Robert H. McNair. With the aid of Senator Robinson the federal government granted Arkansas $411,000 to allow it to complete the normal school year. During the flight back to Arkansas Dyess lost his life when his plane crashed in St. Francis County, killing all thirty-seven passengers aboard. Hopkins selected Floyd Sharp to replace Dyess.[24]

In 1936 Attorney General Bailey, an open opponent of Futrell, announced his candidacy for governor. A liberal by Arkansas standards, Bailey favored redistribution of national wealth. He claimed that southern resources had been exploited by northern capitalists. The attorney general had been instrumental in the prosecution of A. B. Banks of the American Trust and Exchange Bank. In addition, Bailey had pressed the politically powerful Arkansas Power and Light Company to lower its rates. In April Bailey's image was enhanced when he was publicly praised by New York prosecutor Thomas E. Dewey for turning down a $50,000 bribe and for returning Charles "Lucky" Luciano to New York for trial.[25] Bailey won the primary with only 31.9 percent of the vote.

Although Bailey professed to be a New Dealer, he was to clash with the federal government, and especially with Floyd Sharp. The two men became involved in the schism that divided Arkansas between the "state gang" and the "federal gang," a bitter feud that divided Arkansas politics for over a decade. In contrast to Futrell's fears of too much state spending— especially on education—Bailey promised a host of reforms. He called for the solving of the problem of farm tenancy, for rural electrification, for prison reform, and for state-provided school books. Moreover, he advocated the establishment of a state civil service system. The governor also urged the state to refund the highway debt at a lower interest rate. Even Bailey's detractors confessed that the Governor was a sophisticated student of Arkansas's economy.[26] Nevertheless, Bailey's aggressive manner alienated many potential supporters.

Although Bailey promised to serve his full term in office, he attempted to take over Robinson's seat after the Senate majority leader's sudden death in July 1937. Homer Adkins, collector of internal revenue for Arkansas and chief of the so-called "federal gang" because of their control of patronage, sought to defeat Bailey. After sounding out the entire Arkansas congressional delegation, Adkins decided to support Congressman John E. Miller of Searcy. Although Arkansas politics tended to divide on the basis of "friends and neighbors" rather than of ideology, Miller gained conservative support. Both Miller and Bailey tried to get the approval of the national Democratic administration, but Roosevelt steered clear of the election. In the special election held on October 18, Miller carried 61 of the 75 counties and defeated the Governor by 22,000 votes. Bitterly, Bailey blamed the patronage control by Adkins and Sharp for his defeat. To retaliate, Bailey voided the charter to the Dyess colony on a technicality. However, the WPA, rather than see its showplace disintegrate, obtained a new state charter. Even so, after the 1937 election Bailey never relented in his attacks upon the Dyess colony, Sharp, and the New Deal. Bailey became involved with the southern governors movement to rectify the Interstate Commerce Commission railroad transportation rate structure. This movement was the South's answer to Roosevelt's charge that the South was the "nation's number one economic problem." By 1939 Bailey had embraced the theory that Arkansas was in economic fiefdom to northern capitalists.[27]

In 1938 Bailey was reelected governor, as Arkansas had the tradition of giving incumbents a second term. This was due partially to the fact that the "federal gang" concentrated its efforts on helping Hattie Caraway win reelection to the United States Senate.[28]

Bailey in his second term emphasized his objective of solving the highway debt. In 1939 the legislature passed Bailey's refunding bill, but it was promptly invalidated by the Arkansas Supreme Court. Bailey attempted to repass the bill with an emergency clause supported by two-thirds of the state legislature. Attorney General Jack Holt ruled the action invalid. The need for a new funding plan was clear, since Arkansas had had no new money for highways since 1934. Nevertheless, opposition to the refunding plan forced the issue to be placed before the voters in a referendum.[29]

In 1940 Adkins defeated Bailey in his bid for a third term. Since Adkins's differences with Bailey were personal rather than ideological, many policy initiatives were continued. The new governor proposed a refunding plan in 1941 that the legislature promptly passed. After a series of court tests Adkins's plan was declared constitutional. The RFC purchased the entire refunding issue at a lower rate.[30]

Problems of relief and recovery also continued to plague the Bailey administration. In 1937 the Welfare Commission had only enough money to support 6,000 persons. Despite the expenditure of over $40 million by the FERA, Arkansas still lacked the power to generate its own recovery. As long as agricultural prices remained depressed, the state continued to be almost totally dependent upon federal money to deal with unemployment. In 1937 the WPA cut employment rolls in Arkansas from 32,000 to 18,000. This reduction, coupled with the national economic downturn, caused Arkansas's per capita income to fall from $247 to $226 by 1938. As late as the spring of 1941 the WPA remained the state's largest employer, with over 33,000 people on its rolls. Significant achievements of the WPA included the completion of the Martineau road program, the building of schools, stadiums, libraries, and even a zoo and a golf course in Little Rock.[31] The campus of the University of Arkansas was transformed by the construction of five buildings and a football stadium. Never before had counties and municipalities had the opportunity to strengthen and improve their physical plants so significantly.

The WPA perpetuated many of the flaws of the defunct Emergency Relief Administration. No individuals administering the program had experience in social work; consequently an estimated 70 out of 75 county agencies were staffed by political appointees. Like its predecessor, the WPA mirrored the prevailing social mores. One black tenant farmer applying for aid was told to catch rabbits until the first of March when the planters would "furnish" him. The applicant claimed that, while he was in the office a planter appeared and successfully negotiated aid for "his" Negroes. Letters to federal officials often reflected variations of this type of discrimination complaint. WPA rolls were adjusted seasonally to ensure adequate manpower for chopping and picking cotton. As a result, attempts to unionize sharecroppers and day laborers by creating a temporary labor shortage were undermined. Not surprisingly, many clients felt they were being manipulated in order to ensure a continuation of the prevailing low wage scale.[32]

Overall, federal relief did accomplish its primary objective—the prevention of starvation. Furthermore, Arkansas received unprecedented assistance to strengthen its economic infrastructure. By 1943 the WPA had spent over $161 million in Arkansas and had built 11,471 miles of highways, 467 schools, and 44 new parks; it had provided over 19 million meals. No other program in the state's history had such an impact.

Arkansas in comparison to other southern states had been treated quite well.

Although relief was not the only New Deal program in Arkansas, it had been the most important visible federal program. Nevertheless, other administration programs had some effect upon the state. The National Recovery Administration, which proposed regulating every aspect of industrial production, had little effect upon Arkansas. With little industry except for coal and timber, the majority of Arkansas's labor force was not touched. Business-dominated small towns were under little pressure to comply with regulations. Its passing in 1935 had little impact on the state.

The New Deal's creation of the Social Security System in 1935 was opposed by Arkansas's congressional delegation because of the matching clause in the bill. In contrast to the congressional antagonism, old people flocked to join the Townsend Clubs with their promise of $200 a month pension. Dr. C. L. Orgon, the state coordinator of the thirty-six Townsend Clubs, estimated that 100,000 people would be eligible for the proposed program. After enactment of the bill Little Rock attorney A. L. Rotenberry offered a bill which would have allocated a portion of the sales tax to provide pensions of $50 per month to all persons over 60 who did not owe over $500 in personal property tax or $2,000 in real estate tax. The newspapers and public school teachers vigorously condemned the plan. After a court challenge in 1936 the Rotenberry amendment was removed from the ballot on the ground that it was misleading in its wording.[33] Not discouraged, Rotenberry created a Social Security League to continue to press for state aid. State welfare commissioner Gussie Haynes asserted that Arkansas could not afford the projected outlay of $2.1 million. Despite this opposition, Rotenberry gathered the necessary 30,000 signatures to place the amendment on the ballot in 1938. The Arkansas Supreme Court once more struck down the initiative on the grounds that the petition contained fraudulent signatures. Recognizing public pressure for old age assistance, the legislature passed an act written by Dr. W. H. Abington of White County to grant pensions of $3 to $9 per month to the indigent.[34]

The Abington Act had major flaws. First, the bill referred to pensions as "public assistance," a term the federal government found objectionable. Second, the amounts to be given in each county were to be determined by the county relief boards. Finally, the county boards were charged with the determination of eligibility. Angered at the changes in the relief setup, state Welfare Commissioner Gussie Haynes resigned. In March 1939 Governor Bailey was informed by the Social Security Board that Arkansas must comply with congressional guidelines or face a suspension of federal matching payments. Rather than become embroiled in a confrontation, Bailey suspended the Abington Act. However, to ensure his political control over relief Bailey appointed his friend Eli Collins to head the state's Social Security Board. Relief remained a political football.[35]

Arkansas also attracted national attention because of its agricultural difficulties during the depression. The impact of the Agricultural Adjustment Administration (AAA) upon the sharecroppers was widely publicized. In 1935 approximately 60 percent of Arkansas's quarter million farm operators were either rent or share tenants who earned an average of $280 a year. Their desperate poverty was deepened by the decision to withdraw cotton land from production. Agricultural economists saw reduced acreage as the only means to balance supply and demand. Consequently, many landowners refused to rent to sharecroppers, in order to limit production.

In the northeastern section of Arkansas where displacement of croppers was most extensive, the Socialist Party of America helped organize the Southern Tenant Farmers Union (STFU) under the leadership of Harry Leland Mitchell and Clay East, to dramatize the plight of the sharecropper. The STFU gained national publicity in 1935 when Ward Rogers, a graduate of Vanderbilt University and a young Methodist minister, was arrested after addressing an STFU meeting in Marked Tree, Arkansas, on the grounds of advocating the overthrow of the state government. The trial attracted media attention, including that of Raymond Daniell of the *New York Times*. In March Norman Thomas toured Arkansas to investigate conditions in the delta. At the little town of Birdsong in Mississippi County, Thomas was forcibly stopped from speaking by an armed mob of planters and their friends. Appealing to President Roosevelt, Thomas demanded that the eviction of sharecroppers cease and that croppers receive a portion of AAA parity money. Meanwhile, spurred by reports of abuses and planter violence, the Agriculture Department sent Mary Conners Myers, a lawyer in the legal division, to survey the situation. After Mrs. Myers confirmed STFU accusations, Chester Davis, the chief of the production division in the AAA, decided to suppress her politically sensitive report. Feeling that the STFU was composed of troublemakers, Arkansas believed that the northern media were trying to give the state a negative image.[36]

In the fall of 1935 the STFU called a strike during picking time in order to try to raise the base rate to $1.00 per hundred pounds of cotton. Despite violence, planters were willing to raise the base rate to 75¢. In the fall planters evicted suspected union members from their farms. To spotlight the croppers' plight the STFU organized a tent colony near Parkin, Arkansas. On visiting the colony to examine conditions, Governor Futrell warned the tenants against the wiles of agitators. Aubrey Williams asked William Rooksberry, the state director of the National Employment Service, to get jobs for the displaced tenants. In reply Rooksberry claimed that, given the statewide situation, little could be done. Similarly, Floyd Sharp stated that the WPA had too many projects and not enough money to help the tenants.[37]

In the spring of 1936 the STFU called another strike, of cotton choppers who hoed the weeds among cotton plants. The union demanded $1.50 per day rather than the 50 cents they were paid. Because of the planned visit of President Roosevelt to Arkansas for its centennial celebration, state officials were embarrassed by the strike. Futrell sent twenty-five national guardsmen and state rangers into the strike area. David Benson, a union organizer from Florida, was arrested outside Forrest City and hastily tried and convicted for interfering with labor. Clay East, who attended the trial, was threatened by mob action.

As a result of the pressure for outside investigation of the events in Arkansas, Homer Cummings sent Sam Whittiker of Chattanooga, Tennessee, to investigate the situation. Although Whittiker found no grounds for complaints that Negroes were being treated poorly, he criticized Crittenden County Deputy Sheriff Paul D. Preacher for working prisoners on his farm. With this exoneration of Arkansas officials, Roosevelt on June 10 during his visit to the state could praise Arkansas officials—in particular Senate Majority Leader Joseph T. Robinson. A delegation from the STFU attempted to meet with Roosevelt in Little Rock, but only succeeded in seeing his secretary, Marvin McIntyre.[38]

The situation in Arkansas was to get renewed national attention when, after a sharecroppers' meeting on June 8 near Earle, Arkansas, Frank Weems, a Negro tenant farmer, disappeared. To dramatize the continuing violence in northeastern Arkansas, the STFU decided to hold a funeral. Claude Williams, the Presbyterian minister active in union work, accompanied by Willie Sue Blagden, a daughter of an important Memphis family and a socialist, went to visit Weem's supposed widow. In Earle they were accosted by six men who forced them to drive out of town. The men flogged Williams and struck Miss Blagden several times. (Later Weems would be found in Chicago.) The ensuing publicity resulted in a new investigation. Attorney General Homer Cummings suggested that Governor Futrell should act. In August a federal grand jury indicted Paul D. Preacher, the deputy sheriff in Crittenden County, for peonage. Later found guilty, Preacher was sentenced to three years in jail and fined $3,500. In 1938 Arkansas outlawed the practice of hiring prisoners out to planters.[39]

On August 15 Governor Futrell announced that a state commission would be established to recommend legislation to help the tenant farmer. As a consequence of hearings held before the Arkansas Commission on Tenancy, the conclusion was reached that the tenants needed federal assistance in order to become independent farmers. In addition, the commission called for written contracts between tenants and landlords and impartial arbitration of their disputes. In 1939 Arkansas acted upon the commission's principal recommendations by allowing tenants to acquire land that had reverted to the state for nonpayment of taxes.

In 1937 Roosevelt established a presidential committee on farm tenancy to report on proposed federal legislation. As a result of this study, Congress enacted the Bankhead-Jones Farm Tenant Act, creating the Farm Security Administration to lend money to farmers as well as to establish experimental farm colonies throughout the South. Eventually five such colonies were created in the delta area of Arkansas. Although the Farm Security Administration never had the funding to deal with the enormity of the tenant problem, it does reflect the concern of the New Deal for the plight of the truly dispossessed.[40]

By 1939 Arkansas's economic conditions still had not reached the 1929 level. Despite these disappointing results, Arkansas had undergone major changes. The combination of increased mechanization and acreage resulted in a reduction of farm labor. Between 1930 and 1940 tenant farming had declined by one-third. As a result of the change, farm income went up. In 1933 Arkansas farmers received a gross income of $113 million, which by 1940 had climbed to $180 million. Despite the millions spent by various New Deal agencies during this period, Arkansas did not make a complete recovery until the greater economic stimulation of the second World War. War manufacturing facilities financed by both private and public funds totaled $245 million. By 1945 per capita income in Arkansas had reached $722—more than twice the 1921 figure but still well below the national average of $1,234.[41]

In conclusion, the needs of Arkansas were so great that probably no single combination of federal programs could have brought the state to the national income average. The events of the Great Depression brought national attention to many of Arkansas's deep-rooted economic difficulties. The New Deal had worked comparatively well with the state administration as long as the former did not threaten the existing social pattern. Only when the federal government threatened to funnel money to classes of people that normally were not recipients of such assistance, did opposition develop. Letters from individuals to the national administration reflected the belief that the federal government was being foiled by local officials. The common complaint was that the intent of the federal programs was being subverted. Nevertheless, given the basic conservative philosophy that permeated the state, the New Deal's programs probably worked as well as could be expected. Certainly, if outsiders had been brought in to administer the programs the resentment that would have been experienced would have created major difficulties. Today Arkansas still reflects the legacy of the New Deal in its schools, parks, libraries, and roads.

WILLIAM J. BROPHY

8.

BLACKS TEXANS AND THE NEW DEAL

From 1930 to 1940 significant changes occurred within the black community of Texas. Spurred by the collapse of the cotton economy, tens of thousands of blacks left the farm. Complicating the fate of the state's Negroes were the changes wrought by the depression on black business establishments and the black nonfarm labor force. By 1937, for example, only two black-owned banks in the state were still operating. The once viable fraternal insurance industry was all but destroyed by the economic crisis. In 1927 the Odd Fellows had $12,847,023 of insurance in force; the reported figure in 1936 was $507,525. During the same time period membership in the organization fell from 26,578 to 2,017. Alwyn Barr reported in his *Black Texans* that by 1937 only two black insurance companies in Texas had survived the depression. Unemployment rates for nonfarm black workers were staggering even before the election of Franklin Roosevelt. In 1931-32 blacks accounted for 35.6 percent of the unemployed in Austin. The unemployment rate among blacks in Houston exceeded 35 percent as early as January 1931. Conditions such as those mentioned above and the programs initiated during the New Deal fundamentally and irreversibly altered the Negro population of Texas.[1]

Although certain New Deal programs discriminated against the poor, the accomplishments of the national government from March 1933 to the coming of World War II were considerable. True, the Agricultural Adjustment Administration's (AAA) payment plans discriminated against tenants and croppers. The National Recovery Administration (NRA) indirectly led to the displacement of Negroes by whites, and both the Civilian Conservation Corps (CCC) and the National Youth Administration (NYA) operated on a segregated basis. Assistance to the elderly and general relief payments to whites were normally larger than the payments to blacks. Because Negroes were concentrated in agricultural and domestic service jobs, many of them were excluded from the old-age and survivors' insurance program. Such forms of discrimination were unfortunate, and in a world of absolutes, inexcusable, but the existence of discrimination was not surprising. The amazing factor, and the more significant one, was the degree to which Negroes were able to obtain benefits provided through federal legislation.[2]

Throughout the years of the New Deal the proportion of Texans receiving benefits from federally financed programs who were black usually exceeded the percentage of Negroes in the state's population. The first federal agency to have a positive impact upon the economically disadvantaged was the Federal Emergency Relief Administration (FERA). In October 1933 416,174 Texans were receiving FERA payments: 75,535 of these people were Negroes. The percentage of Texans on relief who were black slightly surpassed the proportion of Negroes in the Texas population. According to the 1930 census 14.7 percent of all Texans were Negro. In October 1933 18.1 percent of the relief population was black. By March 1935 Negro families constituted 27.0 percent of all urban and 15.1 percent of all rural Texas families receiving relief. In relation to their relative strength in the population, more blacks than whites were on the relief rolls. Too, Negroes were the only group in the state in which the proportion of females on relief exceeded the proportion of males. The female relief phenomenon among blacks reflected the fragmentation of the black family.[3]

Although Negroes received relief in excess of their proportion of the population, a pattern of discrimination against blacks existed in Texas. Counties with high percentages of Negroes in their populations did not receive relief comparable to that elsewhere in the state. In 1940 there were twenty-seven Texas counties with populations at least 30 percent Negro. These counties contained 10.9 percent of the state's 1940 population. In December 1939 only $4,252 was spent on relief in the twenty-seven counties; this equaled 4.2 percent of the statewide general relief expenditures for the month. Across Texas the average general relief payment for December was $7.57. In the high percentage black counties the average was $6.69, but seven of the twenty-seven counties did not participate in general relief programs. Of the 697,646 residents in the twenty-seven counties, only 711 were the recipients of relief. Discrimination in these counties was not limited to Negroes, but applied to poor people in general.[4]

Among rural Negroes the primary form of discrimination concerned the distribution of work and direct relief. Blacks to a greater degree than whites received direct relief. But whites were more fortunate than blacks in receiving the combination of work and direct relief. Mean financial compensation as direct relief was significantly lower than the average compensation for either work or work-direct relief. Too, the average Negro family obtaining funds from a specific type of relief was granted less money than the typical white family (see table 1).

On the average, the rural black recipient families in the western cotton area studied by the WPA received 72.7 percent as much money as the

TABLE 1

Mean Amount of General Relief for Rural Families in the Western Cotton Area by Race and Type of Relief for June 1935

	Work relief		Direct relief		Work and direct relief	
	Number of families	Mean amount	Number of families	Mean amount	Number of families	Mean amount
Total	3,616	$11	2,408	$7	868	$14
Negro	674	10	898	6	168	12
White	2,942	11	1,510	7	700	15

Source: Calculated from Carle C. Zimmerman and Nathan L. Whetten, *Rural Families on Relief,* Works Progress Administration, research monograph no. 17 (Washington, 1938), 143. The Western Cotton Area consisted of two counties in Oklahoma and the Texas counties of Bastrop, Cass, Collin, Houston, Karnes, McLennan, Montgomery, Shelby, Terry, and Wilbarger.

mean white family on relief. Whereas 57 percent of the white families received between $1 and $9, over 72 percent of the black families were in the $1-$9 category. In May 1935 Negro families receiving general relief in Houston were given a benefit of $12.67; white families averaged $16.86.[5]

Although rural dwellers did not derive the same benefits as those living in urban areas, there apparently was not any attempt to single out rural blacks for differential treatment. Table 2 provides data on both the percentage of blacks in the relief population and the proportion of Negro WPA workers for rural and urban areas. In the rural counties 26.1 percent of the relief population were Negro, and in the urban counties 29.8 percent of the relief recipients were black. The proportion of Negro WPA workers from the rural counties was 16.9, and in the urban counties 15.1 percent of the WPA workers were Negro. Slight variations existed between the rural and urban counties, but the differences were not statistically significant. Since the proportion of blacks and whites residing in rural and urban areas was approximately the same, the evidence suggests that Negroes were not denied either direct relief or WPA work because they resided in rural areas.

Accompanying the general relief programs which embraced the spectrum of the nation's needy were a group of New Deal-devised schemes designed to benefit specific segments of the population. The first New

TABLE 2

Negroes as a Percent of the Relief Population in March 1935, and as a Percent of WPA Workers in May 1940

Negroes on relief in Texas	Negro WPA workers in Texas	Rural Negroes on relief	Rural Negroes on WPA	Urban Negroes on relief	Rural Negroes on WPA
27.8	15.9	26.1	16.9	29.8	15.1

Source: Calculated from Richard Sterner, *The Negro's Share: A Study of Income, Consumption, Housing, and Public Assistance* (New York, 1943), 416.

Deal agency created to meet the needs of young adults was the Civilian Conservation Corps. While the CCC enabling bill was being debated in Congress, Representative Oscar De Priest, a Negro Republican from Illinois, secured the passage of an amendment prohibiting discrimination in the CCC on the basis of race, color, or creed. De Priest's amendment undoubtedly aided blacks by assuring that they would receive the same pay as whites. The amendment did not, however, prevent other forms of discrimination.[6]

By May 1933 W. Frank Persons, the CCC selection director, had received complaints that statewide directors of the CCC in the South were refusing to accept Negro enrollees. Persons responded by threatening to withhold a state's quota if blacks were not accepted. The responsible officials yielded to Persons's pressure. Negroes were able to join the CCC but only on the basis of a quota system which prevented them from obtaining CCC jobs in proportion to their needs.[7]

The unfairness and inadequacy of the racial quota system were well illustrated in Texas during July and August 1935. In July the state director of the CCC, Neal A. Guy, urged young men to register for the CCC with their county relief administrator. Negroes responded to the call, but there were insufficient vacancies in the state's Negro camps to place all black applicants. As the total Texas quota had not been attained, Persons ordered Guy to accept all enrollees, including Negroes, until the quota was reached. A possible solution would have been to establish more Negro camps, but Robert Fechner, the national director of the CCC, was under pressure from white Texans not to permit the establishment of additional Negro camps. With the unofficial support of President Roosevelt, Fechner prohibited Persons from selecting more blacks in Texas until vacancies existed in the Negro camps. This policy was applied nationally, and after July 1935 Negroes were accepted into the CCC only when a vacancy existed in a black camp. Fechner's limited selection policy continued until his replacement by James McEntee in 1941.[8]

As a relief agency, black Texans found the CCC to be of limited value. By 1935 the CCC had accepted only 300 Negroes into its Texas camps. After 1935 Negroes normally participated in the program in approximate proportion to their numbers in the population but not in proportion to their needs. In July 1939 only 2,753 black Texans were enrolled in the CCC. The limited number of Negro participants prevented the CCC from being an economically meaningful relief agency for the state's Negroes.[9]

Beyond the limited help provided by the CCC, young Negroes of both sexes received aid from the NYA. On a segregated basis the NYA conducted programs to benefit men and women between the ages of 15 and 25. In Texas the first director of the NYA, Lyndon B. Johnson, was fair to blacks. Johnson's selection as statewide director proved to be beneficial to the NYA in Texas, to the state's Negroes, and to the career of the future president. Johnson assumed his position in August 1935, and within a few months the NYA was functioning in Texas. By the end of 1935 Johnson and Dr. R. T. Hamilton, the chairman of the Texas Emergency Advisory Council for Negroes, had discussed and then established an NYA center for black women. The camp offered an intensive course on home economics, health education, and workers' education.[10]

Early in the fall semester of 1935 368 Negro college students in Texas were each receiving $35.30 per month from NYA-funded campus jobs. Black high school students were also drawing paychecks from the NYA.

At Prairie View Normal and Industrial College the NYA operated two dormitories for the sons and daughters of Negro tenant farmers. NYA training programs at Prairie View emphasized personal health, poultry raising, dairying, and the home preservation of food. After the involvement of the United States in World War 2, the NYA offered black youths instruction in machine tool work and welding.[11]

Blacks were not discriminated against by the NYA (see table 3). Negroes constituted 9.9 percent of the secondary school population in the state and 11.1 percent of all high school aid students. Similarly, the

TABLE 3

Number and Percent of Negroes in Selected NYA Programs in Texas in December 1939, and Negroes as a Percent of the Component Population

	Total number in the NYA in Texas	Number of blacks in the NYA in Texas	Percent of blacks in the program in Texas	Percent of blacks in the selected population in Texas
School aid	14,838	1,647	11.1	9.9
College aid	6,264	590	9.4	7.1
Out-of school aid	18,059	3,480	19.3	14.7

Sources: Sterner, *The Negro's Share*, 264–66; U.S. Bureau of Census, *Vital Statistics Rates in the United States, 1940–1960* (Washington, 1968), 843. The percentage of Negroes in the selected population figures for the out-of-school aid group was obtained by calculating the percentage of Negroes in the 15-through-24 age bracket on April 1, 1940.

proportion of blacks receiving NYA college and out-of-school employment exceeded the percentages of blacks in the college and 15-through-24-year-old populations. If the records of the NYA camp at Itasca (Hill County) are representative, the individual black received direct economic benefit from the agency. The Itasca center was opened on October 16, 1939, and offered training in domestic work, landscaping, gardening, and general construction skills. A newspaper story published in early 1941 indicated that over 90 percent of the youths trained at Itasca found employment in the private sector.[12]

The Federal Emergency Relief Administration, the Works Progress Administration, and the Agricultural Marketing Administration also sponsored programs which affected education. During the year beginning on July 1, 1937, thirty-four WPA teachers in five central Texas counties taught 754 illiterate Negroes to read and write. A few years earlier the FERA paid 2,182 unemployed teachers in Texas to attend a federally financed training program. Of those accepted for the program, 465 were Negroes. For students coming from poverty backgrounds the Agricultural Marketing Administration initiated the Community Lunch Program in 1935; in 1941 approximately 84,000 black children in Texas received free lunches.[13]

With the passage of the Social Security Act of 1935, the national government initiated an old age assistance program. Unfortunately, employment categories with major concentrations of black workers, such as agricultural and domestic service employees, were excluded from the insurance plan's coverage. Also, Negroes were concentrated in the poorest paying jobs and therefore contributed the least amount of money to the Social Security fund. As a result of smaller contributions, the average black recipient of a Social Security check in 1939-40 received $11.39 per month; the typical white recipient received $13.81.[14]

Among those most severely injured by the economic impact of the Great Depression were the cotton producers of the South. Indicative of the cotton economy's plight were the declining wages paid to cotton pickers and the high level of unemployment in rural areas. Following 1929 the per hundredweight wage paid to cotton pickers fell from $1.11 to 60¢. As late as 1937 Texas cotton pickers were only receiving 65¢ per hundred pounds.[15]

Rural relief rolls reflected the widespread economic destitution in the cotton belt of Texas. In the Western Cotton Area Negroes, in relation to their proportion of the total population, were overrepresented on the relief rolls (see table 4). The disproportionate share of blacks on relief was common to both rural and town families. Negroes comprised 19.6 percent of the rural families in the sample and 31.4 percent of the rural relief families. Town blacks constituted 28.0 percent of the families and 48.6 percent of those families on relief. Most of the families surveyed, however, were located in rural areas. The higher ratio in the towns probably reflected the movement of unskilled blacks from the farms to the towns and the impact of cheap cotton on the economy of towns located in the cotton belt.

Within the Department of Agriculture the leading agricultural economists who advised Secretary of Agriculture Henry A. Wallace were committed to the concept of aiding farmers through acreage reduction.

One cannot doubt Wallace's desire for rural reform, the hope of Senator John H. Bankhead of Alabama to aid all types of farmers involved in the cotton culture, or President Roosevelt's Jeffersonian dream of transforming the South into a region of yeoman farmers.[16] Unfortunately, the dreams and schemes of honest men frequently became counterproductive programs to the tenants and sharecroppers of the South.

After the passage of the Agricultural Adjustment Act of 1933, the

TABLE 4
Negroes as a Proportion of the Relief Population in the Western Cotton Area, February 1935

	Total number	Percent Negro	Percent white
Families in the sample	70,396	20.0	80.0
Relief families in the sample	16,320	32.4	67.6
Rural families in the sample	66,252	19.6	80.4
Rural relief families	15,133	31.4	68.6
Town families in the sample	4,144	28.0	72.0
Town relief families	1,169	48.6	51.4

Source: A. R. Mangus, "The Rural Negro on Relief, February, 1935," *FERA Research Bulletin, October 17, 1935* (Washington, 1935), 7–8.

Department of Agriculture encouraged landowners to plow under between 25 and 50 percent of their cotton acreage. Participating farmers were to receive a subsidy of between 6¢ and 8¢ a pound for cotton not produced. The payment went directly to the landowner and not to the tenant farmer. In theory, the landowner was to split the payment with tenants whose acreage had been plowed under. A cash tenant was to receive the entire subsidy. A sharecropper was to receive 50 percent of the payment, and a third or a fourth tenant was to receive 75 percent of the sum. The Cotton Acreage Reduction Contract utilized in 1933-34, however, was signed solely by the landowner. Under the terms of the contract the landowner was encouraged to keep his tenants, but no legal enjoinment required the landlord to do so. Landowners frequently retired land formerly worked by tenants and planted cotton on the land where the landlord had traditionally planted his crop. This system enabled the landowner to displace his tenants, produce cotton, and collect a subsidy. The director of the Commodities Division of the AAA, Cully Cobb of Georgia, was sympathetic to the landowners and to the pattern of race relations in the South.[17]

From the perspective of the lowly cropper the AAA was an abysmal failure. The literature of the New Deal is replete with reports of landlords evading the spirit of the law by refusing to deal fairly with their tenants and croppers. The 1934 cotton contracts, for example, authorized the landlords to dispose of tenants who were considered to be problems, and various landlords used the provision as justification for forcing people off the land.[18]

Although complaints began to reach the Department of Agriculture in late 1933, the 1934-35 cotton contracts rendered massive injustice to all classes of tenants. Under the 1934-35 contracts participating cotton farmers were entitled to a 3.5¢ per-pound subsidy payment plus a penny parity payment. Landlords were entitled to the entire 3.5¢ subsidy and between one-fourth and one-half of the parity payment. Under this system a sharecropper who had formerly received half of the money from the sale of cotton obtained only one-ninth part of the government subsidy for cotton not being produced. Obviously, the national government's primary agriculture program was detrimental to the economic interests of those people most in need.[19]

The method in which the Department of Agriculture handled complaints and the impact of mechanization compounded the difficulties of tenants and croppers. Complaints received by the Department of Agriculture were forwarded to the state administrators of the AAA for settlement. State administrators normally sent the complaints to county agents, who gave them to the particular landlord involved in the statement. The probable fate of the complaint is obvious. The impact of mechanization was illustrated by the behavior of Ward Templeman of Navasota. By using government subsidy payments and the profits received from the sale of his mules, Templeman acquired the necessary capital to purchase tractors. He retained only those tenants who were skilled tractor drivers; the other tenants became victims of modern farming. Like the drought and the depression, mechanization forced black and white sharecroppers, tenants, and small farmers who could not compete off the land.[20]

The major New Deal farm agencies that attempted to uplift the sharecropping and tenant classes were the Resettlement Administration (RA) and its successor the Farm Security Administration (FSA). One of the forms of assistance rendered by both the RA and the FSA was the rural rehabilitation loan. The RA under Rexford G. Tugwell, and the FSA with the white southern liberal Will W. Alexander at its helm, were committed to fair treatment for Negroes. In Texas Negro families received a reasonable proportion of the rehabilitation loans. From 1935 through 1938 approximately 21 percent of the families accepted as rural rehabilitation borrowers were Negro.[21]

Although variations existed from state to state, the proportion of Afro-Texan families obtaining rural rehabilitation loans was comparable to the South's average. In 1939 there were 25,020 active rural rehabilitation borrowers in Texas of whom 4,254 or 17 percent, were Negro. Forms of discrimination did, however, enter into the rural rehabilitation loan program. The average loan to a Negro family in the South was $606; white families averaged $659. Too, the policy of the FSA was to grant loans on the basis of the farmer's potentiality to be rehabilitated. The FSA saw rehabilitation and the probability of a loan being paid back to the government as being closely associated. Negroes were not considered by the FSA to be good loan risks. But even with the inequity in the average loan and the inability of blacks to borrow in proportion to their needs, the record of the FSA was commendable.[22]

Another plan designed to meet the needs of the poor was one authorizing the FSA to make loans to sharecroppers, farm laborers, and tenant families who hoped to purchase family-sized farms. The program was created in 1937 through the Bankhead-Jones Farm Tenant Act and operated primarily in the South. From 1937 until June 30, 1940, the tenant-purchase plan loaned money to 8,988 southern farm families. In Texas 162 of the 991 families benefiting from the program were black. Texas was among the few states in the South in which the percentage of Negro borrowers approximated the proportion of black tenants in the state.[23]

The intentions of the FSA were noble but of little value to those in economic distress. Typical of the FSA's visionary and antiquated Jeffersonianism was the homestead plan. The homestead plan stemmed from the activities of the Department of Interior's Division of Subsistence Homesteads, the rural rehabilitation plans of the FERA, and Tugwell's RA. As of March 1, 1940, a total of 14,835 units were located on homestead projects encompassing 876,233 acres. A total of twelve projects involving 920 families were initiated in Texas. Of the twelve Texas projects two were for Negroes. Under the plan ninety-five landless black families were able to obtain relatively small farms. Sabine Farms, the larger of the two Negro projects in Texas, was located in Harrison and Panola counties. In these two counties the government purchased 9,786 acres on which eighty families were resettled. The other project, initiated by the Texas Farm Tenant Security Administration, had 111 units scattered over sixteen counties. Fifteen Negro families were resettled on parts of this land.[24]

In general, the plans of the RA and the FSA were poorly funded, inadequate, and outdated. The RA and the FSA made no appreciable improvement in the total picture of rural southern poverty. Even adequate financing would not have enhanced the success story of their programs. At a time when expensive machinery and the beginnings of agribusiness made large land resources a virtual prerequisite to profit on the farm, Tugwell, Alexander, and others were advocating plans to create a new class of yeomen farmers.

Of deep concern to black leaders was the inadequate housing in which innumerable low-family-income Negroes were forced to live. Negro leaders saw in the Public Works Administration's Housing Division and its successor, the United States Housing Authority (USHA), federal plans which would bring immediate, tangible relief to needy blacks. In May 1935 the Rev. Maynard H. Jackson of the Dallas Interdenominational Ministerial Alliance and Dr. R. T. Hamilton met with white officials to discuss two proposed PWA housing projects for Dallas. Late in July the mayor of Dallas, George Sergeant, announced that two projects, one for whites and one for blacks, consisting of 320 units each, would be constructed in Dallas.[25]

The Dallas projects were the first of several major public housing developments in Texas. Houston, Dallas, Fort Worth, Austin, and even the small town of Pelly obtained federally financed housing projects. The projects ranged in size from one designed to house thirty families to a massive effort in North Dallas consisting of 626 units. The only complaint voiced by black leaders concerning the policies of the USHA was the failure of the agency to guarantee that a satisfactory percentage of the skilled workers employed to construct the projects were Negro. Although the labor complaint was valid, the housing benefits derived by the black community partially offset the impact of job discrimination. The average monthly rental rate of $6.59 for the USHA units in Austin provided blacks with decent housing.[26] In all probability the typical Negro who was not directly affected by USHA job discrimination overlooked the problem and was elated to receive a low monthly rent.

Data comparing the distribution of relief and welfare funds among blacks in Texas with Negroes elsewhere in the South provide a mixed picture. The level of benefits obtained by the black community in any particular state must be considered in relation to the proportion of Negroes in the state's population. Table 5 contains the percentage of Negroes in the populations of eleven southern states in 1940. Of these

TABLE 5

Negroes as a Percentage of the Population in Eleven Southern States, 1940

State	Percent Negro	State	Percent Negro
Alabama	34.8	Mississippi	49.5
Arkansas	24.8	North Carolina	28.2
Florida	27.0	South Carolina	43.0
Georgia	34.7	Tennessee	17.3
Louisiana	36.0	Texas	14.4
		Virginia	24.8

Source: Sterner, *The Negro's Share,* 11.

states Texas had the lowest percentage of Negroes in its population. In May 1940 Texas was, with the possible exception of Virginia, the sole former Confederate state in which the percentage of blacks employed by the WPA exceeded the proportion of Negroes in the state's population (see table 6). The other southern states that approximated the record of Texas were Louisiana, North Carolina, and Tennessee. Louisiana had 34.4 percent of its WPA workforce from the Negro community and a population that was 36 percent black. North Carolina was 28.2 percent black and 27.4 percent of her WPA workers were Negro. The respective figures for Tennessee were 17.3 and 13.2 percent.

The record of aid to Negro farmers in Texas by the RA and FSA was not so favorable as that of the WPA. Tables 7 and 8 provide data on the extent of the rural rehabilitation loan and resettlement programs in the South. The norm in the South was for Negroes to obtain rural rehabilitation loans in excess of their proportion of the farm population. Texas, Alabama, Florida, North Carolina, South Carolina, and Virginia conformed to the prevailing pattern. In Louisiana the percentage of Negroes in the farm population and the proportion of black families among rural rehabilitation borrowers were approximately identical. The remaining four states in the sample manifested overt discrimination against blacks seeking to borrow from the RA and the FSA.

In Texas and in most other southern states, Negroes did not participate in the resettlement program in proportion to their relative numerical strength in either the farm or the total population. Blacks constituted 14.4 percent of the Texas population and 12.6 of the state's farm population. Only 10.3 percent of the resettlement units were designated for Negroes. The four states in which the percentage of proposed resettlement units

TABLE 6

Negroes as a Proportion of WPA Workers in
Ten Southern States, May 1940

State	Percent Negro	State	Percent Negro
Alabama	27.2	Mississippi	24.2
Arkansas	15.1	North Carolina	27.4
Florida	18.7	South Carolina	33.8
Georgia	26.8	Tennessee	13.2
Louisiana	34.4	Texas	15.9

Source: Sterner, *The Negro's Share*, 416. Data on Virginia could not be located by the author. The material on Texas was based on twenty-nine counties in East Texas with cities of more than 10,000 population and eighty-eight East Texas counties without cities of at least 10,000 people. Since the vast majority of the Negro population in Texas is located in these counties, the sample is valid.

exceeded the proportion of Negroes in the farm population were Georgia, North Carolina, South Carolina, and Virginia. North Carolina, South Carolina, and Virginia, provided a more equitable distribution of both rural rehabilitation loan funds and resettlement units than Texas.

The allocation of NYA secondary school aid to Negroes throughout the South provided blacks with a disproportionate percentage of the funds. In each of the eleven states surveyed the percentage of Negro high school youths receiving NYA aid exceeded the percentage of blacks in the secondary school population (see table 9). Of the southern states, Texas had the least commendable record. The percentage distance between NYA aid to Negroes and their school enrollment was 1.2 percent. In neighboring Louisiana the difference was 17.4 percent and in Georgia the disparity was 27 percent. Consideration of NYA funds distribution in Texas, however, must be placed in somewhat different context from the apportionment of NYA aid in those southern states with considerable percentages of blacks in their populations. A greater percentage of black youths of high school age in Texas attended school than did Negro youths in the high black density states.

College level NYA assistance and Negro college enrollment reflect essentially the high school picture. In each of the states except South Carolina the proportion of blacks obtaining NYA college support surpassed the percentage of Negroes in the state's population (see table 10). Also, the 2.3 percent difference in Texas between the percentage of

TABLE 7

Negroes as a Proportion of the Farm Population in 1940 and as a Percentage of Rural Rehabilitation Borrowers in Eleven Southern States, 1935-39

State	Average Percentage of Negro rural rehabilitation loans	Negroes as a Percent of the farmers
Alabama	37	31.7
Arkansas	14	26.3
Florida	17	15.7
Georgia	24	27.4
Louisiana	39	39.7
Mississippi	31	54.8
North Carolina	29	21.7
South Carolina	50	44.6
Tennessee	7	11.1
Texas	20	12.6
Virginia	25	20.1

Sources: Calculated from Sterner, *The Negro's Share*, 421; U.S. Bureau of the Census, *Sixteenth Census of the United States: 1940, Agriculture: General Report*, 3: 161-63.

Negroes in the college population and the proportion of blacks obtaining NYA college aid was not great. Only the Carolinas had a closer relationship than Texas between the percentage of blacks in the college population and on NYA assistance. Once more the proportion of college-aid Negroes attending school in Texas was higher than in most other southern states.

A consideration of the actual need of black as compared to white youths does not reflect well upon Texas. The Negro community was less affluent than the white community. Negroes also had a greater necessity for an educated class than did whites. Under these conditions black

Texans should have received a significant disproportion of the available funds. Conversely, one may look at the apportionment of NYA money throughout the South, consider the prevailing racist attitudes of the region and the nation, and see genuine progress in the level of equity which existed. Certainly, those Negroes of school age received a more just distribution of funds than did their grandparents and great-grandparents who were the recipients of old age assistance.

TABLE 8

**Negroes as a Proportion of Families on Proposed Resettlement
Projects and as a Percent of the Farm Population
in Eleven Southern States, 1940**

State	Percent Negro of proposed resettlement families	Negroes as a percent of farmers
Alabama	14.3	31.7
Arkansas	22.2	26.3
Florida	14.7	15.7
Georgia	33.6	27.4
Louisiana	38.3	39.7
Mississippi	13.6	54.8
North Carolina	23.1	21.7
South Carolina	55.6	44.6
Tennessee	9.3	11.1
Texas	10.3	12.6
Virginia	48.0	20.1

Sources: Calculated from Farm Security Administration, *Farm Security Administration Homesteads*, 1–5; Sterner, *The Negro's Share*, 423; *Sixteenth Census of the United States: 1940, Agriculture: General Report*, 3: 161–63.

In terms of dollars received, both white and black Texans who were eligible for old age assistance did better than a majority of other southerners. Indeed, the average monthly old age assistance check paid to blacks in Texas exceeded the mean amount received by whites in Arkansas, Georgia, Mississippi, North Carolina, South Carolina, Tennessee, and Virginia (see table 10). As indicated by the percentages in table 10, however, the relative difference between the payments made to whites and blacks was not exceptional in Texas. Black Texans received 82.5 percent as much money per month in old age assistance as did whites. Negroes in Alabama, Arkansas, North Carolina, Tennessee, and Virginia were in closer relationship to whites in their respective states than were Negroes in Texas. Nevertheless, the greater wealth of Texas and generally higher wages received in Texas produced higher old age assistance checks.

TABLE 9

Negroes as a Percentage of the Recipients of NYA Aid to High School and College Students in Eleven Southern States, December 1939

State	Percent black on school aid	Percent black in school	Percent black on college aid	Percent black in college
Alabama	29.3	14.6	19.4	19.1
Arkansas	13.5	8.6	18.9	5.9
Florida	30.9	13.1	21.5	13.2
Georgia	38.9	11.9	20.1	15.4
Louisiana	31.4	14.0	17.5	10.7
Mississippi	16.8	13.0	13.4	6.8
North Carolina	25.1	18.2	16.5	16.3
South Carolina	43.7	17.8	18.0	18.7
Tennessee	15.9	11.7	21.9	14.3
Texas	11.1	9.9	9.4	7.1
Virginia	25.1	13.9	19.3	14.6

Source: Sterner, *The Negro's Share,* 264–65. Percentages of high school students was based on 1937–38. The percentage of college students was based on 1935–36.

For the American people the 1930s was a pivotal decade in the field of race relations. To be sure, Franklin D. Roosevelt and the New Dealers did not embark upon a racial crusade. The New Dealers did, however, enact into law relief and welfare measures that were guided by national and not state or regional standards. In most instances black Texans derived economic benefits from national programs in excess of their percentage of the state's population, but the benefits obtained by Negroes were not in proportion to their actual needs.

The importance of national standards can best be appreciated by reflecting upon those aspects of Negro life in which there was no positive action from the federal government. What type of educational system had state and local government in Texas provided Negroes? Which jobs did Negroes get from the employers in the private sector of the state's

TABLE 10
Average Monthly Old Age Assistance Payment by Race in Fiscal 1939–40 for Eleven Southern States

State	Average white	Average Negro	Average difference	Negro percent of white
Alabama	$20.30	$16.81	-$3.49	82.5
Arkansas	6.78	6.36	- .42	93.8
Florida	12.66	9.37	- 3.29	74.0
Georgia	7.13	5.70	- 1.43	79.9
Louisiana	13.76	10.61	- 3.15	77.1
Mississippi	11.09	7.17	- 3.92	64.6
North Carolina	10.25	8.87	- 1.38	86.5
South Carolina	9.80	7.60	- 2.20	77.6
Tennessee	9.61	9.00	- .61	93.7
Texas	13.81	11.39	- 2.42	82.5
Virginia	9.65	8.86	- .79	91.8

Source: Calculated from Sterner, *The Negro's Share,* 276. The figures for Alabama are probably higher than those actually paid.

economy? How many Negroes had been condemned to the life of a sharecropper? In what manner were black Texans accused of crime treated by the white people and the courts of Texas? The answers to these and other questions demonstrate the importance of national standards. The New Deal marked the beginning of what has since become an extensive commitment—a commitment by the body politic to ensure a better life for all Americans.

NOTES

1. HENDRICKSON, CCC in the Southwestern States.

1. John A. Salmond, *The Civilian Conservation Corps, 1933-1942: A New Deal Case Study* (Durham, N.C., 1967) 1–23; Hubert H. Humphrey, "In a Sense Experimental: The Civilian Conservation Corps in Louisiana," *Louisiana History* 5 (1964): 351.

2. Materials on the origin of the CCC are to be found in record group 35, data reference file 6, National Archives. Hereafter cited as NARG 35, data ref. 6.

3. Salmond, 27-29; interview with Dean A. Snyder, May 29, 1973, Department of Health, Education and Welfare, Washington, D.C.

4. This assessment is based upon an evaluation of correspondence to be found in NARG 35, 95, 114, and 408.

5. This assessment of relations with the Army is based upon the selection director's correspondence for the states included in this study, NARG 35, file 55.

6. For the origins of the educational program, see NARG 35, data ref. 6; also see Salmond, 48-53, 162-68, 219.

7. Based upon the selection director's correspondence for the states included in this study, 1933-40, NARG 35, file 55.

8. Humphrey, 353; *Happy Days,* December 22, 1934; *Albuquerque Journal,* April 8, 1933.

9. *Arkansas Democrat, New Orleans Times-Picayune, Austin American, Fort Worth Star-Telegram, Baton Rouge Times, Daily Oklahoman, Albuquerque Journal,* April-June 1933.

10. *Baton Rouge Times,* April 10, 1933.

11. *Albuquerque Journal,* April 14, 1933; *Daily Oklahoman,* April 14, 1933; *Happy Days,* October 14, 1933.

12. CCC general correspondence file, NARG 35.

13. Fred Morrell to E. O. Siecke, director, Texas State Forest Service, May 12, 1933; R. Y. Stuart to Robert Fechner, May 15, 1935; NARG 35, sec. 144.

14. See, for example, Reid A. Holland, "The Civilian Conservation Corps in Oklahoma, 1933-1942" (M.A. thesis, Oklahoma State University, 1969), 16-21.

15. Salmond, 30-37.

16. The development of the selection process and its attending problems can be pieced together through an examination of the files of the selection director's cor-

respondence for the states included in this study, April-September 1933, NARG 35, file 55. Also see the files of *Happy Days,* April-September 1933.

17. Ibid. Also see the statistical summaries for the states included in this study, CCC, April 1933–April 1942, NARG 35, file 80.

18. Correspondence of Guy, Johnson, Sweeney, Murchison, Persons, and Snyder, 1936–40, CCC, Texas, NARG 35, file 55; Neal Guy, report of field visit to Texas, November 4–7, 1939; ibid., file 77.

19. Correspondence of Bethune, Haynie, Snyder, and Persons, 1937–40, CCC, Arkansas, NARG 35, file 55.

20. Snyder to Persons, report of field visit to Arizona, October 26–27, 1937; report of field visit to New Mexico, December 4, 1937, CCC, Arizona and New Mexico, NARG 35, file 77.

21. See, for example, Rufus Miles to Persons, report of field visit to Oklahoma, February 3–4, 1938, for discussion of the allotment question. Also see report of the Oklahoma Department of Welfare, CCC selection, 1942, both in NARG 35, file 55.

22. J. L. Hill to W. Frank Persons, January 25, 1941, CCC, Oklahoma; J. S. Murchison to Persons, February 25, 1941, CCC, Texas; NARG 35, file 55.

23. Edward Bethune to Persons, April 20, 1941, CCC, Arkansas, NARG 35, file 55.

24. Hill to Persons, July 12, 1941, CCC, Oklahoma; Adam R. Johnson to Snyder, March 9, 1949, CCC, Texas; NARG 35, file 55.

25. Salmond, 150–55; *Congressional Record,* 75th Cong., 1st Sess., vol. 81, pt. 4, 4374–75.

26. *Arkansas Democrat,* April 6, 1937.

27. Thomas P. Gore to James J. McEntee, July 17, 1934, CCC monthly camp reports, Oklahoma; Bronson Cutting to Fechner, August 9, 1934; McEntee to Cutting, August 13, 1934; ibid., New Mexico; NARG 35, file 12.

28. R. E. Smee to Armstrong Evans, July 21, 1936; Charles T. Evans to Fechner, July 24, 1936; J. S. Billups to McEntee, August 10, 1936; CCC monthly camp reports, Arkansas; ibid.

29. Statistical summaries for the states considered in this study, April 1933-April 1942, NARG 35, file 80.

30. CCC statistical summary, Arizona, April 1933–April 1942, ibid.; *Happy Days,* August 3, 1940; *Dallas Morning News,* April 4, 1937; Holland, 27; Humphrey, 357–59.

31. Interview with Dean A. Snyder, May 28, 1973.

32. Based upon an examination of the files of testimonial letters, CCC, general correspondence, NARG 35.

33. Maude Barrett to Fechner, August 17, 1933, CCC, Louisiana, NARG 35, file 55.

34. Monthly camp and personnel reports, records of Camp SCS-20, Yukon, Oklahoma, 1938, CCC, Oklahoma; monthly camp and personnel reports, records of Camp SCS-10, Wynnewood, Okla. NARG 35, file 12.

35. J. C. Reddock to C. H. Kenlan, August 28, 1940, monthly camp and personnel reports, records of Camp NP-1, Marathon, Tex.; A. M. Stockman to James J. McEntee, July 3, 1939, monthly camp and personnel reports, records of Camp SCS-15-N, Whitewater, N.M.; ibid.

36. Acie Cole to Senator Caraway, May 9, 1933; Persons to Roy Wilkins, May 27, 1933; Persons to W. A. Rooksberry, May 27, 1933; Rooksberry to Persons, June 2, 1933; Fechner to Congressman John E. Miller, July 5, 1933; CCC, Arkansas, NARG 35, file 55.

37. M. J. Miller to Persons, January 14, 1935; Persons to Miller, January 21, 1935; John Eddleman to Persons, May 8, 1935; Eddleman to Fechner, February 19, 1935; Paul J. Glass to Persons, n.d., 1935; M. C. Simmons to Eddleman, April 7, 1935; Ceph Shoemake to Jacobs, April 7, 1935; Wylla C. Leonard to Jacobs, April 22, 1935; ibid.

38. Margaret Woodson to Persons, May 10, 1933; Maude Barrett to Fechner, August 7, 1933; H. J. Early to Persons, March 26, 1935; Clarence A. Laws, New Orleans Urban League, to Charles Taylor, October 12, 1940; CCC, Louisiana, ibid; statistical summary, Louisiana, October 1, 1937, NARG 35, file 80.

39. Fechner to Persons, July 17, 1935; Persons to Frances Perkins, July 30, 1935; Persons to Fechner, July 25, 1935; Neal Guy to Persons, July 30, 1935; Fechner to Persons (telephone conversation), August 1, 1935; McEntee to Persons, August 17, 1935; Col. J. O. Steger to Adam R. Johnson, August 17, 1935; Snyder to Persons, September 9, 1935; Persons to Sweeney, August 26, 1941; CCC, Texas; Persons to Bethune, August 26, 1941; Bethune to Persons, October 8, 1941; CCC, Arkansas, NARG 35, file 55; *Arkansas Gazette, Arkansas Democrat,* October 8, 1941.

40. Jimme Lee Robinson to President Roosevelt, September 21, 1935, monthly camp and personnel reports, records of Camp SP-14, Palo Duro Canyon, CCC, Texas, NARG 35, file 12.

41. J. S. Billups to Charles Taylor, September 9, 1937; Mrs. Chester Cage to Fechner, August 7, 1937; monthly camp and personnel reports, CCC, Louisiana, records of Camp SCS-2, ibid.

42. Smith to Fechner, July 24, 1938; McEntee to adjutant general, July 19, 1938; report of J. S. Billups, August 20, 1938; Glenn E. Riddell to Major G. C. Graham, March 15, 1940; monthly camp and personnel reports, CCC, Arkansas, records of Camp SCS-10, ibid.; David Beede to "Dear Dad," Pawhuska, Oklahoma, June 6, 1936; Persons to Faye Guthrie, December 11, 1937; monthly camp and personnel reports, CCC, New Mexico, records of Camp NM-1-N, ibid.

43. Neal Guy to Persons, December 4, 1937, report of field visit to New Mexico, NARG 35, file 55.

44. M. J. Bowen to Charles H. Kenlan, June 16, 1941; monthly camp and personnel reports, records of Camp F-64, NARG 35, file 12.

45. *Happy Days,* April 6, 1935; Donald L. Parman, *The Navajos and the New Deal* (New Haven, 1976), 32–35.

46. MacArthur to Roosevelt, November 22, 1933; C. M. Granger, acting forester, to X, November 2, 1933; Granger to J. P. Wright, November 23, 1933; NARG 95, file 144. Also see NARG 35, data ref. file 6, vol. 3.

47. Documents relative to this conflict are in NARG 35, data ref. 6; NARG 95, sec. 144; and NARG 407, sec. 8.

48. Monthly camp and personnel reports, records of Camp SP-43-T, 1935-41, NARG 35, file 12.

49. SCS camp narrative reports, CCC, Arizona, records of Camp SCS-11, NARG 114.

50. *Happy Days,* November 3, 1934. Also see J. L. Hill to Persons, January 25, 1941, CCC, Oklahoma, NARG 35, file 55.

51. Col. James Totten, C.O.H.Q., 8th C.A., to adjutant general, May 22, 1933; NARG 407.

52. *Pauls Valley Democrat,* November 6, 1941.

53. Bethune to Snyder, July 15, 1937; Snyder to Bethune, August 20, 1937; Palmer Patterson, Arkansas State Employment Service, to Bethune, July 28, 1949; Persons to Charles Ketchum, January 27, 1939; CCC, Arkansas, NARG 35, file 55; *Arkansas Democrat,* October 1, 1937; *San Antonio Express,* July 9, 1937; *Little Rock Gazette,* August 16, 1940.

54. James J. McEntee, "The CCC and National Defense," *American Forests,* July 1940, n.p.

55. Report of the Oklahoma Department of Public Welfare, 1941; Donald Galehouse to Persons, April 22, 1940; Jewell Adams to J. B. Harper, n.d.; Persons to Charles Sweeney, October 7, 1940; Bethune to Persons, February 28, 1941; NARG 35, file 55; records of Camp BR-12, Yuma, Arizona, March 12, 1942, NARG 35, file 12.

56. Salmond, 216–17; *Washington Post,* April 16, 17, 1942.

57. *Fort Worth Star-Telegram,* June 6, 1942; *Albuquerque Journal,* July 2, 1942.

2. NALL, The Struggle to Save the Land

1. U.S. Department of Agriculture (hereafter cited as USDA), *Crops against the Wind on the Southern Great Plains,* by Glenn K. Rule, Farmers' Bulletin 1833 (Washington, 1939), 5; U.S. Bureau of the Census, *Fifteenth Census of the United States: 1930, Agriculture,* vol. 2, pt. 2 (Washington, 1932), 1468-87; H. L. Gantz, "Practicing a Super-Farming System," *Farm and Ranch* 49 (August 23, 1930): 1, 4, 13; Lewis Hewes, *The Suitcase Farming Frontier* (Lincoln, Neb. 1973), 12-16.

2. H. F. Choun, "Duststorms in the Southwestern Plains Area," *Monthly Weather Review* 64 (June 1936); 196, 198-99, Everett C. Greene to Franklin D. Roosevelt, April 11, 1935; Mrs. George L. Aycock to H. H. Bennett, March 28, 1935; National Archives and Records Service, General Services Administration, Washington, record group 114 (Soil Conservation Service, general files, September 1933-October 1935). (National Archives and record groups hereafter cited as NARG.)

3. H. A. Hildwein, Clovis, N.M., to Senator Bronson Cutting, March 21, 1935, NARG 114.

4. F. W. Roddy to H. H. Finnell, August 5, 1935, ibid.

5. Deaf Smith County, Texas, plan of work for soil conservation, July 1, 1936 to June 30, 1937, conservation legislation, ibid.

6. Fort Hays, Kansas, Experiment Station No. 3, progress report, 1934, 103, ibid.

7. USDA, *Crops against the Wind,* 52; USDA, *Soil Conservation Reconnaissance Survey of the Southern Great Plains Wind-Erosion Area,* by Arthur H. Joel, Technical Bulletin 556 (Washington, January 1937), 28.

8. Robert J. Morgan, *Governing Soil Conservation: Thirty Years of the New Decentralization* (Baltimore, 1965), 4; Fred Floyd, "A History of the Dust Bowl," (Ph.D. dissertation, University of Oklahoma, 1950), 36-37; Donald C. Swain, *Federal Conservation Policy, 1921-1933* (Berkeley, 1963), 151-54.

9. Memorandum to the secretary of agriculture from H. H. Bennett, August 22, 1933; memorandum to Harry L. Hopkins from H. H. Bennett, September 28, 1933; NARG 114.

10. Morgan, 10-12.

11. Erosion Control and Work Relief Project for the Southwestern Drought Area, by H. V. Geib; Geib to H. H. Bennett, May 25, 1934; proposed emergency wind erosion control plan for Oklahoma Panhandle, NARG 114.

12. H. V. Geib to H. H. Bennett, April 4, 1934, ibid.

13. Floyd, 34, 36; H. H. Finnell to H. H. Bennett, September 26, 1934; NARG 114.

14. Albert H. Law, "Returning Protection to the Land," *Farm and Ranch* 54 (January 15, 1935): 1, 4, 16; C. W. Mullen, "High Plains Will Bloom Again," *Farmer-Stockman* 48 (April 1, 1935): 3, 18; Albert H. Law, "The 'Dust Bowl' Comes Back," *Farm and Ranch* 55 (February 15, 1936): 1, 10.

15. F. L. Duley to George A. Barnes, March 21, 1935; Carl E. Wagner to A. E. McClymonds, March 29, 1935; NARG 114.

16. *Amarillo Daily News,* March 19, 1935; *Dalhart Texan,* March 19, 1935 "A Plan for Providing Temporary Immediate Relief from Wind Erosion over the Entire South Plains Area," NARG 114.

17. Telegram, H. H. Bennett to John E. Hill, March 25, 1935; G. R. Quesenberry to M. L. Wilson, May 18, 1935; F. A. Anderson to W. C. Warburton, April 24, 1935; D. P. Trent to M. L. Wilson, April 27, 1935; telegram, H. H. Bennett to H. H. Finnell, April 3, 1935; NARG 114.

18. D. P. Trent to Rexford G. Tugwell, May 11, 1935; G. R. Quesenberry to Senator Carl A. Hatch, May 24, 1935; ibid.

19. Morgan, 20-23.

20. Joseph M. Ray, ed., *Marvin Jones Memoirs* (El Paso, 1973), 106-8; C. B. Manifold to H. H. Finnell, August 17, 1935; NARG 114.

21. Annual report for Region 6 for fiscal year ending June 30, 1936, Soil Conservation Service, H. H. Finnell correspondence, 1935-41, confidential, NARG 114.

22. USDA, *Crops against the Wind,* 67-72; Hugh Hammond Bennett, *Soil Conservation* (New York, 1939), 754-56.

23. USDA, *Sand-Dune Reclamation in the Southern Great Plains,* by Charles J. Whitfield and John A. Perrin, Farmers' Bulletin 1825 (Washington, 1939), 1-13; "From Sand Dunes to Pasture," *The Cattleman* 31 (June 1944): 19-20.

24. Annual report, 1936, Soil Conservation Service, p. 43, NARG 114; USDA, *Report of the Chief of the Soil Conservation Service, 1937,* 14-15; id., *1941,* 16.

25. Report of ECW Camp SCS-14-T, Memphis, Tex., March 31, 1936, NARG 114; USDA, *Crops against the Wind,* 65-66; report of agronomic programs of Memphis camp area, July 1935 to May 1937; NARG 114; Wilmon H. Droze, "The New Deal's Shelterbelt Project, 1934-1942," *Essays on the New Deal* (Austin, 1969), 33; *Amarillo Daily News* March 19, 1935.

26. Morgan, 41-42; interpretation of regulations relative to new AAA as they may affect SCS cooperators, Soil Conservation Service, Civilian Conservation Corps, Memphis, Tex., NARG 114.

27. The first five years of the Regional Agricultural Council for the southern Great Plains states, 1941, pp. 15-18, NARG 114; "To Lay the Dust," *Extension Service Review* 9 (March 1938): 43.

28. U.S. Great Plains Committee, *The Future of the Great Plains* (Washington, D.C., 1936), 106.

29. W. C. Lowdermilk to H. H. Finnell, May 16, 1935; Finnell to Lowdermilk, May 24, 1935; memorandum of understanding, May 21, 1935, Soil Conservation Service, counties legislation; NARG 114.

30. A coordinated program and plan of operation for the prevention and control of wind erosion for the area represented by the counties wind erosion conservation districts in Texas, p. 5, Soil Conservation Service, Civilian Conservation Corps, Memphis, Tex., subject files L-R, NARG 114; H. H. Finnell to H. H. Bennett, December 22, 1936; Finnell to D. S. Myer, March 25, 1937; NARG 114.

31. Morgan, 50, 58-64, 66, 72-76.

32. U.S. Great Plains Committee, *Future of the Great Plains,* 159-71.

33. Annual report, 1939-1940, Region 6, Soil Conservation Service, USDA, pp. 9-10, NARG 114.

34. Aid available to farmers in controlling wind erosion, May 27, 1938, secretary of agriculture, soil, NARG 114; 1939 Sherman County, Tex., Agricultural Conservation Program, Southern Region Bulletin 301, counties legislation, NARG 114; Edwin R. Henson to H. H. Finnell, May 21, 1940; memorandum for C. Luker from D. A. Dobkins, July 25, 1940, NARG 114.

35. U.S. Resettlement Administration, *First Annual Report* (Washington, 1936), 21; E. D. G. Roberts, "The Land Utilization Program in the Southern Great Plains," *Science* 88 (1938): 291-92; USDA, *Report of the Chief of the Soil Conservation Service, 1939,* 68.

36. Conditions justifying the acquisition of land and the execution of the development plan proposed on the southwest Kansas Land Use Adjustment Project, LK-KA 1, land utilization project files, 1934-1939, Kansas, NARG 114; Southern Otero County Land Adjustment Project LA-CO 4, land utilization project files, 1934-39, Colorado, NARG 114; New Mexico submarginal land purchase to project proposal A-4, land utilization project files, 1934-1939, New Mexico, NARG 114; USDA, *Report of the Chief of the Soil Conservation Services, 1941,* 16.

37. Aid available to farmers in controlling wind erosion, May 27, 1939, secretary of agriculture, soil, NARG 16.

38. Annual report, 1939-1940, Region 6, Soil Conservation Service, 15-15, NARG 114; USDA, *Report of the Chief of the Soil Conservation Service, 1941,* 24-25.

39. F. R. Kenney, "Water for the West," *Land Policy Review* 1 (September-

October, 1938): 1–5; USDA, *Report of the Chief of the Soil Conservation Service, 1941,* 16.

3. LAMBERT, Cattlemen, Government, and Depression

1. John T. Schlebecker, *Cattle Raising on the Plains, 1900–1961* (Lincoln, Neb., 1963), 72–119; Lewis Nordyke, *Great Roundup: The Story of Texas and Southwestern Cowmen* (New York, 1955); Texas Drought Committee to Herbert Hoover and Arthur Hyde, August 29, 1930, file 1-E/113, Herbert Hoover Presidential Library (hereafter cited as HHPL).
2. Schlebecker, 90–122.
3. *The Cattleman,* June 27, 1940, 18.
4. D. A. Fitzgerald, *Livestock under the AAA* (Washington, D.C. 1934), 20; Schlebecker, 104–15; Grover B. Hill, "Report and History of Cattle Buying Drouth Relief Program," February 6, 1935; (Texas) National Archives, record group 145 (hereafter cited as NARG).
5. Hill; Fitzgerald, 20-22; Louis H. Bean, "Agriculture and the World Crisis," USDA, *Yearbook of Agriculture, 1933* (Washington, 1935), 93–94.
6. Texas Drought Committee to Herbert Hoover and Arthur M. Hyde, August 29, 1930; J. G. Puterbaugh to Herbert Hoover, January 1, 1931, file 1-E/113; Fred C. Croxton to Pierce Williams, Colorado file; HHPL.
7. C. Roger Lambert, "Hoover and the Red Cross in the Arkansas Drought of 1930," *Arkansas Historical Quarterly,* spring 1970, 3–19.
8. Mark Brown, "A Family Farm History: 'The McAdams Place,'" (manuscript in possession of the author), 6; Louis McHowe, memorandum to the secretary of agriculture, August 14, 1934, official files, Franklin D. Roosevelt Library (hereafter cited as FDRL); C. Roger Lambert, "Drought Letters," *Mid-South Folklore,* spring 1975, 21–23; F. P. Holmes to editor, *Arkansas Gazette,* August 2, 1934.
9. Irvin Marion May, "The Paradox of Agricultural Abundance and Poverty: The Federal Surplus Relief Corporation, 1933–35," (doctoral dissertation, University of Oklahoma, 1970), 118; C. Roger Lambert, "Texas Cattlemen and the AAA," *Arizona and the West,* summer 1972, 142–43.
10. *Producer,* September 1933, 14, 16; November 1933, 13; February 1934, 17; Harry Petrie to Frank Mehling, December 26, 1933; NARG 145.
11. Irvin M. May, "Cotton and Cattle: The FSRC and Emergency Work Relief," *Agricultural History,* July 1972, 408-9; Lambert, "Texas Cattlemen," 141-42.
12. W. P. H. McFaddin, president of the Southeast Texas Live Stock Association, urged the government to use the method to remove 3 or 4 million cattle, for "it would remove the surplus cattle in less than 90 days, employ thousands of people and supply a market for a class of cattle that have not been possible to sell through any other sources; and, at the same time, supply food for the needy." McFaddin to Harry Petrie, February 9, 1934, NARG 145; Lambert, "Texas Cattlemen," 141; Hill.
13. Jay Taylor to Marvin Jones, October 25, 1933, NARG 145; *Producer* November 1933, 13; F. E. Mollin, "Agriculture Adjustment Program As Cattle-Producers View It," *Producer,* November 1933, 5–8.
14. Lambert, "Texas Cattlemen," 143-47; C. Roger Lambert, "Drought Relief for Cattlemen: The Emergency Purchase Program of 1934–35," *Panhandle-Plains Historical Review* 1972, 24.
15. Lambert, "Drought Relief," 21-35; Lambert, "Texas Cattlemen," 144.
16. C. Roger Lambert, "The Drought Cattle Purchase, 1934–35: Problems and Complaints," *Agricultural History,* April 1971, 86–88; Lambert, "Texas Cattlemen," 147-48.
17. Lambert "Drought Relief for Cattlemen," 27–28; Lorena Hickok to Harry L. Hopkins, June 25, 1934, Hopkins files, FDRL.
18. Ibid.

19. "The Drought of 1934-35," 50-57; Lambert, "Drought Relief for Cattlemen," 24-26.

20. May, "Cotton and Cattle," 409-10; Lambert, "Drought Cattle Purchase," 89.

21. Theodore Saloutos, "The New Deal and Farm Policy in the Great Plains," *Agricultural History,* July 1969, 348.

22. Lambert, "Drought Relief for Cattlemen," 29-30; *Kansas City Star,* August 14, 19, 21, September 5, 9, 1934; "Drought of 1934-35," 56-60; Lambert, "Texas Cattlemen," 149-51.

23. L. J. Allen to chief of Bureau of Animal Industry, January 30, 1923, NARG 124; Lambert, "Drought Relief for Cattlemen," 32-34; Lambert, "Texas Cattlemen," 151.

24. Lambert, "Texas Cattlemen," 151-52, 148-49.

25. *Fort Worth Star-Telegram,* March 6, 1934; "Drought of 1934-35," 90-110.

26. E. O. Pollock to W. A. Wheeler, May 16, 1935; minutes of President's Drought Committee, tentative proposal of policy statements by Eric Englund, May 25, 1935, NARG 16; "Drought of 1934-35," 111-16; Paul H. Appleby to Calvin B. Hoover, July 18, 1936; Cattle Purchase Committee; memorandum for J. W. Tapp, November 27, 1936, NARG 16; May, "Cotton and Cattle," 403-5; Lewis C. Gray, "Federal Purchases and Administration of Submarginal Land in the Great Plains," *Journal of Farm Economics,* February 1939, 123-26; Alfred Sears, "The Desert Threat in the Southern Great Plains; The Historical Implications of Soil Erosion," *Agricultural History* January 1941, 2-7; C. H. Wasser, "Early Development of Technical Range Management," *Agricultural History* January 1977, 74-75.

27. Hurt, "Agricultural Technology," 7; "Narrative Report of Soil Conservation Progress in the Tenth Texas Congressional District," USDA, Soil Conservation Service, May 29, 1946, House of Representatives files, Lyndon Baines Johnson Library; Vance Johnson, *Heaven's Tableland: The Dust Bowl Story* (New York, 1947), 155-213; memorandum from the White House to Rexford G. Tugwell, July 7, 1936, OF/FDRL.

28. Press release, July 21, 1934, USDA, memorandum for Aubrey Williams from Franklin D. Roosevelt (in drought file for 1936-1937—no other date), OF/FDRL.

29. Ed. R. Mayer to Franklin D. Roosevelt, August 17, 1936, report of the Great Plains Drought Area Committee, August 1936; summary of the final report of the Great Plains Committee on the Future of the Great Plains (n.d.); Morris L. Cooke to Franklin D. Roosevelt, February 15, 1945 (summary of letter), FDRL; narrative report of Soil Conservation progress in the Tenth Congressional District, USDA, Soil Conservation Service, May 29, 1946, House of Representatives files, Lyndon Baines Johnson Library; Peter K. Simpson, "The Social Side of the Cattle Industry," *Agricultural History,* January 1965, 46-47.

30. James A. Farley to Marvin H. McIntyre, September 1, 1936; Malcolm Miller to Aubrey Williams, July 21, 1936 (transcript of telephone conversation); FDRL; Presidential Drought Conference for Oklahoma, held at the State House, Des Moines, Ia., September 3, 1936 (transcript), OF/FDRL.

31. Richard Kleberg to Stephen Early, November 14, 1939; Stephen Early to Richard Kleberg, December 1, 1939; OF/FDRL.

32. C. Roger Lambert, "Drought, Texas Cattlemen and Eisenhower," *Journal of the West,* January 1977, 66-70.

33. E. J. Kyle, "Important Changes in Our Livestock Industry," *The Cattleman,* July 1940, 25-27; interview with Herman Walker, December 23, 1977.

4. MALONE, Country Music in the Depression

1. Archie Green has discussed the origin of the linkage between the term "hillbilly" and the southern white rural music in "Hillbilly Music: Source and Symbol," *Journal of American Folklore* 78 (July-September 1965); 204-8; an overview of country music history is Bill C. Malone's *Country Music, USA* (Austin, 1968).

2. Eck Robertson and Carl Sprague are discussed in Norm Cohen's "Early Pioneers," and Dalhart is discussed by Walter Darrell Haden in "Vernon Dalhart," both in Bill C. Malone and Judith McCulloh, eds., *Stars of Country Music* (Urbana, Ill., 1975), 11–14, 37–39, 64–86.

3. Early commercial records concentrated on the southeastern United States, possibly because of the romantic lure of the southern mountains, or perhaps because it was easier for New York recording men to reach the southeastern states.

4. Any edition of the *Texas Almanac* contains statistics on tenantry and farm ownership in that state during this century. Additional material on other states is located in Charles S. Johnson, Edwin R. Embree, and William W. Alexander, *The Collapse of Cotton Tenancy: A Summary of Field Studies, 1933-35* (Chapel Hill, N.C., 1935).

5. The "Young People's Page" was composed largely of letters sent to the newspaper by correspondents. Many farm families, such as my own, faithfully clipped the songs and pasted them in old books (often called "ballet books"). William A. Owens discusses the practice in his own household in *Texas Folk Songs* (Dallas, 1950), 16.

6. Interview with Cecil Gill, Arlington, Texas, August 7, 1977. See also the liner notes to his LP "The Yodeling Country Boy," Bluebonnet BL114.

7. A recent biographical study of Rodgers is Chris Comber and Mike Paris, *Jimmie the Kid: The Life of Jimmie Rodgers* (London, 1977). The most astute student of Rodgers, however, is Nolan Porterfield, who is working on a biography. Porterfield has made a preliminary statement in "Stranger through Your Town: The Background and Early Life of Jimmie Rodgers," *John Edwards Memorial Foundation Quarterly* 13 (summer 1977), 4–16.

8. Rodgers's appearances were often mentioned in the entertainment trade magazine *Billboard*. The following include only a sampling of the references made to Rodgers: 40 (December 29, 1928): 30; 41 (February 16, 1929): 3; 42 (April 5, 1930): 30; 44 (March 26, 1932): 42.

9. Interview with Floyd Tillman, Bacliff, Texas, May 31, 1974.

10. Bob Coltman, "Across the Chasm: How the Depression Changed Country Music," *Old Time Music*, winter, 1976/77, 6–12; George T. Simon, *The Big Bands* (New York, 1967); Albert McCarthy, *Big Band Jazz* (New York, 1974).

11. The best history of the Grand Ole Opry is Charles K. Wolfe, *The Grand Ole Opry: The Early Years, 1923-35* (London, 1975); post-1935 developments are surveyed in Malone.

12. Interview with Herald Goodman, Carrollton, Tex., December 29, 1967; interview with Joe (Shelton) Attlesey, Yantis, Tex., July 31, 1974; Frank Page and David Kent, "The Louisiana Hayride," *Country Gazette* 1 (August 1976): 3.

13. Souvenir brochure, *Gus Foster and the Blue Ridge Mountain Folks* (published by KRLD about 1940); interview with Homer (Bill) Callahan, Dallas, Tex., August 23, 1963. A sampling of the Callahan Brothers' style can be heard on "The Callahan Brothers," Old Homestead OHM90031.

14. Malone, 111–114; some of the transcriptions of the Carter Family performances have been recorded on "The Carter Family on Border Radio," JEMF101 (produced by the John Edwards Memorial Foundation in Los Angeles).

15. Interview with Carr P. Collins (one-time owner of the Crazy Water Crystals Company), Dallas, Tex., April 20, 1962; Pat Ahrens, "The Role of the Crazy Water Crystals Company in Promoting Hillbilly Music," *JEMF Quarterly* 6 (Autumn 1970), 107-9.

16. John Cohen, "Fiddlin' Eck Robertson," *Sing Out* 14 (April-May 1964): 55–59; the larger phenomenon is discussed by Stephen Ray Tucker, "The Western Image in Country Music" (M.A. thesis. Southern Methodist University, 1976).

17. Douglas B. Green, "Gene Autry," in Malone and McCulloh, 142–57; examples of Autry's early style can be heard on "40 Rare Gems," Country Music History CMH 114 and 115.

18. Rogers's story is told by Elise Miller Davis in *The Answer Is God* (New York, 1955); Ritter's life and career are discussed by Johnny Bond in *The Tex Ritter Story* (New York, 1976). A brief discussion of other singing cowboys is found in James Horowitz, *They Went Thataway* (New York, 1976).

19. "Songs from Texas," *Time*, March 24, 1941, 36; Charles Faurot, notes to the LP "Texas Farewell: Texas Fiddlers, 1922-30," County 517; a reissue of Robertson's early recordings, including "Sally Goodin," is "Master Fiddler," Sonyatone STR201.

20. Charles Townsend, *San Antonio Rose: The Life and Music of Bob Wills* (Urbana, Ill., 1976), 1, 3, 16.

21. Bob Pinson, "The Musical Brownies," *Country Directory* no. 4 (n.d.), 11-17; several of the Musical Brownies' original recordings have been released on "Taking Off," String STR804; interview with Bob Dunn, Houston, Tex., July 17, 1966; spinoffs from the Milton Brown organization include Cliff Bruner and the Texas Wanderers, Ocie Stockard and the Wanderers, and Bob Dunn and the Vagabonds. The Musical Brownies continued for a few years under the direction of Milton's brother Durwood.

22. Townsend, 143-52; One example of the faithfulness exhibited by Bob Wills's fans is preserved in a daily log maintained by an unknown listener to KVOO: "Bob Wills and his Texas Playboys on Radio, 1942," *Journal of Country Music* 5 (winter 1974), 135-93.

23. The best general collection of Bob Wills material is "The Bob Wills Anthology," Columbia KG32416.

24. Several important anthologies of recorded Western Swing are available: "Rollin' Along," an Anthology of Western Swing," Tishimingo Tsho 2220; "Beer Parlor Jive," String 801; and three volumes recorded on the Old Timey Label, 105, 116, and 117.

25. I may have been the first writer to apply the term "honky tonk" to a particular style of country music; see Bill C. Malone, "A History of Commercial Country Music in the United States, 1920-1964" (Ph.D. dissertation, University of Texas, 1964).

26. Interview with Floyd Tillman, May 31, 1974, and Joe (Shelton) Attlesey, July 31, 1974.

27. Self-pity is certainly not unique to country music. Lawrence W. Levine argues that the attitude has long been a characteristic of American popular music: Levine, *Black Culture and Black Consciousness* (New York, 1977), 275. The Glen Campbell quotation is from an unsigned article called "The Hip Hick," *Time,* January 31, 1969, 73.

28. Interview with Albert Poindexter (Al Dexter), Denton, Tex., August 26, 1973; Weldon Owens, "Cross Country," *Dallas Times-Herald,* April 22, 1962.

29. Townsend Miller, "Ernest Tubb," in Malone and McCulloh, 222-37.

30. Interview with Albert E. Brumley, Powell, Mo., April 5, 1972; the best printed collection of Brumley songs is *The Best of Albert E. Brumley* (Powell, Mo., 1966).

31. Brumley compositions are still heard with great frequency in bluegrass music. Such singers as Ralph Stanley, Mac Wiseman, and the Sullivan Family regularly perform songs like "Rank Stranger" and "I'd Rather Live by the Side of the Road."

32. These lines are from one of Brumley's most popular songs, "If We Never Meet Again," published in *Divine Praise* (Stamps Publishing House, 1945).

33. The unusual interrelationship between northern radical labor organizers and southern conservative balladeers is explored by Archie Green in the notes to Sarah Ogan Gunning, "Girl of Constant Sorrow," Folk-Legacy FSA26, and in *Only a Miner: Studies in Recorded Coal-Mining Songs* (Urbana, Ill., 1972), 419-22.

34. The best recorded collection of depression songs is the New Lost City Ramblers, "Songs from the Depression," Folkways FA5264.

35. Archie Green, "The Death of Mother Jones," *Labor History* 1 (winter 1960): 1-4.

36. John Greenway, *American Folksongs of Protest* (Philadelphia, 1953), 275-302; Woody Guthrie, *Bound for Glory* (New York, 1943).

37. I am most indebted to Richard A. Reuss for my understanding of Guthrie during the thirties: letter from Richard A. Reuss to author, February 26, 1969. See also Richard A. Reuss, "Woody Guthrie and His Folk Tradition," *Journal of American Folklore* 83 (July-September 1970): 273-303.

38. R. Serge Denisoff, *Great Day Coming* (Urbana, Ill., 1971), 41, 47.

39. Guthrie also recorded his "Dust Bowl Ballads" for Victor: vol. 1, Victor P-27, and vol. 2, Victor P-28.

40. Both songs are discussed by Dorothy Horstman in *Sing Your Heart Out, Country Boy* (New York, 1975), 343-44, 406-8.

41. The term was coined by Douglas B. Green in his essay on Gene Autry, Malone and McCulloh, 151.

5. WHISENHUNT, Search for a Villain

1. Richard Hofstadter, *The Age of Reform* (New York, 1955), 70.

2. Ibid., 71.

3. "Letters from Readers," *Dallas Morning News*, January 14, 1931.

4. Theodore G. Joslin, *Hoover off the Record* (Garden City, N.Y., 1934), 11; Clement Wood, *Herbert Clark Hoover: An American Tragedy* (New York, 1932), 326; Harris Gaylord Warren, *Herbert Hoover and the Great Depression* (New York, 1959), 83.

5. Ralph W. Steen, *Twentieth Century Texas* (Austin, 1942), 23; Democratic National Committee correspondence, 1928-33; Franklin D. Roosevelt Library, Hyde Park, New York, July 20, 1931, box 721 (hereafter cited as FDRL); *Texas Spur* (Spur, Tex.), January 30, 1931.

6. FDRL, November 9, 1932, box 736; *Big Spring News*, as quoted in *Terry County Herald* (Brownfield, Tex.), April 22, 1932; letter, August 4, 1930, gen. correspondence re Texas, 1929-32, Office of the Secretary of Agriculture, USDA, record group 16, National Archives; *Uvalde Leader-News*, June 24, 1931.

7. *Terry County Herald*, August 29, 1930; Ross Sterling files as governor of Texas, correspondence, Texas State Archives, Austin, September 1, 1931, box 176; "Letters from Readers," *Dallas Morning News*, January 7, 1931.

8. Ibid., April 15, 1930; *Lamar County Echo* as quoted in *Dallas Morning News*, November 18, 1930; "Letters from Readers," ibid., November 16, 1930, June 9, 1931; *Galveston Daily News*, March 4, 1930; *Uvalde Leader-News*, February 5, 1932; "Public Opinion," *Amarillo Daily News*, September 18, 1930; "Looking Forward," *Southwest Water Works Journal*, 13 (January 1932): 22.

9. Clipping from *Texarkana Press*, November 30, 1931, in Morris Sheppard Scrapbook, Morris Sheppard Papers, University of Texas at Austin Archives; Wright Patman to Sam Rayburn, June 22, 1932, Sam Rayburn Papers, correspondence, 1932, Sam Rayburn Library, Bonham, Tex.; *Congressional Record*, 72d Cong., 1st Sess., 1932, 75, pt. 5, 4962.

10. Ibid., *Congressional Record* 72 Cong., 1st Sess., 1931, 75 pt. 1, 737, 735; pt. 4, 3998.

11. FDRL, August 3, 1932, September 6, 1932, box 727; "Public Opinion," *Amarillo Daily News*, February 1, 1932; Connally Papers, December 8, 1929, box 7.

12. *Galveston Daily News*, December 30, 1930; *George West Enterprise*, December 27, 1929.

13. *Hebbronville News*, November 18, 1931.

14. *Sterling City News-Record*, January 15, 1932.

15. "Letters from Readers," *Dallas Morning News*, November 12, 1930, June 8, 1932; *Austin Statesman*, August 15, 1931.

16. FDRL, October 22, 1932, box 727.

17. Ibid., November 27, 1929, box 718; April 18, 1932, box 721; July 11, 1932, box 724; December 3, 1932, box 733.

18. Ibid., March 29, 1932, box 720.

19. Ibid., January 14, 1931, box 721.

20. Ibid., January 30, 1933, box 738; Connally Papers, n.d., box 10; February 14, 1931, box 25; "Letters from Readers," *Dallas Morning News*, August 5, 1931.

21. *Fredericksburg Standard*, March 4, 1932; *El Paso Times*, November 22, 1931; Connally Papers, October 6, 1931, box 15; Baker Mercantile Company, correspondence, Southwest Collection, Texas Tech University, September 7, 1931, wholesale letters, 1931-35.

22. Letters, October 3, 1932, November 29, 1929, secretary's correspondence, Department of Commerce Papers, record group 40, National Archives; letters, March 29, 1932, December 30, 1932, Rayburn Papers; letter, October 6, 1931, box 15, Connally Papers; Henry Ansley, *I Like the Depression* (Indianapolis, Ind., 1932), 27-28; FDRL, April 12, 1932, box 722.

23. Wright Patman to Rayburn, June 22, 1932, Rayburn Papers; *Congressional Record*, 72d Cong., 1st Sess., 1932, 75, pt. 4, 3996; *Ferguson Forum*, May 21, 1931.

24. Letter, May 31, 1932, Rayburn Papers.

25. *Weekly Dispatch*, January 30, 1932; J. T. Canales, "Usury," *Lulac News* 1 (July 1932): 5.

26. *Austin Statesman*, October 17, 1931, January 6, 1932; *Bonham Daily Favorite*, May 1, 1931, July 25, 1931.

27. "Musings of Monty," *Monty's Monthly* 13 (January 1931): 34; *Congressional Record*, 72d Cong., 2d Sess., 1932, 76, pt. 1, 1017; *Roby Star-Record*, October 30, 1930; Seth Shepard McKay, *Texas Politics, 1906-1944* (Lubbock, Tex., 1952), 228-29.

28. *Weekly Dispatch*, November 8, 1930; *Dallas Craftsman*, December 27, 1929, March 28, 1930; "Correspondence," *Texas Outlook* 15 (March 1931): 2; FDRL, May 24, 1932, box 722, September 5, 1932, box 727.

29. Letter, March 29, 1932, Rayburn Papers.

30. Canales, 5; FDRL, August 23, 1931, box 720; December 12, 1932, Box 736; February 1, 1933, box 734; letter, October 17, 1931, Sterling Papers, box 180.

31. Letter, January 5, 1932, Rayburn Papers.

32. *Southern Messenger*, May 5, 1932; FDRL, December 10, 1932, box 734; undated newspaper clipping in Norris scrapbook, J. Frank Norris Papers in the possession of Rev. E. Ray Tatum.

33. *Sterling City News-Record*, December 13, 1929; *George West Enterprise*, January 24, 1930; *San Patricio County News*, June 25, 1931; *Canadian Record*, July 14, 1932; *Roby Star Record*, March 25, 1932.

34. FDRL, November 4, 1932, box 735; Connally Papers, n.d., box 12; FDRL, November 1, 1932, box 734.

35. W. L. Clayton, "The World's Economic Tangle," *Acco Press* 9 (April 1931): 22; "The Rights of the Dollar," *West Texas Today* 12 (February 1932): 22; "Behind the Relief," ibid. 13 (December 1932): 8.

36. *Dallas Morning News*, February 5, 1932; Ben F. Miller, *A Presidential Survey from Washington to Hoover Inclusive* (Slaton, Tex., 1932), 120-21; Cyclone Davis, *Memoir* (Sherman, Tex., 1935), 84.

37. *Congressional Record*, 72d Cong., 1st Sess., 1932, 75, pt. 2, 1400.

38. Henry Morton Robinson, *Fantastic Interim* (New York, 1943), 224; Joslin, 182-83.

39. *Dallas Morning News*, February 5, 1932; *Galveston Daily News*, February 5, 1932.

40. U.S. Congress, Senate, Subcommittee of the Committee on Manufactures,

Hearings, Establishment of National Economic Council, 71st Cong., 3d Sess., 1931, 183; *Austin Statesman,* May 25, 1931; *Devil's River News,* November 7, 1930; *Weekly Dispatch,* August 6, 1930; Dr. Edwin A. Elliott, "Economic Depression and Unemployment," *Texas Outlook* 15 (July 1931): 11.

41. FDRL, April 22, 1932, box 722; Connally Papers, n.d., box 20; Wright Patman to Herbert Hoover, August 19, 1930, USDA, correspondence; "Letters from Readers," *Dallas Morning News,* March 14, 1930; *Amarillo Sunday Globe-News,* November 30, 1930.

42. Leonard P. Ayres, *The Economics of Recovery* (New York, 1934), 43-44; *Amarillo Daily News,* February 5, 1932; *Galveston Daily News,* February 6, 1932; *Dallas Morning News,* February 5, 1932; *Terry County Herald,* October 23, 1931; Miller, 209.

43. Ibid., 211; FDRL, January 29, 1933, box 731; *Bonham Daily Favorite,* October 12, 1931; "In Our Opinion," *Editorials of the Month for Texas* 1 (November 1930): 555; FDRL, January 4, 1933, box 735; ibid., November 9, 1932, box 735; "Letters from Readers," *Dallas Morning News,* June 3, 1932.

44. FDRL, January 26, 1933, box 732; September 12, 1932, box 730; *Southern Messenger,* May 5, 1932; FDRL, May 12, 1932, box 721; "Public Opinion," *Amarillo Daily News,* January 20, 1931; "Letters from Readers," *Dallas Morning News,* September 12, 1931.

45. *Hebbronville News,* June 17, 1931.

46. Ibid.

47. "Letters from Readers," *Dallas Morning News,* April 15, 1930; *Amarillo Daily News,* June 16, 1932; D. A. Bandeen, "Don't Try to Tinker with Fundamentals," *West Texas Today* 13 (February 1933): 19.

48. FDRL, January 23, 1932, box 721; September 6, 1932, box 727; "Letters from Readers," *Dallas Morning News,* June 12, 1931; *Hebbronville News,* June 24, 1931; *Huntsville Item,* August 20, 1931; "Free Trade," *The Common Herd* 15 (March 1930), 14-15.

49. FDRL, April 19, 1932, box 722.

50. *Greenville Messenger* as quoted in *Ferguson Forum,* January 29, 1931; *Bonham Daily Favorite,* August 26, 1931; *Weatherford Democrat,* June 12, 1931; *Fredericksburg Standard,* September 11, 1931; *Amarillo Daily News,* June 16, 1932; *Roby Star-Record,* October 30, 1930; Warren, 88.

51. *Congressional Record,* 71st Cong., 3d Sess., 1931, 74, pt. 4, 4384; 72d Cong., 1st Sess., 1931, 75, pt. 1, 733; 72d Cong., 2d Sess., 1932, 76, pt. 1, 991.

52. Ibid., 1017.

53. *The Valley Farmer,* May 20, 1931, 6; "An Open Letter to Our Friends," *Acco Press* 10 (July 1932): 4-5.

54. FDRL, January 7, 1929, box 719; Connally Papers, October 25, 1929, box 6; U.S. State Department Decimal File, 1919-1929, record group 59, National Archives, March 21, 1929, box 6228.

55. FDRL, April 5, 1932, box 718.

56. Secretary's correspondence, individual case file, 1929-1933, Department of the Treasury, record group 56, National Archives, November 4, 1931, box 2; Ansley, 57; *McAllen Monitor,* October 7, 1932; *Huntsville Item,* November 24, 1932; *Pecos Enterprise and Gusher,* January 6, 1933; "Letters from Readers," *Dallas Morning News,* September 12, 1931.

57. Baker Mercantile Company, April 25, 1932, customers' letters, 1931-33.

58. FDRL, November 4, 1932, box 724; December 2, 1932, box 731.

59. Senator Tom Connally, as told to Alfred Steinberg, *My Name Is Tom Connally* (New York, 1954), 135; secretary's correspondence, Treasury Department, October 27, 1931, box 2; April 17, 1932, Rayburn Papers; *Dallas Craftsman,* March 25, 1932.

60. FDRL, September 9, 1932, box 724.

61. *Dallas Morning News,* March 26, 1932; *Hebbronville News,* April 15, 1931;

Canadian Record, May 26, 1932; "In Our Opinion," *Editorials of the Month for Texas* 3 (January 1932); 11; *Austin Statesman,* April 5, 1932; *Roby Star-Record,* January 22, 1932; "Musings of Monty," *Monty's Monthly* 13 (October 1931): 33–34; *Texas Weekly,* February 14, 1931, 6; *The Alcade* 21 (November 1932): 37.

62. FDRL, July 2, 1932, box 723; February 23, 1933, box 738; "Public Opinion," *Amarillo Daily News,* February 17, 1932; *Southern Messenger,* March 3, 1932.

63. *Austin Statesman,* June 3, 1932; Merton L. Dillon, "Religion in Lubbock," Lawrence L. Graves (ed.), *A History of Lubbock* (Lubbock, Tex., 1962), 482; Maury Maverick, *A Maverick American* (New York, 1937), 157; E. Ray Tatum, "Conquest or Failure: A Biographical Study in the Life of J. Frank Norris" (manuscript in the possession of the author at the University Baptist Church, Lubbock, Tex.), 237, 239, 243.

64. *Amarillo Daily News,* August 19, 1931; *Hebbronville News,* July 30, 1930; *Huntsville Item,* October 22, 1931; *San Patricio County News,* July 31, 1930; "Isolation Not Possible," *Dallas* 11 (August 1932): 12.

65. *Tahoka News* as quoted in *Terry County Herald,* July 17, 1931; *Uvalde Leader-News,* June 26, 1931; *Amarillo Daily News,* December 29, 1932; *Dallas Morning News,* October 1, 1931; *Galveston Daily News,* November 12, 1930.

66. *Congressional Record,* 72d Cong., 1st Sess., 1931, 75, pt. 1, 352; pt. 2, 4963; 72d Cong., 2d Sess., 1932, 76, pt. 1, 991; Bascom M. Timmons, *Garner of Texas* (New York, 1948), 132–33; *Galveston Daily News,* December 23, 1931.

67. FDRL, July 13, 1931, box 718; *Ferguson Forum,* June 25, 1931; FDRL, October 23, 1931, box 719; August 10, 1931, box 718.

68. *Ferguson Forum,* February 26, 1931; James A. Clark and Weldon Hart, *The Tactful Texan: A Biography of Governor Will Hobby* (New York, 1958), 171; FDRL, April 8, 1932, box 721; July 4, 1932, box 726; "Letters from Readers," *Dallas Morning News,* January 15, 1932; *Uvalde Leader-News,* February 26, 1932; "Letters from Readers," *Dallas Morning News,* June 24, 1932, December 1, 1932.

69. *Dallas Morning News,* April 11, 1930; *Galveston Daily News,* June 25, 1930; *Fredericksburg Standard,* March 15, 1930; Bureau of Labor Statistics, *Committee for Unemployment Relief,* 9, 12.

70. *Congressional Record,* 71st Cong., 2d Sess., 1930, 72, pt. 11, 12247; 72d Cong., 1st Sess., 1931, 75, pt. 1, 159; Allan A. Michie and Frank Ryhlick, *Dixie Demagogues* (New York, 1939), 62; *Congressional Record,* 72d Cong., 1st Sess., 1931–32, 75, pt. 1, 159, 736; pt. 4, 4407.

71. *Congressional Record,* 71st Cong., 3d Sess., 1931, 74, pt. 4, 4381–87; *Austin Statesman,* October 20, 1929; *Weekly Dispatch,* May 24, 1930; "Letters from Readers," *Dallas Morning News,* February 8, 1930, January 31, 1930.

72. FDRL, January 17, 1933, box 735; Connally Papers, February 2, 1931, box 24; Sterling Papers, September 26, 1931, box 180; *Austin Statesman,* May 30, 1932; *El Paso Times,* June 26, 1932; *Galveston Daily News,* September 2, 1930.

73. *Haskell Free Press,* August 27, 1931; *Hollands,* March, 1931, 5; *Hebbronville News,* November 19, 1930; FDRL, December 16, 1932, box 735; "Letters from Readers," *Dallas Morning News,* August 8, 1931; *Devil's River News,* April 8, 1932; Connally Papers, n.d., 1930, box 12; January 5, 1932, Rayburn Papers.

6. PATENAUDE, Texas and the New Deal

1. Dorothy D. DeMoss, "Dallas, Texas, During the Early Depression: The Hoover Years, 1929–33," (master's thesis, University of Texas at Austin, 1966), 17, 49; William E. Montgomery, "The Depression in Houston during the Hoover Era, 1929–32," (master's thesis, University of Texas at Austin, 1966), 50; Judith G. Jenkins, "Austin, Texas, during the Great Depression, 1929–36," (master's thesis, University of Texas at Austin, 1966), 52.

2. John D. Biggers, *Final Report on Total and Partial Unemployment* (3 vols.; Washington, 1938), 3: 404. Standardized questionnaire submitted to fifty people

in the San Antonio area, fall 1971 (author's possession); Ralph W. Steen, *Twentieth Century Texas* (Austin, 1942), 29–31.

3. *Texas Almanac and State Industrial Guide, 1941-42* (Dallas, 1941), 300; *1940,* 239; *1936,* 129; Harold L. Ickes, *The Secret Diary of Harold L. Ickes: The First Thousand Days, 1933-1936* (3 vols.; New York, 1953), 1: 32; Owen P. White, "Piping Hot," *Colliers,* January 12, 1935, 10–11; see also Barbara T. Day, "The Oil and Gas Industry and Texas Policies, 1930–1935," (Ph.D. dissertation, Rice University, 1973).

4. "The Party and Roosevelt Record of Karl A. Crowley," Franklin D. Roosevelt Papers, President's personal file 2871, Franklin D. Roosevelt Library, Hyde Park, New York (hereafter cited as FDRL); *Dallas Times-Herald,* July 2, 1932; T. W. Davidson to author, October 6, 1952; Bascom H. Timmons to author, December 14, 1972; interview with John Naylor, September 25, 1952; interview with James A. Farley, August 18, 1971; James M. Burns, *Roosevelt: The Lion and the Fox* (New York, 1955), 154, 341; Alexander Shanks, "Sam Rayburn and the Democratic Convention of 1932," *Texana* 3 (winter 1965): 332.

5. Interviews with Jesse Jones, March 6, 1952, Maury Maverick, March 8, 1952, O. H. Cross, September 24, 1952, and Farley, August 18, 1971; George Mahon to author, June 6, 1969; Irving G. Williams, *The Rise of the Vice Presidency* (Washington, D.C., 1956), 175; *Time,* November 17, 1967, 32.

6. Jesse Jones with Edward Angley, *Fifty Billion Dollars: My Thirteen Years with the RFC 1932-1945* (New York, 1951), 510; Clinton W. Gilbert, "Contact Man," *Colliers,* February 18, 1933, 25; Donald Young, *American Roulette: The History and Dilemma of the Vice Presidency* (New York, 1965), 168; *New York Times Magazine,* December 13, 1936, 24; interview with Farley, August 18, 1971; Raymond Moley, *Twenty-Seven Masters of Politics: In a Personal Perspective* (New York, 1949), 245.

7. *New York Times,* November 17, 1961, 28; Neil MacNeil, *Forge of Democracy: The House of Representatives* (New York, 1963), 70; *Business Week,* December 4, 1954, 168.

8. *Fort Worth Star Telegram,* October 8, 1961; Paul F. Healy, "That Are Just Crazy about Sam" *Saturday Evening Post,* November 24, 1951, 71; *Washington Sunday Star,* January 5, 1941; "Leadership in Congress," *Review of Reviews* 95 (January 1937): 49; Moley, 244.

9. *Fort Worth Star Telegram,* October 8, 1961; Booth Mooney, *Roosevelt and Rayburn: A Political Partnership* (Philadelphia, 1971), 100, 106; Arthur Krock, *Memoirs: Sixty Years on the Firing Line* (New York, 1968), 189.

10. Telephone conversation with James A. Farley, August 20, 1970 (first quotation); *New York Times,* April 18, 1934, 5 (second quotation); interview with Farley, August 18, 1971; *Washington Sunday Star,* January 19, 1941; *Dallas Herald,* November 17, 1961.

11. U.S. Congress, *Official Congressional Directory,* 73rd to 75th Congresses; *Washington Daily News,* July 31, 1937; "Garner's Campaign Bomb," *Literary Digest* 114 (August 6, 1932): 8; Eddie Dowling, number 532, Columbia Oral History Project, Columbia University.

12. *Official Congressional Directory,* 73rd to 75th Congresses; Frank Freidel, *F.D.R. and the South* (Baton Rouge, 1965), 2; Raymond Moley, *The First New Deal* (New York, 1966), 234.

13. Arthur M. Schlesinger, *The Age of Roosevelt: The Coming of the New Deal* (3 vols.; Boston, 1965), 2: 6, 426; interview with Marvin Jones, 1952, Columbia Oral History Project, 639–this document was Mr. Jones's personal copy and in his possession in 1971; clipping, Garner scrapbooks, no. 14, University of Texas Archives; "The House of Jesse," *Fortune,* May 1940, 132, 140, 142; Jones, 270; Bascom H. Timmons, *Jesse H. Jones: The Man and the Statesman* (New York, 1956), 256; "Professional SOB," *Forbes,* August 1, 1971, 16.

14. Moley, *The First New Deal,* 350; Schlesinger, 2: 431; Ray Tucker, "Texas Steerer," *Colliers,* September 22, 1934, 16.

15. Interview with Farley, August 18, 1971; Timmons, 273; Garner to Costello, May 24, 1939, Jesse Jones Papers, general correspondence, general miscellaneous—Garner 1932–56, box 10, National Archives.
16. Williams, 157; Michael V. DiSalle with Lawrence G. Blockman, *Second Choice* (New York, 1966), 141; interview with Farley, August 18, 1971; interview with Jesse Jones, March 6, 1952; W. R. Poage to author, June 2, 1969.
17. Interview with Ralph Steen, March 7, 1952; George Mahon to author, June 6, 1969; T. R. Fehrenbach, *Lone Star: A History of Texas and the Texans* (New York, 1968), 652; *Washington Daily News*, n.d., 1937, Jesse Jones Papers, subject file, Democratic-Federal, box 186, NA; interview with Marvin Jones, March 4, 1971.
18. Roosevelt to Garner, September 25, 1934, President's Personal File 1416, FDRL; Garner to Roosevelt, October 1, 1934, Roosevelt to Garner, October 5, 1934, ibid.; "He Can't Fish until Congress Adjourns," *Literary Digest*, August 3, 1935, 7; Krock, 189; Bascom H. Timmons, *Garner of Texas*, 191.
19. *Washington Daily News*, July 3, 1937.
20. Urban congressmen tended to back the administration on social and economic issues, while those from predominantly rural districts were inclined to oppose the administration after 1936. James T. Patterson, *Congressional Conservatism and the New Deal: The Growth of the Conservative Coalition in Congress, 1933–1939* (Lexington, Mass., 1967), 331; *Newsweek*, March 13, 1939, 18.
21. Interview with Jesse Jones, March 6, 1952; Timmons, *Garner of Texas*, 215–16; *Washington Daily News*, November 6, 1938; Garner scrapbooks, no. 17; Jonathan Mitchell, "Garner: Texas Bogey Man," *New Republic*, August 31, 1938, 51; *U.S. News and World Report*, November 21, 1958, 102; clipping, Raymond Clapper Papers, reference file Fr-Ga, box 134, Library of Congress.
22. See Lionel V. Patenaude, "Garner, Sumners and Connally: The Defeat of the Roosevelt Court Bill in 1937," *Southwestern Historical Quarterly* 74 (July 1970); C. Dwight Dorough, *Mr. Sam* (New York, 1962), 260; Kenneth G. Crawford, "The Real John Garner," *Nation*, August 5, 1930, 139; interview with Farley, August 18, 1971; according to Patterson, Texas had ten conservatives in its delegation, more than any other state. See his *Congressional Conservatives and the New Deal*, 344-49, 126; *Washington Daily News*, n.d., 1937, Jesse Jones Papers, subject file, Democratic-Federal, box 186, NA; interview with Marvin Jones, March 4, 1971.
23. Edward J. Webster to Harry Hopkins, November 29, 1934, Harry Hopkins Papers, box 60, FDRL; *Records of the Texas Relief Commission, 1933-35, #10*, p. 30, #43, p. 1, box 2-10-917, Texas State Archives; M. J. Miller to Hopkins, August 24, 1935, Hopkins Papers, box 54, FDRL; James V. Allred, files as Governor of Texas, general files, box 235, Texas State Archives.
24. "Bexar County Reports," *Report of the Texas Rehabilitation and Relief Commission*, September 20, 1933, box 44, Texas State Archives; Works Progress Administration, *The Pecan Shellers of San Antonio* (Washington, 1940), 37; Lorena Hickok to Hopkins, April 17, 1934, Hopkins Papers, box 54, FDRL.
25. Webster to Hopkins, November 25, 28, 29, December 2, 1934, Hopkins Papers, box 60, FDRL; Hickok, April 17, 1934, ibid., box 54.
26. Neal Guy to Frank Persons, report of field trip to Texas, November 4-7, 1939, NARG 35; *American City* 53 (November 1938): 87; Wilborn E. Benton, *Texas: Its Government and Politics* (Englewood Cliffs, N.J., 1966), 473; Webster to Hopkins, November 25, 1934, Hopkins Papers, box 60, FDRL.
27. Jenkins, 109; interviews with W. A. Philpott, September 25, 1952, and Jesse Jones, March 6, 1952; Carter to Louis Howe, June 20, 1933, PPF 1433, FDRL; W. P. Hobby to author, October 22, 1952; Hickok to Hopkins, April 17, 1934, Hopkins Papers, box 54, FDRL; *Texas Weekly*, July 7, 21, 1934; *Texas Business Review*, January 29, 1934, 1.
28. Webster to Hopkins, November 25, 28, 29, 1934, Hopkins Papers, box 60, FDRL; *Texas Weekly*, May 13, 1933, June 25, November 7, 1936.
29. *Texas Weekly*, May 25, June 29, 1935; *Texas Business Review*, September 30, 1935, 2; *Dallas Morning News*, June 20, 1935; Carter to Roosevelt, May 7, 1935,

PPF 1433, FDRL; *Texas Weekly,* February 13, July 24, 1937; *Dallas Morning News,* July 3, 1937; *Texas Industry* 3 (April 1937): 20; *Texas Law Review,* October 1937, 137; Hobby to author, October 22, 1952; interview with Jesse Jones, March 6, 1952; James V. Allred to author, March 23, 1952.

30. Interview with Jesse Jones, March 6, 1952; *Texas Weekly,* April 20, 1935; telegram, Carter to Roosevelt, December 25, 1935, PPF 1433, FDRL; "Texas," *Fortune,* December, 1939, 82, 84; *Dallas Morning News,* November 23, 1937.

31. Sherwood H. Avery to author, October 13, 1952; Hobby to author, October 22, 1952; *Texas Weekly,* April 9, 1938; Fehrenbach, 651; V. O. Key, *Southern Politics in the State and Nation* (New York, 1949), 255.

32. Interview with Jerry R. Holleman, October 27, 1952; Biggers, 3: 403; *Labor Messenger* (Houston), August 4, 25, October 6, 1933; *Proceedings, Texas State Federation of Labor, Thirty-Seventh Convention, Dallas, May 14-17, 1934,* 13; *Weekly Dispatch* (San Antonio), July 20, 1935.

33. *Labor Messenger,* October 26, 1934; interview with Holleman, October 27, 1952; *Union Banner* (Ft. Worth), June 24, 1938.

34. *El Paso Labor Advocate,* December 22, 1933; *Labor Messenger,* October 2, 1936, January 7, 1938; interviews with Ray Harrington, September 23, 1952, and Holleman, October 27, 1952.

35. Interviews with Harrington, September 23, and Holleman, September 27, 1952.

36. Interviews with George Blair and Eugene Butler, September 25, 1952; E. M. Cooke to author, October 3, 1952; A. R. Mangus, *Changing Aspects of Rural Relief* (Washington, D.C., 1938), 127-28; Webster to Hopkins, November 25, 28, 1934, Hopkins Papers, box 60, FDRL; *Texas Almanac, 1941-1942,* 300.

37. Webster to Hopkins, November 25, 28, 1934, Hopkins Papers, box 60, FDRL; *Texas Almanac, 1941-1942,* 300.

38. Owen P. White, *Texas: An Informal Biography* (New York, 1945), 254; *The Cattleman,* January 1933, 9; interview with J. C. Burgen, September 25, 1952; H. G. Lucas to Chester Davies, n.d., AAA, alphabetical correspondence file, 1933-1935, NARG 145; Frank A. Briggs to Chester Davis, ibid.

39. *Congressional Record,* 74th Cong., 2d Sess., 1936, 6935; Marvin Jones to author, October 13, 1952; Cooke to author, October 3, 1952; interview with Butler, September 25, 1952.

40. Interview, E. Dale Odem with Mrs. James V. Allred, May 6, 1968, North Texas State University Oral History Collection, O.H. 10, 12-13; *Dallas Morning News,* September 26, 1959; *Newsweek,* August 8, 1936, 16. See also James V. Allred Papers, box 266, University of Houston, special collections, Houston, Texas.

41. Stuart A. MacCorkle, "State Control over Counties in Texas," *Southwestern Social Science Quarterly* 27 (September 1936): 161; Bryon Utecht, *The Legislature and the Texas People* (San Antonio, 1937), 168; George Mahon to author, June 6, 1969; *San Antonio Express,* September 12, 1934.

42. Interview with Malcolm Bardwell, July 23, 1971.

43. Jeffersonian Democrats Correspondence, folder 3. The papers of this organization were originally housed at the University of Texas Archives in Austin. Later J. Evetts Haley, who had donated them, turned the material over to the Panhandle Plains Historical Society, Canyon, Tex. As of this writing, they are in the possession of Mr. Haley.

44. *The Jeffersonian Democrat,* October 6, 1936; W. P. Hamblen to Haley, August 20, 1936, Jeffersonian Democrats correspondence, folder 11; Haley to author, September 30, 1952.

45. *Journal of the Senate of Texas,* 45th Legislature, Reg. Sess., 1937, 209, 213; *San Antonio Express,* February 10, 1937; *Journal of the House of Representatives* (Texas), 45th Legislature, Reg. Sess., 1937, 374-75. Later the House voted not to take sides on the issue but subsequently supported Roosevelt. See pp. 389, 431-32, 2665-68. *New York Times,* February 10, 1937, 1; *San Antonio Express,*

February 7, 9, 1937; Julian Capers, Jr., to Tom Connally, February 23, 1937, political file, box 96, Tom Connally Papers, Library of Congress; "Proceedings of the Fifty-Sixth Annual Meeting of the Texas Bar Association Held at San Antonio, Texas, July 1,2,3, 1937," *Texas Law Review*, 1937, 137; *Austin Statesman*, July 3, 1937.

46. Interview with Philpott, September 25, 1952; E. Kimbark MacColl, "The Supreme Court and Public Opinion: A Study of the Court Flight of 1937," (Ph.D. dissertation, University of California at Los Angeles, 1953), 364–70.

47. Jimmie Clark, "Austin Labor Angles," *Weekly Dispatch*, February 2, March 12, 1937; *Union Banner*, March 9, 1937; interview with George B. Blair, September 25, 1952; *New York Times*, February 18, 1937, 2; James E. Ferguson to Farley, n.d., PPF 2081, FDRL; memo for record, February 17, 1937, political file, box 92, Connally Papers; Allred to Bibb Graves, May 1, 1937, box 270, Allred Papers; *Dallas Morning News*, March 14, 1937; *Austin American*, March 28, 1937; *San Antonio Express*, March 26, 1937.

48. Allred to author, March 23, 1952; interview with Jesse Jones, March 6, 1952. For background, see Stanley Walker, "The Dallas Morning News," *American Mercury* 65 (December 1947), and Roland W. Melugin, "The Dallas Morning News and the New Deal," (master's thesis, East Texas State University, 1965).

49. Interview with Ralph Steen, March 7, 1952.

7. STRAUSBERG, New Deal in Arkansas

1. United States Department of Commerce, *Personal Income by States since 1929* (Washington, 1956), 142; Donald H. Grubbs, *Cry from the Cotton: The Southern Tenant Farmers Union and the New Deal* (Chapel Hill, N.C., 1971), 10–15; Pete Daniels, *High Water Rising: The Great Mississippi Flood of 1927* (Nashville, 1975); USDA, *Report of the National Drought Committee* (Washington, 1930), 15.

2. Lee Reeves, "Highway Bond Refunding in Arkansas," *Arkansas Historical Quarterly* 2 (winter 1943): 315–18; Benjamin V. Ratchford, *American State Debts* (Durham, N.C., 1941), 386–88; the state had the second lowest per capita expenditure for education in the nation.

3. *Arkansas Gazette* (Little Rock), November 10, 1930.

4. V. O. Key, Jr., *Southern Politics in State and Nation* (New York, 1949), 183; *Arkansas Gazette*, April 4–10, 1932; C. Roger Lambert, "Hoover and the Red Cross in the Arkansas Drought of 1930," *Arkansas Historical Quarterly* 29 (spring 1970): 19.

5. Boyce Alexander Drummond, Jr., "Arkansas Politics: A Study of a One-Party System," (dissertation, University of Chicago, 1957), 199–200; Harry Lee Williams, *Forty Years behind the Scenes in Arkansas Politics* (Little Rock, 1949), 86–87; Bureau of Labor Statistics, Bulletin 11 (1932–33), 23.

6. Harvey Parnell to Reconstruction Finance Corporation, November 17, 1932, Reconstruction Finance Corporation Emergency Loan, box 2, Arkansas, Record Group 234, National Archives, Washington, D.C. (hereafter cited as NARG); *Arkansas Gazette*, February 16, 1933; Floyd Sharp, *Traveling Recovery Road: The Story of Work Relief and Rehabilitation in Arkansas* (Little Rock, 1936), 16; United States Department of Commerce, *Statistical Abstract of the United States in 1935*, 589.

7. *Arkansas Gazette*, January 24, 1933, January 10, 1933, February 23, 1933.

8. Ibid., March 16, 1933.

9. "Study of Relief in Madison and Searcy County," USDA, Bureau of Agricultural Economics, NARG 83.

10. J. M. Futrell to Harry Hopkins, July 1, 1933, records of Projects Administration, Federal Emergency Relief Administration (FERA), Arkansas official, May-December 1933, NARG 69.

11. Aubrey Williams, "Dead Battery," manuscript, Aubrey Williams Papers,

box 44, Franklin D. Roosevelt Library, Hyde Park, N.Y. (hereafter cited as FDRL).
12. Williams to Hopkins, August 6, 1933, records of Projects Administration, FERA, Arkansas official, May-December 1933, NARG 69; transcript of telephone call from Williams to Hopkins, October 14, 1933, FERA, NARG 69.
13. Sharp, 16; *Arkansas Gazette,* December 15, 1933.
14. Ibid., February 15, 1935.
15. Garrett Whiteside (secretary to Senator Hattie Caraway) to Robert T. Lansdale, May 11, 1934; Hopkins to Caraway, May 21, 1934; Gertrude Gates to Williams, June 28, 1934, FERA, state file 400, Arkansas, January-May 1934, NARG 69.
16. William Wilson and W. H. Metzler, *Characteristics of Arkansas Rural Rehabilitation Clients,* Agricultural Experiment Station Bulletin no. 348 (Fayetteville, Ark., 1937), 14; Anne Robertson to John G. McCall, *Report on Madison County,* reports on emergency relief states, USDA, Bureau of Agricultural Economics, NARG 83.
17. John Eakins to Franklin D. Roosevelt, November 8, 1932, Democratic National Committee Papers, Arkansas, box 1, FDRL; Commonwealth College, *Fortnightly,* June 15, 1934; *Southwestern American* (For Smith), October 6, 1934.
18. Floyd Sharp to Nels Anderson, February 15, 1935; file 640.1, Arkansas complaints, FERA, NARG 69.
19. *Arkansas Gazette,* March 2, 1935, March 8, 1935; J. M. Futrell to Hopkins, March 9, 1935, file 400, FERA, NARG 69.
20. Hopkins to Futrell, March 15, 1935, ibid.; *Arkansas Gazette,* March 10, 15, 16, 1935.
21. Ibid., April 14, 1933, June 4, 9, 1935; L. L. Ecker-Racz to Williams, July 19, 1935, file 401.1, FERA, Narg 69.
22. *Arkansas Gazette,* July 16, August 1, 7, 1935.
23. Ibid., April 12, 1933; Winthrop Lane to Williams, July 10, 1935, file 400.1; William R. Dyess to James Smith, April 16, 1934, file 401, FERA, NARG 69; see Donald Holley, *Uncle Sam's Farmers* (Urbana, Ill., 1974) for the story of the Dyess colony.
24. *Arkansas Gazette,* November 27, 1935, January 4, 15, 1936; Sharp, 133; *Arkansas Gazette,* January 17, 1936.
25. Clarence H. Dunhof, "Four Decades of Thought on the South's Economic Problems," in *Essays in Southern Economic Development,* Melvin L. Greenhut and W. Tate Whitman (eds.), (Chapel Hill, N.C., 1964), 31–34; *Arkansas Gazette,* April 7, 1936.
26. Drummond, 138–45; *Arkansas Gazette,* July 4, 1936; interview with Brooks Hays on September 6, 1975, tape in special collections, University of Arkansas, Fayetteville.
27. *Arkansas Gazette,* July 15, 1937; Key, 183–85; *Arkansas Gazette,* July 19, 1937; *Report to the President on the Economic Conditions of the South,* National Emergency Committee (Washington, 1938); Benjamin B. Kendrick, "The Colonial Status of the South," *Journal of Southern History* 8 (February 1942): 19.
28. *Arkansas Gazette,* July 10, 1938.
29. Reeves, 322; Drummond, 207–8.
30. Drummond, 212; Reeves, 329.
31. Report by J. J. Harrison, National Emergency Council director in Arkansas, June 20, 1937, records of the National Emergency Council, Division of Field Operations, 1934–1939, record group 44, Washington National Records Center, Suitland, Md.; Department of Commerce, *Personal Income,* 142; Floyd Sharp, "Final Report of the Arkansas Works Projects Administration," March 1945, Arkansas, box 83, NARG 69.
32. E. J. Webster, report on Missouri, Oklahoma, Texas, Arkansas, Harry Hopkins Papers, box 67, FDRL; "Report on Grant County," Bureau of Agricultural Economics, NARG 83; H. L. Mitchell to Hopkins, June 23, 1938, Southern Tenant Farmers Union Papers, University of North Carolina Library; a repudiation of better

relief wages was given Floyd Sharp in a published speech entitled "The Place of Public Employment in the General Scheme of Public Aid and Social Security," Floyd Sharp Papers, box 9, University of Arkansas special collections.

33.	*Arkansas Gazette,* August 18, 1935; *Fayetteville Times,* June 12, 1935; *Arkansas Gazette,* April 16, October 4, 1936.

34.	*Arkansas Gazette,* September 26, December 12, 1938.

35.	Ibid., June 28, 1939.

36.	The complete story of the STFU is recalled by Donald H. Grubbs, *Cry from the Cotton;* the details of the fight over the AAA can be found in David Conrad's *The Forgotten Farmers: The Story of Sharecroppers in the New Deal* (Urbana, Ill., 1965); *Arkansas Gazette,* March 13, 14, 17, 1935.

37.	Grubbs, 85–86; William to William Rooksberry, February 18, 1936; Sharp to Williams, February 20, 1936, box 68, WPA Papers, NARG 69.

38.	Report by A. G. Albright, superintendent of state police to Governor Futrell, June 11, 1936, J. Marion Futrell Papers, Arkansas Historical Commission, territorial capitol, Little Rock; *Arkansas Gazette,* June 11, 1936; Grubbs, 106.

39.	Cedric Belfrage, *South of God* (New York, 1941), 281–84; *Time,* December 7, 1936, 17; *Arkansas Gazette,* September 13, 1938.

40.	Grubbs, 122–23, 155; Jerold S. Auerbach, "Southern Tenant Farmers: Socialists Critics of the New Deal," *Labor History* 7 (winter 1960): 18.

41.	*Statistical Abstract 1941,* 682, 710; James Emmett Pool Grimer, "The Growth of Manufacturers in Arkansas, 1900–1950," (Ph.D. dissertation, George Peabody College, 1958), 160–61; Department of Commerce, *Personal Income by States,* 142–43.

8. BROPHY, Black Texans and the New Deal

1.	Alwyn Barr, *Black Texans: A History of Negroes in Texas 1528–1971* (Austin, 1973), 153–55; William J. Brophy, "The Black Texan, 1900–1950: A Quantitative History" (doctoral dissertation, Vanderbilt University, 1974), 143–44.

2.	See, for example, Donald H. Grubbs, *Cry from the Cotton: The Southern Tenant Farmers' Union and the New Deal* (Chapel Hill, N.C., 1971), 19–23; George B. Tindall, *The Emergence of the New South, 1913–1945,* vol. 10 of *A History of the South* (Baton Rouge, La., 1967), 544–50; Charles S. Johnson, Edwin R. Embree, and Will W. Alexander, *The Collapse of Cotton Tenancy: Summary of Field Studies and Statistical Surveys, 1933–35* (Chapel Hill, N.C., 1935), 52, 57-58, 60; Charles L. Franklin, "Characteristics and Taxable Wages of Negro Workers, Thirteen Selected Southern States, 1938," *Social Security Bulletin;* (March 1941), 21; Paul S. Taylor, "Power Farming and Labor Displacement in the Cotton Belt, 1937," part 1, *Northwest Texas, Monthly Labor Review* 46 (March 1938): 597.

3.	Brophy, 15, 221–22; statistical data calculated from Federal Emergency Relief Administration, *Unemployment Relief Census, October, 1933.* report no. 1 (Washington, 1934), 52-53.

4.	Calculated from Mary E. Bateman, *Trends in Public Assistance, 1933-1939: Data on Old-Age Assistance, Aid to Dependent Children, Aid to the Blind, and General Relief, by States, 1936-1939, and by Counties, December, 1939,* Federal Security Agency Bureau of Research and Statistics, report no. 8 (Washington, 1940), 90–93.

5.	Carle C. Zimmerman and Nathan L. Whetten, *Rural Families on Relief,* Works Progress Administration, research monograph no. 17 (Washington, 1938), 144; Tindall, 547.

6.	John A. Salmond, *The Civilian Conservation Corps, 1933-1942: A New Deal Case Study* (Durham, N.C., 1967), 23.

7.	Ibid., 88–91, 99.

8.	Ibid., 97–99; Tindall, 548; *Austin American,* July 27, 1935. Fechner's policy applied only to those states that maintained segregated camps.

9.	Barr, 155; *Dallas Express,* July 22, 1939.

10. Alfred Steinberg, *Sam Johnson's Boy: A Close-Up of the President from Texas* (New York, 1968), 93-95.

11. *Negro Labor News* (Houston), July 31, October 23, 1937; *Dallas Express,* October 12, 19, 1937, February 21, 1942.

12. *Dallas Express,* February 8, 1941.

13. *Dallas Morning News,* August 12, 1935; *Dallas Express,* October 31, 1942; *Negro Labor News,* July 2, 1938.

14. Richard Sterner, *The Negro's Share: A Study of Income, Consumption, Housing, and Public Assistance* (New York, 1943), 276; Franklin, "Characteristics and Taxable Wages of Negro Workers," 21.

15. "Wages in Cotton Picking, 1937," *Monthly Labor Review* 46 (March 1938): 756; Brophy, 232.

16. Frank B. Feidel, *F. D. R. and the South* (Baton Rouge, La., 1965), 63-64; Edward L. and Frederick H. Schapsmeier, *Henry A. Wallace of Iowa: The Agrarian Years, 1910-1940* (Ames, Ia., 1968), 196.

17. Grubbs, 18-19; Schapsmeier and Schapsmeier, 197-98; Wolters, *Negroes and the Great Depression,* 10-11.

18. Johnson et al., 57-58; Karl E. Ashburn, "Economic and Social Aspects of Farm Tenancy in Texas," *Southwestern Social Science Quarterly* 15 (March 1935): 305.

19. Grubbs, 19-20; Wolters, 12-13; Schapsmeier and Schapsmeier, 198-99.

20. Johnson et al., 40-43; Taylor, 597.

21. Sterner, 421; Brophy, 237.

22. Sterner, 299-301; Wolters, 64-65; National Resources Planning Board, *Security, Work, and Relief Policies* (Washington, 1943), 160.

23. Sterner, 305-307.

24. Ibid., 423; Farm Security Administration, *Farm Security Administration Homesteads* (Washington, 1940), 5; "New Life for Texas Farmers," *Crisis* 43 (July 1936): 212, 218.

25. *Dallas Express,* June 1, 1935; *Dallas Morning News,* July 23, 24, 1935.

26. *Dallas Express,* December 6, 13, 1941, January 10, July 4, 1942; *Dallas Morning News,* March 4, 11, 25, July 1, 1939; *Negro Labor News,* January 20, June 22, 1940; "Rents Established for P.W.A. Housing," *Monthly Labor Review* 46 (June 1938): 1362-63.

CONTRIBUTORS

William J. Brophy is an associate professor and chairman of the department of history at Stephen F. Austin State University in Nacogdoches, Texas. He was awarded the Ph.D. from Vanderbilt University. His essay in this book is based upon a chapter in his dissertation, "The Black Texan: A Quantitative History." Dr. Brophy has read papers relating to various aspects of black history before state, regional, and national organizations. He has served as a consultant to VISTA and was a delegate to the 1976 Democratic National Convention.

Kenneth E. Hendrickson, Jr. is currently professor and chairman of the Department of History at Midwestern State University at Wichita Falls, Texas. Dr. Hendrickson is a specialist on socialist history, particularly in Pennsylvania and New York, and on various New Deal relief agencies. A native of Iowa, he attended the University of South Dakota, where he received the B.A. and M.A. degrees. He did his doctoral work at the University of Oklahoma, where he received the Ph.D. in history in 1962. Prior to coming to Midwestern State University, he taught at Ithaca College in New York and at Shippensburg State College in Pennsylvania. A prolific scholar, he has presented sixteen scholarly papers and has published twenty-two articles, sketches, and reviews. He has written or contributed to three books, including *Socialism and the Cities* (Kennikat, 1975).

C. Roger Lambert, a native of Texas, attended North Texas State University for the B.A. and M.A. degrees, and the University of

Oklahoma for the Ph.D., where he studied under the eminent historian, Gilbert Fite. He taught at the University of Wichita, Del Mar College, and Angelo State University before assuming his current position in 1966 on the history faculty of Arkansas State University in Jonesboro. An authority on agricultural history, he has presented numerous scholarly papers and has published articles in numerous journals including *Agricultural History*, *The Cattleman*, and *Arkansas Historical Quarterly*.

Bill C. Malone is the unquestioned authority on the history of country music in the United States. His *Country Music, USA* (University of Texas Press, 1968) is the definitive work on the growth and commercialization of country music in the twentieth century. He has also coedited with Judith McCulloh *Stars of Country Music* for the University of Illinois Press and currently has two other book-length manuscripts in preparation. A native of Smith County, Texas, Malone received three degrees from the University of Texas at Austin, including the Ph.D. in history, which was awarded in 1965. He has taught at Southwest Texas State University, Murray State University in Kentucky, and Wisconsin State University at Whitewater. He is currently associate professor of history at Tulane University in New Orleans.

Garry L. Nall, an authority on agricultural history in the twentieth century, has been at West Texas State University in Canyon, Texas, since 1963, where he currently holds the rank of associate professor of history. He received the B.A. and M.A. degrees at the University of Texas at Austin, and the Ph.D. from the University of Oklahoma in 1972. He has published articles on high plains agriculture in the *Panhandle-Plains Historical Review* and the *Red River Valley Historical Review.* He also contributed a chapter to the book *Rural Oklahoma,* edited by Donald E. Green and published by the Oklahoma Historical Society in 1977.

Lionel V. Patenaude is a native of Massachusetts. Following service in World War 2 as a pilot, he entered the University of Texas at Austin, where he received the Ph.D. in 1953 after studying under Dr. Walter Prescott Webb. Recalled into the Air Force in 1951, he served in Korea and other areas of the world. Retiring from the Air Force in 1968, he returned to college teaching and served on the faculties at Georgia Tech and St. Mary's University in San Antonio prior to assuming his present position at the University of Texas at San Antonio.

An authority on Texas in the New Deal, he has published articles in such journals as the *Southwestern Historical Quarterly,* the *Social Science Journal,* and *Texana.* He is currently writing a book to be entitled *Texans and the New Deal.*

Stephen F. Strausberg, a native of Brooklyn, New York, did his undergraduate work at Brooklyn College, and he received the Ph.D. in history in 1970 from Cornell University. A specialist in American economic history, he became interested in the impact of the Great Depression on Arkansas after taking a position as assistant professor of history at the University of Arkansas in 1968. He has several articles in print and has a book now pending publication. Strausberg has been active as a book reviewer, as a public speaker, and in community affairs.

Donald W. Whisenhunt, the editor of this volume, is vice president for academic affairs and professor of history at the University of Texas at Tyler. He has taught history at Murray State University in Kentucky and Thiel College in Pennsylvania. Prior to moving to Tyler in 1977 he was dean of the college of liberal arts and sciences at Eastern New Mexico University in Portales. He is a graduate of McMurry College and took his graduate degrees at Texas Tech University. He is the author of thirty articles and four books, including two for Kennikat: *Delegate From New Jersey: The Diary of John Fell* (1973) and *The Environment and the American Experience* (1974).

INDEX